Modern Hindi Grammar

Omkar N. Koul

Modern Hindi Grammar

Omkar N. Koul

2008
DUNWOODY
PRESS

Modern Hindi Grammar

All inquiries should be directed to:
Dunwoody Press
6525 Belcrest Road, Suite 460
Hyattsville, MD 20782
U.S.A.

ISBN: 978-1-931546-06-5
Library of Congress Control Number: 2004113175
Printed and bound in the United States of America

Table of Contents

3. Morphology

5. Lexicon

Preface

Modern Hindi Grammar aims at providing basic information on various aspects of Hindi phonology, morphology, and syntax along with their unique features or characteristics.

Hindi has a special status in India. It is spoken by the largest population in India. It is the official language of the Union of India and eleven state governments, including Delhi. It is taught as a second language in all the non-Hindi speaking states under the three-language formula. Under this formula, a child is supposed to learn his mother tongue, Hindi, and English. If a child's mother tongue is Hindi, (s)he is expected to learn an additional modern Indian language or a foreign language. Hindi is taught as a foreign language in a large number of countries throughout the world. Besides need-based language learning materials, there is a need for a pedagogically oriented grammar of this language. The present grammar aims to fulfill the need of second/foreign language learners of Hindi in India as well as other countries. A large number of Hindi speakers have settled in non-Hindi speaking states in India, or have migrated and settled abroad. The second generation of these migrants is fast losing contact with their mother tongue in the absence of its use in various domains of their day-to-day life in alien surroundings. They are looking for suitable language learning materials including pedagogically oriented grammars for maintaining the language among their children.

Hindi has a long tradition of grammars and grammatical literature. The existing grammars mentioned in the introduction as well as in references are either too old and do not describe modern spoken and written Hindi, or they are sketchy or too scholarly or detailed. They do not fulfill the needs of second and/or foreign language learners or those native speakers who want to maintain the language in an alien atmosphere.

This grammar is pedagogically oriented. It will be of special interest to Hindi language learners and teachers in different situations. It will also be of interest to linguists and researchers working in the area of language typology, and to general readers as well.

In *Modern Hindi Grammar* we have utilized simple terminology and provided suitable descriptions with tables for grammatical categories, phrases, and sentence types. The introduction gives a survey of the Hindi speaking area and the number of its speakers, its classification and dialects, Hindi-Urdu relationship, the status of Hindi and its use in administration, education and mass media, Hindi grammars, and the objectives of the present grammar. The phonology section describes segmental phonemes, suprasegmentals, and morphophonology. The morphology provides a description of different word classes: nouns, pronouns, adjectives, numerals, adverbs, particles, connectives, and interjections. It deals with inflectional as well as derivational morphology. The syntax describes the structure of phrases, sentence types, complex and compound constructions, special word order variations, and other intricate syntactic features. The lexicon presents a list of useful classified vocabulary which is useful for students and teachers of Hindi as well as general readers. This grammar emphasizes special features of Hindi that set it apart from other Indo-Aryan languages. In short, it will fulfill the needs of the basic language learner as well as provide useful information for the linguist and the general reader.

I would like to take this opportunity to thank Mr. Thomas Creamer, Director, Language Research Center (a division of McNeil Technologies) for asking me to write this grammar and for deciding to publish it. I would like to thank Prof. Anjani Kumar Sinha, and Prof. Kashi Wali for going through the first draft of it and for offering useful comments and suggestions. Finally, I would like to thank my colleagues at the Indian Institute of Language Studies for providing their assistance.

I hope students, researchers, teachers, and linguists will find this book useful.

Omkar N. Koul

Abbreviations

1.	first person
2.	second person
3.	third person
abl	ablative case
adv	adverb
asp	aspirated
aux	auxiliary
caus	causative
cond	conditional
cor	correlative
cp	conjunctive participle
dat	dative
emp	emphatic
erg	ergative
fut	future
gen	genitive case
hon	honorific
imp	imperative
impf	imperfective
inf	infinitive
indef	indefinite
ms	masculine singular
neg	negative
nom	nominative
non hon	non honorific
NP	noun phrase
obl	oblique
part	particle
pass	passive
pl	plural
pol	polite
poss	possessive
postp	postposition
pre	presumptive
prox	proximate
psp	past participle
ptc	participle
q	question particle
refl	reflexive
rel	relative
rem	remote
sbj	subjunctive mood
sg	singular
unas	unaspirated
VP	verb phrase
vd	voiced
vl	voiceless
*	ungrammatical

References

Abbi, Anvita 1980. *Semantic Grammar of Hindi: A Study in Reduplication*. New Delhi: Bahri Publications.
___. 1984. The conjuctive participle in Hindi-Urdu. In *International Journal of Dravidian Linguistics,* 13: 252-63.
Agnihotri, Rama Kant 2007. *Hindi: An Essential Grammar*. London: Routledge.
Bahl, Kali Charan 1967. *A Reference Grammar of Hindi*. Chicago: University of Chicago (mimeographed).
___. 1974. *Studies in the Semantic Structure of Hindi*. Delhi: Motilal Banarsidass.
Bahri, U.S. (ed.) 1981. *Topics in Hindi Linguistics*. vol. 1.New Delhi: Bahri Publications.
Bhatia, Kailash Chandra 1964.Consonant Sequences in Standard Hindi. In *Indian Linguistics*, 25: 206-12.
Bhatia, Tej K.1987. *A History of the Hindi Grammatical Tradition: Hindi-Hindustani Grammar, Grammarians, History and Problems.* Leiden: E. J. Brill.
___. 1993. *Punjabi: A Cognitive-Descriptive Grammar*. London: Routledge.
___. 1995. *Negation in South Asian Languages*. Patiala: Indian Institute of Language Studies.
Comrie, B. and N. Smith 1977. Lingua Descriptive Series Questionnaire. *Lingua* 42,1: 1-71. Special Issue.
Das, Pradeep Kumar 2006. *Grammatical Agreement in Hindi-Urdu and its Major Variations.* Munich: Lincom Europa.
Davison, Alice 2000. Lexical anaphors and pronouns in Hindi/Urdu. In Lust, Barbara C. et.al. (eds.) *Lexical Anaphors and Pronouns in Selected South Asian Languages.* Berlin: Mouton de Gruyter.
Fairbanks, Gordon H. and Bal Govind Misra 1966. *Spoken and Written Hindi*. Ithaca: Cornell University Press.
___. and P.B. Pandit 1965. *Hindi*: *A Spoken Approach*. Poona: Deccan College.
Gambhir, Surendra K. *Spoken Hindi-Urdu* 1978. Madison: University of Wisconsin, Center for South Asian Studies.
Gumperz, John J. and June Rumery 1967. *Conversational Hindi-Urdu*. Devanagri edition by Ripley Moore and S.M. Jaiswal. Delhi: Radhakrishna Prakashan. 2 Volumes.
Guru, Kamta Prasad 1920. *Hindi vya:karan*. Kashi: Lakshmi Narayan Press. (1962 edition).

Hook, Peter Edwin 1974. *The Compound Verb in Hindi*. Ann Arbor: The University of Michigan.

___. 1970. *Hindi Structures: An Intermediate Level*. Ann Arbor: The University of Michigan.

Jagananathan, V. R. 1981. *parayog aur prayog*. New Delhi: Oxford University Press.

Jagannathan, V.R. and Ujjal Singh Bahri 1973. *Introductory Course in Spoken Hindi: A Microwave Approach To Language Teaching* Chandigarh. Bahri Publications.

Kachru, Yamuna and Rajeshwari Pandharipande 1983. *Intermediate Hindi*. Delhi. Motilal Banarsidass.

Kachru, Yamuna 1966. *An Introduction to Hindi Syntax*. Urbana: The University of Illinois. (Mimeographed)

___. 1978. On relative clause formation in Hindi-Urdu. *Linguistics,* 207: 5-26.

___. 1980. *Aspects of Hindi Grammar*. New Delhi: Manohar.

___. 2006. *Hindi.* Amsterdam: John Benjamin.

Kelkar, Ashok R.1968. *Studies in Hindi-Urdu I: Introduction and Word Phonology*. Poona: Deccan College.

Kellog, S. H. 1876. *A Grammar of the Hindi Language*. London: Routledge and Kegan Paul (3rd edition 1963).

Klaiman, M. H. 1976. Topicalization and Relativization in Hindi. In *Indian Linguistics*, 37: 315-33.

Koul, Omkar N. (ed.) 1982. *Topics in Hindi Linguistics* Vol 2. New Delhi: Bahri Publications.

___. 1982. Coordinating Conjunctions in Hindi. In Koul, Omkar N. (ed.) *Topics in Hindi Linguistics* Vol 2.

___. (ed.) 1994. *Topics in Hindi Linguistics* Vol 3. New Delhi: Bahari Publications.

___. 1994a. Use of Indian Languages in Administration. In Koul, Omkar N. (ed.) *Language Development and Administration.* New Delhi: Creative, 109-17.

___. 1994b. Common Bases of Hindi and Urdu. In *Gaveshna* Vol. 63-64: 267-78.

___. 1994c. *Hindi Phonetic Reader*. Patiala: Indian Institute of Language Studies.

___. (ed.) 1999a. *Topics in Hindi Linguistics* Vol 4. New Delhi: Bahri Publications.

___. 1999b. The Use of Particles in Hindi. In Koul, Omkar N. (ed.) *Topics in Hindi Linguistics,* Vol.4, 61-75.

___. 1999c. Interrogative Questions in Hindi. In Koul, Omkar N. (ed.), *Topics in Hindi Linguistics,* Vol.4, 165-187.

___. and Kashi Wali 2006. *Modern Kashmiri Grammar*. Springfield: Dunwoody Press.
Masica, Colin P. 1976. *Defining a Linguistic Area: South Asia.* Chicago: University of Chicago Press.
___. 1981. Identified object marking in Hindi and other languages. In Koul, Omkar N (ed.) 1982.
McGregor, R. S. 1995. *Outline of Hindi Grammar*. Oxford: Oxford University Press. (3rd edition).
Mehrotra, R. C. 1980. *Hindi Phonology: A Synchronic Description of the Contemporary Standard.* Raipur: Bhashika Prakashan.
Mehrotra, R.R. 1977. *Terms of Kinship, Modes of Address and Reference in Hindi*. A Study in Anthropological Linguistics. New Delhi: Motilal Banarsidass.
Mitner, V. 1969. Hindi. In Sebeok (ed.) *Current Trends in Linguistics*, Vol 5 *Linguistics in South Asia*. The Hague: Mouton.
Montaut, Annie 1994. Reflexivisation et focalisation en hinid/oordou. In *Bulletin de la society Linguistique de Paris,* 89: 83-120.
___. 2005. A Grammar of Hindi. Munich: Lincom Europa.
Misra, K.S. 1977. *Terms of Address and Pronominal Usage in Hindi.* A Sociolinguistic Study. New Delhi: Bahri Publications.
Ohala, Manjri 1983. *Aspects of Hindi Phonology*. Delhi: Motilal Banarsidass.
Porizka, Vincenc. 1963. *Hindi Language Course.* Prague. Statni pedagogicke nakladatelstvi (Revised edition 1972).
Pray, Bruce 1970. *Topics in Hindi-Urdu Grammar*. Berkeley: Center for South Asian Studies, University of California.
Rai, A. 1984. *A House Divided: The Origin and Development of Hindi/Hindavi*. Delhi: Oxford University Press.
Rajgopalan, N.V. 1973. *Hindi ka bhashavaigyanik vya:karaṇ*. Agra: Kendriya Hindi Sansthan.
Schmidt, Ruth Laila 1999. *An Essential Grammar of Urdu.* London: Routledge.
Schmidt, Ruth Laila 2003. Urdu. In Cardona, George and Dhanesh Jain (eds.) *The Indo-Aryan Languages.* London, New York: Routledge, 286-350.
Shapiro, Michael C. 1989. *A Primer of Modern Standard Hindi*. Delhi: Motilal Banarsidass.
Shapiro, Michael C. 2003. Hindi. In Cardona, George and Dhanesh Jain (eds.) *The Indo-Aryan Languages.* London, New York: Routledge, 250-285.

Sharma, Aryendra 1958. *A Basic Grammar of Modern Hindi*. New Delhi: Central Hindi Directorate (Fifth Edition 1994).
Shukla, Shaligram 2000. *Hindi Phonology*. Munich: Lincom Europa.
___. 2001. *Hindi Morphology*. Munich: Lincom Europa.
Singh, K.S. (ed.) 1978. *Readings in Hindi-Urdu Linguistics*. New Delhi: National Publishing House.
Singh, Rajendra and Rama Kant Agnihotri 1997. *Hindi Morphology: A Word-Based Description*. Delhi: Motilal Bnarsidass.
Singh, Suraj Bhan 1999. Concept of Semantic Field and Collocation in Hindi/Urdu Lexicography. In Koul, Omkar N. (ed.) *Topics in Hindi Linguistics*, Vol 4, 143-63.
___. 2003. *angrezi-hindi anuva:d vya:karaṇ* (*English – Hindi Translation Grammar*). Delhi: Prabhat Prakashan.
Sinha, Anjani Kumar, 1973. Factivity and relations between main and subordinate clauses in Hindi. In *Papers from the Ninth Regional Meeting of the Chicago Linguistic Society*. Chicago: University of Chicago, Department of Linguistics, 351-58.
Srivastava, R. N. 1968. Theory of monophonematics of aspirated phonemes of Hindi. *Acta Linguistica*, 363-73.
Subbarao, K.V. 1984. *Complementation in Hindi Syntax*. New Delhi: Academic Publications.
Upreti, M. L. 1964. *Hindi mẽ pratyay vica:r*. Agra: Vinod Book House.
Vajpeyi, K. 1958. *Hindi shabdanushasan*. Kashi: Nagri Pracharni Sabha.
Verma, M.K. 1971. *The Structure of Noun Phrase in English and Hindi*. Delhi: Motilal Banarsidass.
Wali, Kashi and Omkar N Koul 1997. *Kashmiri: A Cognitive-Descriptive Grammar*. London: Routledge.

1. Introduction

1.1. Area and Its Speakers

Hindi is an Indo-Aryan language (a branch of the-Indo-European family of languages), spoken primarily in the states of Bihar, Chattisgarh, Delhi, Haryana, Himachal Pradesh, Jharkhand, Madhya Pradesh, Rajasthan, Uttarakhand, and Uttar Pradesh in India. Besides being the official language of these states it is also the official language of government of India along with English. According to the 2001census, it is spoken by 422,048,642 speakers which include the speakers of its various dialects and variations of speech grouped under Hindi. It is also spoken by a large number of people of Indian origin settled abroad.

1.2. Dialects and Classification

Hindi and Urdu languages have their origins in Khariboli spoken in areas around Delhi. Khariboli was adopted by the Afghans, Persians, and Turks as a common language of interaction with the local population during the period of Islamic invasions and the establishment of Muslim rule in the north of India between the eighth and tenth centuries AD. In time, it developed a variety called Urdu with significant borrowings from Arabic and Persian and that uses a Persian script. It was also known as *rexta* "mixed language." As Urdu gained patronage in the Muslim courts and developed into a literature language, the variety used by the general population gradually replaced Sanskrit, literary Prakrits, and Apabhramsas as the literary language. This latter variety looked to Sanskrit for linguistic borrowings and Sanskrit, Prakrits, and Apabhramsas for literary conventions. It is this variety that became known as Hindi.

Hindi and Urdu have a common form known as Hindustani which is essentially a Hindi-Urdu mixed language. This was the variety that was adopted by Indian leaders as a symbol of national identity during the struggle for freedom. Hindi has been used as a literary language since the twelfth century. The development of prose, however, began only in the eighteenth century, which marks the emergence of Hindi as a full-fledged literary language.

Grierson (1906) has divided Hindi into two groups: Eastern Hindi and Western Hindi. Between the Eastern and the Western Prakrits there was an intermediate Prakrit called Ardhamagadhi. The modern representative of the corresponding Apabhamsa is Eastern Hindi and the Shaurasena Apabhramsa of the middle Doab is the parent of Western Hindi. In the Eastern group Grierson discusses three dialects: Awadhi, Bagheli, and Chattisgarhi. In the Western group he discusses five dialects: Hindustani, Braj Bhasha, Kanauji, Bundeli, and Bhojpuri. Eastern Hindi is bounded on the north by the language of the Nepal Himalaya and on the west by various dialects of Western Hindi, of which the principal are Kanauji and Bundeli. On the east, it is bounded by the Bhojpuri dialect of Bihari and by Oriya. On the South it meets forms of the Marathi language. Western Hindi extends to the foot of the Himalayas on the north, south to the Jamna valley, and occupies most of Bundelkhand and a part of central provinces on the east side.

The Hindi region is traditionally divided into two: Eastern Hindi and Western Hindi. The main dialects of Eastern Hindi are Avadhi, Bagheli and Chattisgarhi. The Western Hindi dialects are Haryanvi, Braj Bhasha, Bhundeli, Kanuji and Khariboli. The dialects spoken in the regions of Bihar (i.e., Maithili, Bhojpuri, Maghi etc.) in Rajasthan (i.e., Marwari, Jaipuri, Malvi etc.) and some dialects spoken in the northwestern areas of Uttar Pradesh, and Himachal Pradesh were kept away from the earlier classification. Now, all of these dialects are also covered under the term Hindi. The standard Hindi developed from the Khariboli has borrowed lexical items from Sanskrit and is the vehicle of all official literary and commercial communication. It is intelligible throughout the broad Hindi language region. Another literary style, Urdu, has also developed from Khariboli and it uses the Perso-Arabic script and borrows from Perso-Arabic sources.

1.3. Hindi – Urdu

Historical and cultural processes and the linguistic affinity which exists in Indian languages led to the emergence of Hindi-Urdu or so-called Hindustani as the lingua-franca of major areas of India long before its freedom. In an earlier period, the languages of administration, Sanskrit in the case of the earliest Hindu kingdoms, Persian in the case of the Muslim dynasties, and English in the case of the British regime, have mostly remained confined to the elite.

Beginning with the invasion of Mohammed Ghori in the late 12th century AD, the foreign invaders settled down in India to rule. The Slave, Tughluq, Lodi, and Mughal dynasties used Persian in their administration, but they used the local language spoken in and around Delhi for communicating with the people for their day-to-day needs. This local language was a form of Apbhramsha, which eventually became Khariboli; they called this language Hindi - a language belonging to Hind. Thus, the Hindi language derived its name from the Persian towards the end of the 12th century or beginning of the 13th century. During the Mughal period, the word "Urdu" was derived from the Turkish word "Yurt" or "ordu" that meant "military encampment." This variety was distinguished on the basis of Perso-Arabic influence at the lexical level and was written in the Perso-Arabic script. Hindi-Urdu became the medium of communication between the Muslim rulers and the local people. The southern variety of the speech, best known as Dakhini, also became the medium of literature and socio-religious discourse. This variety is influenced by Dravidian languages as a result of language contact.

Due to a common structural basis, Hindi and Urdu continued to be treated as synonymous for centuries at least up to the period of Mirza Ghalib. Mirza Ghalib called his language "Hindi" on several occasions, though he used the Perso-Arabic script for writing it. He named one of his works "ode-e-Hindi" (perfume of Hindi). Primarily in the domain of different genres of literature, Hindi and Urdu started drifting away from each other not only in the use of two different scripts, but also in literary styles and vocabulary. Hindi started drawing more and more from Sanskrit, and Urdu from Persian and Arabic. The processes continue today.

During British rule, when English was adopted as the official language, local languages were assigned roles for certain functions at lower levels of administration. A competition started between the proponents or supporters of Hindi and those of Urdu for official recognition of their languages. In the first instance, Urdu was recognized by the British in the Northwest and Oudh, Bihar, and the Central Provinces in 1830 AD as the language of the courts. This was followed by the recognition accorded to Hindi in certain areas. Hindi and Urdu were involved in controversy and mutual competition for their recognition in various domains of education and administration. The mutual conflicts intensified at the beginning of the 20th century. On the one hand, there were proponents of Hindi and Urdu who were eager to maintain separate linguistic identities, and, on the other hand, some national leaders wanted to develop Hindustani as a combined linguist identity on the basis of its use by the general population.

1.4. Linguistic Characteristics

Hindi shares major linguistic characteristics with other Indo-Aryan languages. It has ten vowels. The length of vowels is phonemic. All vowels can be nasalized and nasalization is phonemic. The Hindi syllable contains a vowel as its nucleus, followed or preceded by consonants. Words usually have two or three syllables.

Nouns are inflected for number, gender and case. There are two numbers: singular and plural, two genders: masculine and feminine; and two cases: direct and oblique. Nouns are assigned one of the two genders. The gender of inanimate objects is not predictable from the form or meaning. Pronouns are inflected for number and case. Adjectives are of two types: declinable and indeclinable. The first type is uninflected for number, gender, and case, whereas the second type is not.

Verbs are inflected for person, number, gender, tense, mood, and aspect. There are three tenses: present, past, and future; three moods: imperative, indicative, and subjective; two aspects: imperfective and perfective. Hindi is a verb-final language.

Hindi is written in the Devanagari script which originated from Brahmi. The Devanagari script for Hindi is standardized, but certain minor variations still exist. In this grammar we are using Devanagari and Roman scripts for the data from the language.

1.5. Status

As stated above, Hindi is the official language of the Union of India and ten states. It is spoken by the largest number of people in India. It is widely used in administration, education, and mass media.

The use of Hindi in administration at the Union level as well as in the Hindi speaking states is not free from problems (Koul 1994a). There are some serious gaps in the Official Language Policy (OLP), and the rules and procedures which are being followed in its implementation. There are problems related to the development of its administrative register. The main problems related to the development of the administrative register are: (i) an artificial coinage of terminology, (ii) lack of standardization, and (iii) lack of coordination between various agencies and duplication of efforts. Problems related to its practical use include the lack of proper monitoring, lack of encouragement, and absence of strong political will.

The implementation of the OLP at the Union level has become the victim of political indecision, the attitude of its protagonists, the lack of will of the monitoring agencies, and the lack of adherence to the rules and regulations set up for it. Even after its continuous use in administration for more than sixty years, its development is still questioned by critics. There is a need to review the OLP, and the rules and procedures of its implemenation to identify its problems and resolve them.

The Constitution of India adopted in 1950 provides for the use of Hindi in Devanagari script as the official language of the Union. Article 343 states:

The official language of the Union shall be Hindi in the Devanagari script. The form of numerals to be used for the official purpose of the Union shall be the international form of Indian numerals.

Article 351 provides a directive for the development of Hindi as follows:

It shall be the duty of the Union to promote the spread of the Hindi language, to develop it so that it may serve as a medium of expression for all the composite culture of India and to secure its enrichment by assimilating without interfering with its genius, the forms, style and expressions used in Hindustani and in the other languages of India specified in the Eighth Schedule, and by drawing, whenever necessary or desirable, its vocabulary primarily from Sanskrit and secondarily from other languages.

The Hindi language was supposed to replace English in 1965, fifteen years after the adoption of the Constitution of India. The early sixties witnessed resentment and agitation, primarily in the southern states of India, regarding the replacement of English by Hindi. It was argued that Hindi was not developed enough to replace English in its administrative domain. Thus, the Official Language Act (OLA) was passed in 1963 providing for the continuation of English as an associate official language in the Union and also for its use in parliament for an indefinite period of time. The Act dealt with the setting-up of the Committee on Official Language, authorization of the Hindi translation of Central and State acts, optional use of Hindi in judgments of High courts, etc. The passing of the OLA was successful in achieving timely political gains, but it has not been in the interest of the development of Hindi and its use as the sole official language of the Union in the years to come.

The development of Hindi has become a complex concern for the Government of India. The development of Hindi is often linked to the development of other regional languages. The Ministry of Home Affairs (Government of India) Resolution (1968) made some important recommendations in this regard:

1. It is the duty of the Government of India to promote the spread of the Hindi language.
2. The development of Hindi as well as other regional languages is in the interest of the educational and cultural advancement of the country.
3. Efforts should be made to implement the Three-Language Formula.
4. Compulsory knowledge of Hindi or English should be essential for the public service of the Union.
5. Languages of the Eighth Schedule should be used as alternative media for examinations for all-India and higher Central services.

The Resolution adopted by the Ministry of Home Affairs has turned out to be merely a political policy statement. It was not followed by an action plan for the promotion or the spread of the Hindi language in a sustainable manner, although it was rightly realized that the development of Hindi and regional languages is necessary for the educational and cultural advancement of the country. No clear-cut strategies were framed for encouraging their use in education. It did not stop the mushrooming of competing English-medium private schools. Efforts were made to implement the Three-Language Formula, but, in the absence of proper monitoring of its implementation, the Formula itself was diluted by different states, which resulted in its several versions. The Union Public Service Commission (UPSC) has made a provision for the use of languages of the Eighth Schedule as alternative media for competitive examinations, but, in the absence of adequate study materials in Hindi and regional languages, English continues to reign supreme as the only viable medium of examinations. Hindi is taught to the officers and staff of the Central service during their in-service training, but there is no urgency for its use as long as English continues as an associate official language. The Resolution makes important recommendations, but in the absence of an effective action plan and a sense of urgency on the part of the agencies involved, these recommendations are not implemented properly.

Hindi has a significant role in education. It is used as a subject of study as well as a medium of education in India from the primary level to the university level in all the Hindi-speaking states in India. It is also used as a medium for technical education at the lower levels. Various organizations at the Union and state levels are engaged in the preparation of textbooks and supplementary instructional materials in Hindi. English continues to be a preferred medium of instruction for science and technology at the higher levels.

Hindi has a prominent role in both electronic and print media. Hindi is widely used in programs on radio and television and in films. The language style of Hindi used in electronic media is close to the spoken variety of so-called Hindustani. In the print media, styles vary from high Hindi to that commonly understood by the Hindi-Urdu speech community. Whereas a few newspapers and periodicals prefer high Hindi or the Sanskritized style, others prefer to use the Urdu vocabulary. A large number of newspapers, periodicals, and journals are published in Hindi.

1.6. Grammars in Hindi

Beginning in the eighteenth century, Hindi has a long tradition of grammatical literature which falls under the categories of (a) traditional grammars, (b) comparative and historical grammars, and (c) modern linguistic grammars. Bhatia (1987) provides a critical survey of the Hindi grammatical tradition. Traditional grammars describe the language using the traditional framework of Sanskrit grammars. Comparative and historical grammars are mostly concerned with presenting the diachronic description of the grammatical features at different linguistic levels, especially phonology and morphology. They are useful for historical linguists and those interested in the comparative linguistics of Indo-Aryan languages.

Modern linguistic grammars in Hindi have been written with various objectives. Most of the modern linguistic grammars deal with some aspects of syntax at length and tend to apply the western theoretical models and raise theoretical issues. They are useful for linguists interested in theoretical discussions and are of little use to the language learners and teachers of Hindi or to general readers. It is important to mention a few grammars here.

Aryendra Sharma (1958) prepared first detailed descriptive grammar of modern Hindi in English. It has been revised and printed several times. Though written in a traditional format it presents a good description of Hindi. Different linguistic aspects of Hindi have been described in various dissertations and independent grammatical studies lately. I will specially mention three recent works: Mountaut (2005), Kachru (2006), and Agnihotri (2007) written with different objectives.

Moutaut (2005) provides a functional description of Hindi from a typological perspective. She provides a brief phonological outline of standard Hindi, its morphological analysis, an analysis of simple clauses and complex sentences. The final section provides representative features of standard Hindi, its various dialects with special reference to other neighboring Indo-Aryan languages. She presents review of the earlier works on the subject and uses examples from various written texts. It is a first linguistic grammar of Hindi written from a typological point of view and is useful for linguists working in the area of linguistic typology with special reference to Indo-Aryan languages.

Kachru (2006) describes the structure of modern Hindi keeping in view primarily the sociolinguistic context of language use. She provides description of sounds, devices of word formation, rules of phrases, and sentence constructions and conventions and practices of language use in spoken and written texts keeping in view recent linguistic theories. She also deals with the information and discourse structure of the current use of Hindi. This is quite useful for linguists and language learners of Hindi in various situations.

Agnihotri (2007) is a practical reference guide to the core structures and linguistic features of Hindi. He provides brief description of various simple, compound and complex structures of Hindi. Word morphology, phonology, and issues related to Devanagari script are dealt with adequate examples. It is useful for linguists and students of Hindi for reference.

There is a scope for a pedagogically oriented grammar which provides essential information for the use of Hindi language learners as well as teachers. The present *Modern Hindi Grammar* is an effort in this direction. It is pedagogically oriented; utilizing simpler terminology and authentic data from standard spoken and written Hindi; providing useful descriptions and tables of grammatical categories as well as simple descriptions of phrases, and sentence types designed for the use of language learners, teachers of Hindi at various levels. The Phonology describes segmental phonemes (vowels, consonants), suprasegmentals (length, stress, intonation), and morphophonology (alternations, deletion and insertion, allomorphs). The Morphology provides descriptions of nominal morphology (noun inflection, gender, number, case, postpositions, pronouns, adjectives), verb morphology (types of verbs, verb inflections, voice, tense, aspect, mood, non-finite verb forms), and adverbs. The Syntax describes the structure of phrases, sentence types, complex and compound constructions, other syntactic constructions among other items. The Lexicon presents a classified vocabulary of Hindi under 12 sub-sections. It is followed by Index.

2. Phonology

2.1. Phonological Units (Segmental)

The pulmonic egressive airstream mechanism is involved in the production of all phonetic segments of the language.

2.1.1. Distinctive Segments

The inventory of the distinctive segments of Hindi is as follows:

Vowels

	Front	Central	Back
High	i:		u:
Lower High	i		u
Mid	e		o
Lower Mid	ɛ		ɔ
Low		a a:	

The nasalization is phonemic in Hindi. It is represented by the nasal sign ˜ written above the vowel signs as given below:

	Front	Central	Back
High	ĩ:		ũ:
Lower High	ĩ		ũ
Mid	ẽ		õ
Lower Mid	ɛ̃		ɔ̃
Low		ã ã:	

Consonants

	Bilabial	Labio-dental	Alveolar	Dental	Retroflex	Palatal	velar	Glottal Stops
vl.unasp	p			t	ṭ		k	
vl.asp	ph			th	ṭh		kh	
vd.unsap	b			d	ḍ		g	
vd.asp	bh			dh	ḍh		gh	
Affricates								
vl.unas						c		
vl.asp						ch		
Vd.unas						j		
vd.asp						jh		
Nasal	m			n	ṇ		η	
Trill				r				
Flap								
unasp					ṛ			
asp					ṛh			
Lateral				l				
Fricative								
vl		f	s			š	x	
vd			z					h
Semivowel		v				y		

2.1.2. Description of Phonemes

2.1.2.1. Vowels

Oral Vowels

There is a contrast in the position of the tongue, the height of the tongue, and the rounding of the lips in the articulation of vowels.

/i:/	(high front unrounded long vowel):		
	ईद	i:d	Eid
	नीर	ni:r	water
	जल्दी	jaldi:	hurry

/i/	(high front unrounded short vowel):		
	इमारत	ima:rat	building
	गिरना	girna:	to fall
	पति	pati	husband
/e/	(mid front unrounded long vowel):		
	एक	ek	one
	रेत	ret	sand
	जूते	ju:te	shoes
/a/	(low central unrounded short vowel):		
	अगर	agar	if
	पर	par	but
	न	na	no
/a:/	(low central unrounded long vowel):		
	आम	a:m	mango
	आराम	a:ra:m	rest
	अच्छा	accha:	good
/u/	(high back rounded short vowel):		
	उठना	uṭhna:	to rise
	पुत्र	putr	son
	किंतु	kintu	but
/u:/	(high back rounded long vowel):		
	ऊन	u:n	wool
	सूद	su:d	interest
	भालू	bha:lu:	bear
/o/	(mid back rounded long vowel):		
	ओस	os	dew
	रोटी	roṭi:	bread
	दो	do	two
/ɛ/	(lower mid unrounded front vowel)		
	ऐनक	ɛnak	mirror
	गैर	gɛr	stranger
	लै	lɛ	tune
/ɔ/	(lower mid rounded back vowel)		
	औरत	ɔrat	woman
	दौलत	dɔlat	wealth
	सौ	sɔ	hundred

Nasal Vowels

Nasalization is phonemic in Hindi. All the vowels can be nasalized.

/ĩ/	इंच	ĩc	inch
	पिंजरा	pĩjra:	cage
/ĩ:/	ईंट	ĩ:ṭ	brick
	सींचना	sĩ:cna:	to irrigate
	नहीं	nahĩ:	no
/ẽ/	भेंट	bhẽṭ	meeting
	में	mẽ	in
/ã/	अँगूठा	ãgu:ṭha:	thumb
	ठंड	ṭhãḍ	cold
/ã:/	आँगन	ã:gan	courtyard
	माँग	mã:g	demand
	माँ	mã:	mother
/ũ/	उँस	ũs	ounce
	मुँह	mũh	face
/ũ:/	ऊँट	ũ:ṭ	camel
	सूँघना	sũ:ghna:	to smell
	जूँ	jũ:	louse
/õ/	ओंठ	õṭh	lip
	गोंद	gõd	gum
	सरसों	sarsõ	mustard
/ɛ̃/	ऐंठना	ɛ̃ṭhna:	to tighten
	भैंस	bhɛ̃s	buffalo
	मैं	mɛ̃	I
/ɔ̃/	औंधा	ɔ̃dha:	upside down
	चौंतीस	cɔ̃ti:s	thiry-four
	भौं	bhɔ̃	eyebrow

2.1.2.2. Consonants

Consonants are classified into different groups on the basis of their manner and place of articulation. Examples of phonemic consonantal segments of Hindi are presented in minimal or near minimal pairs. Non-phonemic phonetic segments are also exemplified. The examples given below represent their phonetic transcription.

Stops and Affricates

In the production of stops, air coming out of the lungs is stopped at the point of articulation and then released with plosion. Stops occur at initial, medial, and final positions of words.

/p/	(voiceless unaspirated bilabial stop):		
	पल	pal	moment
	कपड़ा	kapṛa:	cloth
	साँप	sã:p	snake
/ph/	(voiceless aspirated bilabial stop):		
	फल	phal	fruit
	सफल	saphal	successful
	साफ	sa:ph	clean
/b/	(voiced unaspirated bilabial stop):		
	बल	bal	strength
	अंबर	ambar	sky
	सब	sab	all
/bh/	(voiced aspirated bilabial stop):		
	भालू	bha:lu:	bear
	सभा	sabha:	meeting
	लाभ	la:bh	profit
/t/	(voiceless unaspirated dental stop):		
	तार	ta:r	wire
	कातना	ka:tna:	to spin
	रात	ra:t	night
/th/	(voiceless aspirated dental stop):		
	थाली	tha:li:	palate
	हाथी	ha:thi:	elephant
	हाथ	ha:th	hand
/d/	(voiced unaspirated dental stop):		
	दरवाज़ा	darva:za:	door
	वर्दी	vardi:	uniform
	बंद	band	closed
/dh/	(voiced aspirated dental stop):		
	धन	dhan	wealth
	आधा	a:dha:	half
	दूध	du:dh	milk
/ṭ/	(voiceless unaspirated retroflex stop):		
	टोकरी	ṭokri:	basket

	काटना	ka:ṭna:	to cut
	कोट	koṭ	coat
/ṭh/	(voiceless aspirated retroflex stop):		
	ठग	ṭhag	cheat
	मिठाई	miṭha:i:	sweets
	आठ	a:ṭh	eight
/ḍ/	(voiced unaspirated retroflex stop):		
	डाली	ḍa:li:	branch
	निडर	niḍar	fearless
	साँड	sã:ḍ	bull
/ḍh/	(voiced aspirated retroflex stop):		
	ढोल	ḍhol	drum
	गढा	gaḍha:	ditch
/k/	(voiceless unaspirated velar stop):		
	कान	ka:n	ear
	लकड़ी	lakṛi:	wood
	नाक	na:k	nose
/kh/	(voiceless aspirated velar stop):		
	खोदना	khodna:	to dig
	देखना	dekhna:	to see
	राख	ra:kh	ashes
/g/	(voiced unaspirated velar stop):		
	गर्दन	gardan	neck
	अगर	agar	if
	आग	a:g	fire
/gh/	(voiced aspirated velar stop):		
	घर	ghar	home
	सूँघना	sũ:ghna:	to smell
	बाघ	ba:gh	tiger

In the production of affricates, air coming out of the lungs passes with friction when the articulator is released gradually. Affricates occur in the initial, medial and final positions of words.

/c/	(voiceless unaspirated palatal stop):		
	चार	ca:r	four
	बच्चा	bacca:	child
	कांच	kã:c	glass
/ch/	(voiceless aspirated palatal affricate):		
	छे	che	six

	मछली	machli:	fish
	कुछ	kuch	some
/j/	(voiced unaspirated palatal affricate):		
	जान	ja:n	life
	गाजर	ga:jar	carrot
	ताज	ta:j	crown
/jh/	(voiced aspirated palatal affricate):		
	झंडा	jhā̃ḍa:	flag
	सुझाव	sujha:v	suggestion
	साँझ	sā̃:jh	evening

Fricatives

There are alveolar and glottal fricatives. They occur at all positions.

/f/	(voiceless labio-dental fricative)		
	फ़र्ज़	farz	duty
	नफ़रत	nafrat	dislike
	सिर्फ़	sirf	only
/s/	(voiceless alveolar fricative):		
	सात	sa:t	seven
	सस्ता	sasta:	cheap
	दस	das	ten
/z/	(voiced alveolar fricative):		
	ज़बान	zaba:n	language
	बाज़ार	ba:za:r	market
	गज़	gaz	yard
/š/	(voiceless alveolar fricative):		
	शक	šak	suspicion
	आशा	a:ša:	hope
	नाश	na:š	destruction
/x/	(voiceless velar fricative):		
	ख़बर	xabar	news
	अख़बार	axba:r	newspaper
	शाख़	ša:x	branch
/h/	(voiceless glottal fricative):		
	हाथी	ha:thi:	elephant
	बहार	baha:r	spring
	राह	ra:h	way

Nasals

There are bilabial, alveolar, and velar nasals. The velar nasal occurs in medial and final positions only.

/m/	(voiced bilabial nasal):		
	माथा	ma:tha:	forehead
	कमरा	kamra:	room
	आराम	a:ra:m	rest
/n/	(voiced alveolar nasal):		
	नाक	na:k	nose
	लाना	la:na:	to bring
	धान	dha:n	paddy
/ṇ/	(voiced retroflex nasal)		
	अणु	aṇu	atom
	प्राण	pra:ṇ	life
/ŋ/	(voiced velar nasal):		
	रंगना	raŋna:	to dye
	रंग	raŋ	color

Trill

There is a voiced alveolar trill which occurs in all positions.

/r/	(voiced alveolar trill):		
	रस्सी	rassi:	rope
	नर्म	narm	soft
	तार	ta:r	wire

Flaps

/ṛ/	(voiced unaspirated retroflex flap):		
	सड़क	saṛak	road
	भीड़	bhi:ṛ	crowd
/ṛh/	(voiced aspirated retroflex flap):		
	पढ़ना	paṛhna:	to read
	धाढ़	dha:ṛh	jaw

Lateral

There is a voiced alveolar lateral which occurs in all positions.

/l/	(voiced alveolar lateral):		
	लोग	log	people
	कला	kala:	art
	जाल	ja:l	net

Semi-vowels

/v/	(voiced labio-dental semi-vowel):		
	वादा	va:da:	promise
	दवाई	dava:i:	medicine
	नाव	na:v	boat
/y/	(voiced palatal semi-vowel):		
	याद	ya:d	memory
	साया	sa:ya:	shade
	राय	ra:y	opinion

2.1.2.3. Distribution of Phonemes and Allophones

The retroflex voiced aspirated stop ढ /ḍh/ does not occur in the final position of words. The velar nasal ङ /ɳ/, and the retroflex flaps ड़ /ṛ/and ढ़ /ṛh/ do not occur in the word-initial positions.

The nasal phoneme न /n/ has dental, retroflex, palatal, and velar allophones: न [n], ण [ṇ], and ङ [ɳ]. Palatal and velar nasals are not assigned any phonemic status in Hindi. Phonetically they are pronounced in the speech only when they are followed by palatal and velar voiced consonant phonemes. They occur before homorganic voiced consonants.

2.2. Phonotactics

2.2.1. Vowel Sequences

In Hindi only two vowel sequences are permissible.

ai:	नाई	nai:	new
ia:	दिआ	dia:	lamp
ie	चलिए	calie	let's go
ui:	सुई	sui:	needle
uã:	कुँआ	kuã:	well
oi:	रोई	roi:	wept
oe	खोए	khoe	lost

2.2.2. Consonant Clusters

2.2.2.1. Word-initial Consonant Clusters

Word-initial consonant clusters are not as frequent as the word-medial consonant clusters.

ky	क्या	kya:	what
kr	क्रम	kram	order
gy	ग्यारह	gya:rah	eleven
gr	ग्रंथ	granth	book
jy	ज्येष्ठ	jyešṭh	elder
jv	ज्वर	jvar	fever
ṭr	ट्रेन	ṭren	train
ḍy	ड्योडा	ḍyoḍa:	two and a half times
ḍr	ड्रामा	ḍra:ma:	drama
ty	त्याग	tya:g	sacrifice
tv	त्वचा	tvaca:	skin
dhy	ध्यान	dhya:n	attention
py	प्यार	pya:r	love
pr	पृथ्वी	prithvi:	earth
br	ब्रह्मा	bramha:	*Brahma*
by	ब्याह	bya:h	marriage
šy	श्याम	šya:m	Shyam
šr	श्रम	šram	labor
sv	श्वास	šva:s	breath

sy	स्यार	sya:r	jackal
zy	ज़्यादा	zya:da:	more
nr	नृत्य	nraty	dance
ny	न्याय	nya:y	justice
mr	मृग	mrig	deer
vy	व्यक्ति	vyakti	person
hr	हृदय	hriday	heart

Initial three-consonant clusters

str	स्त्री	stri:	woman
skr	स्क्रीन	skri:n	screen
smr	स्मृति	smriti:	remembrance

2.2.2.2. Word-medial Consonant Clusters

Consonant clusters occur frequently in the medial position. Most of these clusters are formed across syllable or morpheme boundaries. There are some restrictions in the formation of consonant clusters as follows: (i) two aspirated consonants do not combine to form a consonant cluster, (ii) /ch/ is not combined to form a consonant cluster, (iii) /ḍ/ does not occur as the second member of a consonant cluster. Examples of the consonant clusters are given below.

pt	कप्तान	kapta:n	captain
ps	वापसी	va:psi:	return
fs	अफसोस	afsos	sorry
fl	गफ़्लत	gaflat	mistake
fr	नफ़रत	nafrat	hate
fv	अफ़्वा	afva:	rumor
bn	शब्नम	šabnam	dew
bz	सब्ज़ी	sabzi:	vegetable
tm	आत्मा	a:tma:	soul
dt	बद्तर	badtar	very bad
dm	बदमाश	badma:š	rouge
kb	मक्बूल	makbu:l	popular
kt	मक्तब	maktab	school
kṭ	अक्टर	akṭar	actor
kd	हक़्दार	hakda:r	rightful owner/entitled
kr	इक़रार	ikra:r	acceptance

ks	नुक्सान	nuksa:n	loss
gv	भगवान	bhagva:n	God
ck	अचकन	ackan	a long button-up coat
mb	अंबर	ambar	sky
md	नम्दा	namda:	a carpet
mjh	सम्झना	samjhna:	to understand
mv	हम्वार	hamva:r	smooth
nd	अंदर	andar	inside
nṭ	गंटी	ganṭi:	a bell
nḍ	ठंड़ा	thãḍa:	cold
nkh	पंखा	pãkha:	fan
nj	रंजिश	rãjiš	anger
ns	इंसाफ	insa:ph	justice
nz	मंज़िल	manzil	destination
nv	जानवर	ja:nvar	bird
sp	अस्पताल	aspata:l	hospital
sb	कस्बा	kasba:	town
st	सस्ता	sasta:	cheap
sd	हस्दी	hasdi:	jealous
sv	तस्वीर	tasvi:r	picture
št	कुश्ती	kušti:	wrestling
šm	दुश्मन	dušman	enemy
šv	रिश्वत	rišvat	bribe
lt	गल्ती	galti:	mistake
lṭ	उल्टा	ulṭa:	opposite
lk	हल्का	halka:	light in weight
lm	फिल्मी	filmi:	related to film
ls	आल्सी	a:lsi:	lethargic
lz	मुल्ज़िम	mulzim	accused
rb	गुर्बत	gurbat	poverty
rd	गर्दन	gardan	neck
rx	कारख़ाना	ka:rxa:na:	factory
rz	मर्ज़ी	marzi:	consent
rh	सरहद	sarhad	frontier
rv	दरवाज़ा	darva:za:	door
zm	आज़माना	a:zma:na:	to try
hb	रहबर	rahbar	guide
ht	मोहताज	mohta:j	dependent
hs	तहसील	tahsi:l	*tehsil* (subdivision)
hl	मोहल्ला	mohlla:	*mohalla* (dwelling ward)

yd	पायदार	pa:yda:r	strong
yv	पयवंद	payvand	grafting

Medial three consonant clusters

mjhn	समझना	samjhna:	to understand
pgr	उपग्रह	upgrah	satellite
tpr	उत्प्रोक्ष	utprokš	metaphor
tthr	पत्थरीला	patthri:la:	stony
cct	उच्चता	uccta:	height
kšp	पक्षपात	pakšpa:t	partiality
jjv	उज्जल	ujjval	bright
ndr	अन्दरूनी	andru:ni:	internal
ndhk	अंधकार	andhka:r	darkness
ndg	बंदगी	bandgi:	worship
nsk	संस्कार	sanska:r	rites
ndn	वंदना	vandna:	prayer
nyv	धन्यवाद	dhanyva:d	thanks
rtk	नर्तकी	nartki:	dancer (f)
rkht	मूर्खता	mu:rkhta:	foolishness
rmc	कर्मचारी	karmca:ri	worker
ršn	दर्शनीय	daršni:y	worth seeing
rvj	सार्वजनिक	sa:rvjanik	public
syt	सदस्यता	sadasyta:	membership
stm	अस्थमा	asthma:	breathing problem
šṭr	राष्ट्रीय	ra:šṭri:y	national

Medial four-consonant clusters

ntrt	स्वतंत्रता	svatantrta:	independence
ndrv	पंद्रहवाँ	pandhrva:	fifteenth

2.2.2.3. Word-final Consonant Clusters

Consonant clusters occur less frequently in the word-final position.

pp	गप्प	gapp	gossip
pn	स्वप्न	svapn	dream
tm	ख़त्म	xatm	finish
tn	यत्न	yatn	try

ṭṭh	लट्ठ	laṭṭh	stick
cc	उच्च	ucc	high
cch	स्वच्छ	svacch	clean
kt	रक्त	rakt	blood
mp	लम्प	lamp	lamp
nt	सन्त	sant	saint
nk	बंक	bank	bank
nkh	शंख	šankh	conch
st	मस्त	mast	carefree
št	गश्त	gašt	take a round
šṭ	कष्ट	kašṭ	trouble
rth	अर्थ	arth	meaning
rkh	मूर्ख	mu:rkh	fool

Final three-consonant clusters

ntr	मंत्र	mantr	hymn
ndr	इंद्र	indr	name of God
str	अस्त्र	astr	weapon

2.2.3. Syllable Structure

Hindi has a (C)(C)V(C)(C) syllable structure. The assignment of the medial units to syllables does not depend on morphological structure. The first consonant of the medial cluster is assigned to the preceding syllable and the remaining elements of the unit to the following syllable. In the following examples, the syllable boundary is marked with [+] sign.

नक् + शा	नक्शा	nak+ša:	nakša:	map
सुन् + दर	सुंदर	sun+dar	sundar	beautiful
किस् + मत	किस्मत	kis+mat	kismat	fate

The vowel-initial syllables are found only in the initial position of words.

आकाश	a:ka:š	sky
अमृत	amrit	nectar
इमारत	ima:rat	building
इलाज	ila:j	treatment

There are different types of syllables.

Monosyllable:		
माँ	mã:	mother
चाय	ca:y	tea
घर	ghar	house
Di-syllable:		
फ़ायदा	fa:ida:	profit
शोला	šola:	flame
कागज़	ka:gaz	paper
Tri-syllable:		
नसीयत	nasi:hat	advice
हिरासत	hira:sat	arrest
हकीकत	haki:kat	fact
Quadra-syllable:		
हिंदुस्तानी	hindusta:ni:	Indian
मुकाबला	muka:bila:	competition
इंसानियत	insa:niyat	humanity

2.3. Suprasegmental Features

Nasalization, length, stress, intonation, and juncture are suprasegmental features.

2.3.1. Nasalization

Nasalization is an important suprasegmental feature in Hindi. All the vowels can be nasalized. Nasalization is distinctive so it has phonemic status.

सास	sa:s	mother-in-law		साँस	sã:s	breath
काटा	ka:ṭa:	cut		काँटा	kã:ṭa:	thorn
पूछ	pu:ch	ask		पूँछ	pũ:ch	tail
गोद	god	lap		गोंद	gõd	gum
थी	thi:	was		थीं	thĩ:	were

2.3.2. Length

Length is phonemic in Hindi. There are three pairs of short and long vowels: /i/ and /i:/; /a/ and /a:/; /u/ and /u:/. The following minimal pairs illustrate the contrast in the length of these vowels.

मिल	mil	mix		मील	mi:l	mile
दस	das	ten		दास	da:s	servant
उन	un	they (obl)		ऊन	u:n	wool

2.3.3. Stress

Stress is not a distinctive feature of Hindi; it is not in phonemic contrast. Hindi is a syllable-timed language, sometimes individual words are stressed for emphasis only. Usually, the syllable preceding the consonant cluster gets stress.

बुद्धि	buddhi	intelligence
सत्य	saty	truth

The initial cluster of the word also gets stress.

प्रेम	prem	love
स्पष्टता	spašṭta:	clarity

In di-syllabic words where both syllables have long or short vowels, the first syllable is stressed.

अक्सर	aksar	always
अंदर	andar	inside
आकार	a:ka:r	figure
आसमान	a:sma:n	sky

In di-syllable words wherein the first syllable contains low front or back vowels, the first syllable is stressed.

फ़ौजी	fɔji:	soldier
कैदी	kɛdi:	prisoner

The second syllable is stressed when the first syllable has a short vowel and the second has a long vowel.

नसीब	nasi:b	fate
किताब	kita:b	book

In tri-syllable words, the first syllable is stressed if the first syllable has a long vowel, the second has a short vowel, and the third has a long vowel.

बेहया	behaya:	shameless
बेवकूफ़	bevaku:ph	stupid

The last syllable is stressed if the first syllable has a short vowel and the last two have long vowels.

हिंदुस्तान	hindusta:n	India
बनजारा	banja:ra:	nomad

In words of more than three syllables, the stress is always on the penultimate syllable.

समझदारी	samajhda:ri:	understanding

2.3.4. Intonation

There are four major types of intonational patterns: (1) high-fall, (2) high-rise, (3) rise-and-fall, (4) mid-level. Intonations have syntactic rather than emotional content. Statements have a high-fall intonation pattern. Intonation peaks are generally positioned on the penultimate word or on the negative particle if there is one.

1. वह किताब पढ़ रहा है।
   vah kita:b paṛh raha: hɛ.
   he book read-pr is
   He is reading a book.

2. कागज़ अलमारी में नहीं हैं।
   ka:gaz alma:ri: mẽ nahĩ: hɛ̃
   papers almirah in neg are
   The papers are not in the almirah.

Yes-no questions and tag questions have a high-rise intonation.

3. क्या वह कल आया?
kya: vah kal a:ya:?
Q he yesterday came-Q
Did he come yesterday?

Information questions have a rise-and-fall intonation. The rise in intonation is registered on the question word and the fall is attained gradually.

4. आप कब बाज़ार गए?
a:p kab ba:za:r gaye?
you when market went
When did you go to the market?

5. मोहन किससे मिला?
mohan kisse mila:?
Mohan who-dat met-3s
Who did Mohan meet?

Commands generally follow the mid-level intonational pattern.

6. दरवाज़ा बंद करो।
darva:za: band karo.
door close do-imp
Close the door.

Contrastive and Emphatic Intonation

The contrastive and emphatic intonations are the same as they employ more than the average stress on the constituents of a sentence. The element to be contrasted carries a slightly higher stress than the emphasized segment. For example, any of the elements can be emphasized in the following sentence depending on the degree of emphasis. The emphasis is indicated by bolding different elements.

7a. **आप** दिल्ली जाइए।
a:p *dilli: ja:ie.*
you Delhi go-fu-2p
You go to Delhi.

7b. आप **दिल्ली** जाइए।
a:p ***dilli:*** *ja:ie.*
You go to Delhi.

7c. आप दिल्ली **जाइए**।
a:p dilli: ***ja:ie.***
You go to Delhi.

2.3.5. Juncture

Juncture is functional in Hindi. Internal juncture may be considered as phonemic juncture. Mostly, the medial clusters have juncture because those sequences of sounds do not occur in the same syllable.

मुश्किल	muškil	difficult
अनजान	anja:n	ignorant
कुर्ता	kurta:	shirt
बदमाश	badma:š	rogue

The following minimal pairs indicate the phonemic status of internal juncture:

खाना	kha:na:	food
खा + ना	kha: + na:	to eat
कलाई	kala:i:	wrist
कल + आई	kal + a:i:	came yesterday
सिर्का	sirka:	vinegar
सिर + का	sir + ka:	of the head

There are two types of juncture: (i) internal juncture and (ii) external juncture. The internal juncture (+) reduces words into phrases or compound words in the sentences.

8a. ज़िंदगी + मौत का क्या भरोसा
zindagi: + mɔt ka: kya: bharosa:
life death-gen what guarantee
There is no guarantee of life or death.

External juncture (#) occurs between each word and the words joined by this juncture retain their separate identity.

8b. ज़िंदगी # मौत का क्या भरोसा
zindagi: # mɔt ka: kya: bharosa:
There is no guarantee of life or death.

2.4. Morphophonemics

Various morphological processes can be marked as loss, addition, and replacement of phonemes.

2.4.1. Loss of Phoneme

The vowel /a/ in the last syllable is dropped when the suffix /-õ/ is added to the word.

औरत	ɔrat	woman
औरतों	ɔratõ	women (obl)
पागल	pa:gal	mad
पागलों	pa:glõ	mad persons (obl)

The consonant न /n/ of a numeral system is lost before any numeral suffix beginning with /त t-, र r-, ह h-/ is added.

तीन ti:n three	+	रह rah ten marker	=	तेरह terah thirteen

2.4.2. Addition of Phoneme

The vowel ए /-e/ is added to the root before the suffixes are added to it.

तिर tir	+	पन pan	=	तिरेपन tirepan fifty-three
तिर tir	+	सठ saṭh	=	तिरेसठ tiresaṭh sixty-three

When different suffixes are added to the root, the an addition of a consonant takes place.

ब ba	+	तीस ti:s	=	बतीस batti:s thirty-two
शक šak	+	ई i:	=	शकी šaki: one who doubts

2.4.3. Alternations

The long vowel ओ /o/ of the verb root changes to a short vowel उ /u/ when the suffix -ला */-la:/* is added to the verb roots.

खोल khol open	+	ला la:	=	खुला khula: opened
रो ro weep	+	ला la:	=	रुला rula: to make weep?

The long vowel ई */i:/* of the verb root becomes the short इ */i/* when the suffix अ *-a:* is added to the verb root.

पी pi: drink	+	ला la:	=	पिल pila: make drink
सीख si:kh learn	+	आ a:	=	सिखा sikha: teach

When the suffixes ला */-la:/* or आ */-a:/* are attached to the monosyllabic verbal stems their vowels ए /e/ and आ /a:/ change into इ /i/.

दे de give	+	ला la:	=	दिला dila: cause to give
खा kha: eat	+	ला la:	=	खिला khila: cause to eat
देख dekh see	+	आ a:	=	दिखा dikha: cause to see

In certain morphophonemic changes, some consonants are replaced by others.

तीन ti:n three	+	पन pan	=	तिरेपन trepan fifty-three
इक ik one	+	चालीस ca:li:s	=	इकतालीस ikta:li:s forty-one

Morphophonemic changes at junctural points or sandhi are very common in Hindi. They usually takes place in compound words.

सूर्य su:rya sun	+	आदि a:di etc.	=	सूर्यादि su:rya:di sun and the like.
चंद्र candr moon	+	उदय uday rise	=	चंद्रोदय candroday moonrise

3. Morphology

This chapter deals with the morphological structure of different word classes, describing their inflectional and derivational forms. Word classes described include nouns, pronouns, adjectives, verbs, adverbs, particles, connectives, and interjections.

3.1. Nouns

3.1.1. Noun Inflection

Nouns in Hindi are inflected for gender, number, and case. There are three declensions of nouns; Declension I includes आ */a:/* ending masculine nouns; Declension II includes all other masculine nouns; and Declension III includes all feminine nouns.

3.1.1.1. Gender

There are two genders in Hindi: masculine and feminine. Besides the natural gender of animate nouns, every inanimate noun is assigned a gender. Though the gender of a large number of inanimate nouns can be predicted by their endings, there are no hard and fast rules for assigning the genders. Masculine forms are traditionally taken as basic. The gender formation involves (a) suffixation, (b) phonological changes, and (c) suppletion. We can make some general observations as follows.

(i) Most of the आ /a:/ ending masculine nouns have their feminine forms ending in ई /i:/.

लड़का	laṛka:	boy	लड़की	laṛki:	girl
चाचा	ca:ca:	uncle	चाची	ca:ci:	aunt
बिल्ला	billa:	he cat	बिल्ली	billi:	she cat
बच्चा	bacca:	child (m)	बच्ची	bacci:	child (f)
दादा	da:da:	father's father	दादी	da:di:	father's mother
नाना	na:na:	mother's father	नानी	na:ni:	mother's mother
साला	sa:la:	wife's brother	साली	sa:li:	wife's sister
पगला	pagla:	a mad man	पगली	pagli:	a mad woman

In the above examples, the final -आ /*-a:*/ in the masculine nouns is replaced by - ई /*-i:*/ in their feminine forms.

(ii) Most of the - ई /*-i:*/ ending animate masculine nouns have their feminine forms ending in -अन /*-an*/.

Masculine			Feminine		
धोबी	dhobi:	washerman	धोबन	dhoban	washerwoman
तेली	teli:	oilman	तेलन	telan	oilwoman
माली	ma:li:	gardener (m)	मालन	ma:lan	gardener (f)
जोगी	jogi:	saint (m)	जोगन	jogan	saint (f)

(iii) Some nouns ending in - आ /*-a:*/ form their feminine (diminutive) by
replacing -आ /*-a:*/ with - इया /*-iya:*/.

डबा	ḍaba:	box	डिबिया	ḍibiya:	a small box

(iv) Most of the -आ /*-a:*/ ending inanimate nouns are masculine and - ई /*-i:*/ ending inanimate nouns are feminine.

Masculine			Feminine		
पंखा	pankha:	fan	पंखी	pankhi:	a small fan
सोटा	soṭa:	a big stick	सोटी	soṭi:	a small stick
कटोरा	kaṭora:	a bowl	कटोरी	kaṭori:	a small bowl
कोठा	koṭha:	a room	कोठरी	koṭhri:	a small room

In the above examples, the final -आ /a:/ in the masculine forms is replaced by the suffix -ई /i:/.

(v) The suffix -नी /-ni:/ is added to the masculine nouns to form the feminine.

Masculine			Feminine		
शेर	šer	lion	शेरनी	šerni:	lioness
मोर	mor	peacock	मोरनी	morni:	peahen
मास्टर	ma:sṭar	teacher (m)	मास्टरनी	ma:sṭarni:	teacher (f)
ऊँट	ũ:ṭ	camel	ऊँटनी	ũ:ṭni:	she-camel
नौकर	nɔkar	servant (m)	नौकरानी	nɔkra:ni:	servant (f)

(vi) The suffix -ई */-i:/* is added to the masculine nouns to form the feminine.

Masculine			Feminine		
दास	da:s	servant	दासी	da:si:	maid
पुत्र	putr	son	पुत्री	putri:	daughter
सुंदर	sundar	beautiful	सुंदरी	sundri:	beautiful woman

3.1.1.2. Number

There are two numbers: singular and plural.

(i) The -आ */-a:/* ending masculine nouns (including pronouns and adjectives), with a few exceptions change into -ए */-e/* ending forms in the plural.

Singular			Plural		
लड़का	laṛka:	boy	लड़के	laṛke	boys
घोड़ा	gho:ṛa:	horse	घोड़े	ghoṛe	horses
मेरा	mera:	my	मेरे	mere	my
काला	ka:la:	black	काले	ka:le	black

The following -आ /-a:/ ending masculine nouns do not change in their plural form.

पिता	pita:	father/fathers
नेता	neta:	leader/leaders
दरिया	dariya:	river/rivers

(ii) All other consonant and/or other vowel-ending nouns do not change in their plural forms.

मोर	mor	peacock(s)
कोट	koṭ	coat(s)
ग्राम	gra:m	village(s)
हाथी	ha:thi:	elephant(s)
रुमाल	ruma:l	handkerchief/handkerchiefs
धोबी	dhobi:	laundry man/ laundry men

(iii) The feminine plurals are formed by adding the suffix -एं /ẽ/ to the consonant-ending singular forms.

किताब	kita:b	book	किताबें	kita:bẽ	books
मेज़	mez	table	मेज़ें	mezẽ	tables
गाय	ga:y	cow	गायें	ga:yẽ	cows

(iv) The plural suffix -इयाँ -iyã: is added to the -ई -i: ending feminine nouns.

लड़की	laṛki:	girl	+ इयाँ -iyã:	=	लड़कियाँ	laṛkiyã:	girls
कुर्सी	kursi:	chair	+ इयाँ -iyã:	=	कुर्सियाँ	kursiyã:	chairs
कहानी	kaha:ni:	story	+ इयाँ -iyã:	=	कहानियाँ	kaha:niyã:	stories

Notice that when the suffix is added the final vowel of the stem is deleted.

3.1.1.3. Case

The syntactic and semantic functions of noun phrases are expressed by case-suffixes, postpositions and derivational processes. There are two cases: direct and oblique. Case-suffixes and postpositions are used to express syntactic and semantic functions. Case suffixes are defined as bound suffixes, which do not occur independently as words and are added only to the noun phrases. Case suffixes added to the oblique forms of nouns agreeing in number and gender.

Case	Masculine		Feminine	
	Sg	Pl	Sg	Pl
Direct	Ø	Ø	Ø	Ø
Oblique	-ए -e	**-ओं** -õ	**-इ** -i	**-ओं** -õ
Vocative	-ए -e	-ओ -o	-इ **-i**	-ओ -o

The vocative address forms may be preceded by the vocative morphemes ओ *o/* हे *he/* अरे *are*. The role of case-suffixes and postpositions is explained in the paradigms of लड़का *laṛka:* 'boy' and लड़की *laṛki:* 'girl' given below.

Case	Noun + Marker			
	Masculine		Feminine	
	Sg	Pl	Sg	Pl
Direct	लड़का	लड़के	लड़की	लड़कियाँ
	laṛka:	laṛke	laṛki:	laṛkiyã:
Oblique	लड़के	लड़कों	लड़की	लड़कियों
	laṛke	laṛkõ	laṛki:	laṛkiyõ

Vocative	ओ o/ हे he/ अरे are लड़के	laṛke	Oh boy
	ओ o/ हे he/ अरे are लड़को	laṛko	Oh boys
	ए e/ हे he/ अरे are लड़की	laṛki:	Oh girl
	ए e/ हे he/ अरे are लड़कियो	laṛkiyo	Oh girls

Case-suffixes followed by postpositions indicate various relationships between the noun phrases and the verb phrases.

3.1.2. Postpositions

Postpositions have specific semantic functions. They express the semantic dimensions of a noun such as benefaction, manner, or location. The main postpositions are: ने *ne* 'ergative marker'; को *ko* 'to'; के लिए *ke liye* 'for'; पर *par* 'on'; में *mẽ* 'in'; से *se* 'from'; से *se* 'with'; का /के /की *ka/ke/ki:* 'of'.' The postpositions are written as separate words with nouns (अमित ने *amit ne*, उमा को *uma: ko*), but they are tagged to pronouns (मैंने *mɛ̃ne* उसको *usko,* किसका *kiska:*).

3.1.2.1. The Postposition ने *ne*

The postposition ने *ne* is used with subject noun phrases usually with the transitive verbs in the past tense. The verb agrees with the object.

1. मैंने पत्र लिखा।
mɛ̃ne patr likha:
I-erg letter wrote
I wrote a letter.

1a. *मैंने पत्र लिखा।
**mɛ̃ patr likha:*

2. उसने कपड़े धोए।
usne kapṛe dhoye
he-erg clothes washed
He washed clothes.

2a. वह कपड़े धोया।
**vah kapṛe dhoya:*

Whenever the objects are followed by the dative postposition को *ko*, the verb remains in masculine singular form.

3. मोहन ने बहिन /बहनों को बुलाया।
mohan ne bahin/bahnõ ko bula:ya:
Mohan-erg sister/sisters-dat called
Mohan called (his) sister/sisters.

4. हमने लड़के / लड़कों / लड़की /लड़कियों को पढ़ाया।
hamne laṛke/laṛkõ/laṛki:/ laṛkiyõ ko paṛha:ya:
we-erg boy/boys/girl/girls-dat taught
We taught the boy/boys/girl/girls.

The ने *ne* postposition is not used with the subjects of the following transitive verbs: लाना *la:na:* 'to bring,' खेलना *khelna:* 'to play,' बोलना *bolna:* 'to speak,' भूलना *bhu:lna:* 'to forget,' and बकना *bakna:* 'to chatter.'

5. उमा कमीज़ लाई।
uma: kami:z la:i:
Uma-nom shirt brought
Uma brought a shirt.

5a. *उमा ने कमीज़ लाई।
**uma: ne kami:z la:i:*

6. लड़का बोला।
laṛka: bola:
boy said
The boy said.

6a. *लड़के ने बोला।
**laṛke ne bola:*

7. वह रास्ता भूला।
voh ra:sta: bhu:la:
he way forgot
He forgot/lost the way.

7a. *उसने रास्ता भूला।
**usne ra:sta: bhu:la:*

8. वह काफी देर बका।
vah ka:phi: de:r baka:
he-nom lot duration chattered
He chattered for a long time.

8a. *उसने काफी देर बका।
**usne ka:phi de:r baka:*

The postposition ने *ne* is used with the following intransitive verbs: छींकना *chĩ:kna:* 'to sneeze'; खाँसना *khã:sna:* 'to cough'; नहाना *naha:na:* 'to take a bath'; and थूकना *thu:kna:* 'to spit'.

9. उसने घर से निकलते समय छींका।
usne ghar se nikalte samay chĩ:ka:
he-erg house-abl from set out-ptc time sneezed
He sneezed as he was leaving the house.

10. बीमार व्यक्ति (ने) ज़ोर से खाँसा।
bi:ma:r vyakti (ne) zo:r se khã:sa:
ill person-erg loudly coughed
The ill person coughed loudly.

11. मैंने गरम पानी से नहाया।
mɛ̃ne garm pa:ni: se naha:ya:
I-erg hot water with bathed
I took a bath in hot water.

12. तुमने सड़क पर क्यों थूका?
tumne saṛak par kyõ thu:ka:?
you-erg road on why spit-past
Why did you spit on the road?

It is not used in constructions using the modal verbs लगना *lagna:*, चुकना *cukna:*, and सकना *sakna::*

13. वह सेब खाने लगा।
vah seb kha:ne laga:
he apple eat-inf-obl started
He started eating apples.

13a. *उसने सेब खाने लगा।
**usne seb kha:ne laga:*

14. मैं यह काम कर चुका।
mɛ̃ yah ka:m kar cuka:
I this work do completed
I finished this work.

14a. *मैंने यह काम कर चुका।
**mɛ̃ne yah ka:m kar cuka:*

15. वह चिट्ठी लिख सका।
vah ciṭṭhi: likh saka:
he letter write could
He could write a letter.

15a. *उसने चिट्ठी लिख सका।
**usne ciṭṭhi: likh saka:*

In the case of a few transitive verbs like समझना *samjhna:* 'to understand' and खेलना *khelna:* 'to play,' the use of this postposition is optional.

16. मैंने उसकी बात समझी।
mɛ̃ne uski: ba:t samjhi:
I-erg his/her matter understood
I understood what he said.

16a. मैं उसकी बात समझा।
mɛ̃ uski: ba:t samjha.:
I his/her matter understood
I understood what he said.

17. मैं समझा वह बीमार है।
mɛ̃ samjha: voh bi:ma:r hɛ.
I understood he sick is
I thought he was sick.

17a. मैंने समझा वह बीमार है।
mɛ̃ne samjha: voh bi:ma:r hɛ.

18. वह हाकी खेला।
vah ha:ki: khe:la:.
he hockey played
He played hockey.

18a. उसने हाकी खेली।
usne haki: khe:li:.
he-erg hockey played
He played hockey.

The use of the postposition ने *ne* is invariably found in compound verb constructions with the verb समझना *samjhna:* 'to understand' as the main verb.

19. मैंने बात समझ ली।
mɛ̃ne ba:t samajh li:
I-erg matter understand took
I understood the matter.

19a. *मैं बात समझ ली।
**mɛ̃ ba:t samajh li:*

3.1.2.2. The Postposition को *ko*

The postposition को *ko* is used in different types of sentences and is placed after nouns. It is optional when used with object nouns which are followed by conjunct verbs with an adjective or adverb and the verb.

1. मेज़ (को) साफ करो।
mez (ko) sa:f karo
table (dat) clean do-imp
Clean the table.

2. काम (को) खत्म करो।
ka:m (ko) xatm karo
work (dat) finish do-imp
Finish the work.

3. कार (को) तेज़ करो।
ka:r (ko) tez karo.
car (dat) fast do-imp
Speed up the car.

4. कागज़ (को) दूर रखो।
ka:gaz (ko) du:r rakho.
paper (dat) away do-imp
Keep the paper away.

5. संदूक (को) इधर/ उधर/ ऊपर/ नीचे रखो।
sandu:k (ko) idhar/udhar/upar/ni:ce rakho
box (dat) here/there/up/down do-imp
Keep the box here/there/up/down.

In the object +को *ko*+verb construction, the verb may be transitive or causative.

6. मैंने पत्र (को) पढ़ा।
mɛ̃ne patr (ko) paṛha:
I-erg letter (dat) read
I read the letter.

7. उसने किताब को बेचा।
usne kita:b ko beca:
he-erg book-dat sold
He sold the book.

7a. उसने किताब बेची।
usne kita:b beci:
He sold the book.

8. उसने बच्चे को सुलाया।
usne bacce ko sula:ya:
he-erg child-dat sleep-caus
He made the child sleep.

8a. उसने बच्चा सुलाया।
usne bacca: sula:ya:

In the subject + को *ko* + complement + verb constructions, the verbs express the state of mind, physical experience, involuntarily actions, feelings, obligations, and emotions (9-12).

9. सुनीता को बुखार है।
suni:ta ko bhukha:r hɛ
Sunita-dat fever is
Sunita has fever.

10. अमर को दुख हुआ।
amar ko dukh hua:
Amar-dat pain felt
Amar felt pain.

11. मोहन को खाँसी आई।
mohan ko hãsĩ: a:i:
Mohan-dat laugh came
Mohan laughed.

12. बच्चे को डर लगा।
bacce ko ḍar laga:
child-dat fear struck
The child was afraid.

The postposition को *ko* is used in the secondary object + को *ko* + main object + verb constructions.

13. मैं अपने भाई को पत्र लिख रहा हूं।
mɛ̃ apne bha:i: ko patr likh raha: hũ:
I self-obl brother-dat letter write-prog am
I am writing a letter to my brother.

Pronouns + को *ko* have alternate forms as follows:

वह	*vah*	+	को *ko*	=	उसको/ उसे *usko/use*
यह	*yah*	+	को *ko*	=	इसको/ इसे *isko/ise*
इन	*in*	+	को *ko*	=	इनको/ इन्हें *inko/inhẽ*
उन	*un*	+	को *ko*	=	उनको/ उन्हें *unko/unhẽ*

In the उसे *use*/इसे *ise*/इन्हें *inhẽ*/उन्हें *unhẽ* forms, there is an inherent को *ko*. It is possible to use these forms along with nouns + को *ko.*

14. उसे/उन्हें मोहन को दे दो।
use/unhẽ mohan ko de do.
that/those-dat Mohan-dat give-imp
Give that/those to Mohan.

15. इसे ले जाओ।
ise le ja:o.
this-dat take-imp
Take this.

The postposition को *ko* is not normally used with time adverbials.

16. वह आज आएगा।
vah a:j a:ega:.
he today come-fut
He will come today.

16a. *वह आज को आएगा।
**vah a:j ko a:ega:*

17. वह कल जाएगा।
vah kal ja:ega:.
he tomorrow go-fut
He will go tomorrow.

17a. *वह कल को जाएगा।
**vah kal ko ja:ega:.*

But in certain contexts, को *ko* can be used with कल *kal,* not to indicate 'tomorrow,' but to denote an indefinite time in the future.

18. कौन जाने कल को क्या होगा।
kɔn ja:ne kal ko kya: hoga:.
who know-obl tomorrow-obl what happen-fut
Who knows what will happen tomorrow?

19. अगर कल को उन्हें कुछ हो गया तो...
agar kal ko unhẽ kuch ho gaya: to...
if tomorrow-obl he-obl something happenened then ...
If anything happens to him tomorrow then ...

The postposition को *ko* can be used optionally with time adverbs, like रात *ra:t* 'night,' शाम *ša:m* 'evening,'and दुपहर *dupahar* 'afternoon.'

20. आज शाम/शाम को आप मेरे घर आइए।
a:j ša:m/ša:m ko a:p mere ghar a:iye.
today evening/-dat you mine house come-imp.pol
Please come to my house today in the evening.

The postposition को *ko* is not used with place adverbs like यहाँ *yahã:* 'here'; वहाँ *vahã:* 'there'; ऊपर *upar* 'above'; नीचे *ni:ce* 'under'; आगे *a:ge* 'in front'; and पीछे *pi:che* 'behind.'

21. मैं यहाँ आऊँगा।
mɛ̃ yahã: a:ũ:ga:
I here come-fut
I will come here.

21a. *मैं यहाँ को आऊँगा।
**mɛ̃ yahã: ko a:ũ:ga:*

22. वे ऊपर पहुँचे।
ve u:par pahũce
they top reached
They reached up (the stairs).

22a. *वे ऊपर को पहुँचे।
*ve u:par ko pahũce

The postposition को *ko* is added to the subject noun/pronoun if it is followed by an object and the verb चाहिए *ca:hiye* 'need/want' or the modal 'should' (i.e., subject + को *ko* + object + चाहिए *ca:hiya*).

23. उसको यह अखबार चाहिए।
usko yeh akhba:r ca:hiye
he-obl this newspaper wants
He wants this newspaper.

24. उसको यह काम करना चाहिए।
usko yah ka:m karna: ca:hiye
he-obl this work do-inf should
He should do this work.

The verbal noun + को *ko* (as complementizer) construction shows purpose.

25. उसे आने को कहो।
use a:ne ko kaho.
he-dat come-inf-obl tell-imp
Tell him to come.

26. उठने को दिल करता है।
uṭhne ko dil karta: hɛ
rise-inf-obl pp heart want-ptc be
One would like to get up.

27. हम दफ़्तर जाने को तैयार हैं।
ham daftar ja:ne ko tɛya:r hɛ̃.
we office go-inf-obl pp ready are
We are ready to go to the office.

28. आपके पास पीने को क्या है?
a:pke pa:s pi:ne ko kya: hɛ?
you-gen-obl near drink-inf-obl pp what is
What do you have to drink?

The postposition को *ko* can be used for emphasis as well.

29. जाने को क्या, मैं कभी भी जा सकता हूँ।
ja:ne ko kya:, mɛ̃ kabhi: bhi: ja: sakta: hũ:.
go-inf-obl dat what, I anytime go can be
What is there, I can go anytime.

को *ko* can also be used to denote an object of a verb requiring a predicate.

30. अमित गरीबी को पाप समझता है।
amit gari:bi: ko pa:p samajhta: hɛ.

Amit poverty sin consider-ptc is
Amit considers poverty a sin.

31. कपड़ों को गंदा मत करो।
kapṛõ: ko ganda: mat karo.
clothes dirty neg do-imp
Don't dirty your clothes.

It is used to denote time. When it is used with time adverbials it denotes specificity like दोपहर को *dopahar ko* or मंगलवार को *maŋalva:r ko* but not जनवरी को *janva:ri ko* or आज को *a:j ko*, कल को *kal ko*.

32. वह दोपहर को आएगा।
vah dopahar ko a:yega:.
he noon come-fut
He will come at noon.

33. मैं मंगलवार को दिल्ली जाऊँगा।
mɛ̃ maŋalva:r ko dilli: ja:ũ:ga:.
I Tuesday Delhi go-fut
I'll go to Delhi on Tuesday.

3.1.2.3. The Postposition से *se*

The postposition से *se* is used to indicate association or mutual dealing.

1. मैं उससे बात करता हूँ।
mɛ̃ us-se ba:t kar-ta: hũ:.
I he-obl-with talk do-ptc am
I talk with him.

2. वह पड़ोसी से लड़ा।
vah paṛosi: se laṛa:.
he neighbor with quarreled
He quarreled with his neighbor.

3. नेहरू बच्चों से प्यार करते थे।
nehru: baccõ se pya:r karte the.
Nehru children-obl with love do-ptc was
Nehru used to love children.

4. मुझसे झूठ न बोलो।
mujh-se jhu:ṭh na bolo.
me-obl-with lie neg say-imp
Don't lie to me.

5. उससे मज़ाक न करो।
usse maza:k na karo.
he-obl-post joke don't do-imp
Don't joke with him.

6. वह पड़ोसी से नफरत करता है।
vah paṛosi: se nafrat karta: hɛ.
he neighbor with hate do-ptc is
He hates his neighbor.

7. मैं आपसे प्रार्थना करता हूँ।
mɛ̃ a:pse pra:rthna: karta: hũ:.
I you-post request do-ptc am
I request you.

8. सरकार से माँग की जाती है।
sarka:r se mã:g ki: ja:ti: hɛ.
government with request do aux is
The government is requested.

9. मैं ऐसे लोगों से दूर रहना पसंद करता हूँ।
mɛ̃ ɛse logũ: se du:r rahna: pasand karta: hũ:.
I this type people from far remain-inf like do-ptc am
I like to be away from this kind of people.

It is used to indicate a sense of separation or keeping away from something.

10. दिल से क्रोध निकालो।
dil se krodh nika:lo
heart from anger remove-imp
Remove anger from your mind.

11. वह दफ़्तर से निकला।
vah daftar se nikla:.

he office from came out
He set out from the office.

It represents cause, reason and origin.

12. वह बुख़ार से कमज़ोर हुआ।
vah bukha:r se kamzor hua:.
he fever from weak became
He became weak by fever.

13. बीज से पौधा निकलता है।
bi:j se pɔdha: nikalta: hɛ.
seed from plant comes out
The plant grows out of a seed.

14. बात से बात निकलती है।
ba:t se ba:t nikalti: hɛ.
talk from talk comes out
One thing comes out of the other.

15. लकड़ी से मेज़ें बनती हैं।
lakṛi: se mezẽ banti: hɛ̃.
wood from tables make-ptc are
The tables are made of wood.

16. मिट्टी से बर्तन बनते हैं।
miṭṭi: se bartan bante hɛ̃.
clay from pots make-ptc are
Pots are made of clay.

It indicates the starting point, place, time, and direction.

17. मुझे दफ़्तर से तार मिला ।
mujhe daftar se ta:r mila:.
I-obl office from telegram got
I got a telegram from the office.

18. यहाँ से शहर बहुत दूर है।
yahã: se šahar bahut du:r hɛ.
here from city very far is
The city is far away from here.

19. कल से आज अच्छी धूप है।
kal se a:j acchi: dhu:p hɛ.
yesterday from today good sunshine is
It is more sunny today than yesterday.

It indicates time.

20. वह देर से गया।
vah der se gaya.:
he late went
He went late.

It is used to indicate the difference or comparison in quality and quantity.

21. वहाँ से यहाँ अधिक गरमी पड़ती है।
vahã: se yahã: adhik garmi: paṛti: hɛ.
there from here more heat fall-ptc is
This place is hotter than that place.

22. वह दो साल से बीमार है।
vah do sa:l se bi:ma:r hɛ.
he two year from sick is
He has been sick for the last two years.

23. पीछे से आवज़ आई।
pi:che se a:va:z a:yi:.
behind from call came
Someone called from behind.

It is used to indicate means, instrument, or agency.

24. चाकू से सब्ज़ी काटो।
ca:ku: se sabzi: ka:ṭo.
knife with vegetable cut-imp
Cut vegetables with the knife.

25. कलम से पत्र लिखो।
kalam se patr likho.
pen with letter write-imp
Write a letter with the pen.

26. हम हाथ से खाना खाते हैं।
ham ha:th se kha:na: khate hɛ̃.
we hand with food eat-ptc are
We eat our meals with our hands.

27. पौधों को पानी से धो लो।
pɔdhõ: ko pa:ni: se dho lo.
plants-obl to water with wash-imp
Wash the plants with water.

28. वह बारिश से भीग गया।
vah ba:riš se bhi:g gaya:
he rain with wet became
He was drenched in the rain.

29. उसने अक्ल से काम किया।
usne akl se ka:m kiya:
he-erg wit with work did
He worked with wit.

It indicates manner.

30. मेरी बात ध्यान से सुनो।
meri: ba:t dhya:n se suno.
my talk attention with listen-imp
Listen to what I say with attention.

31. वह तेज़ी से आया।
vah tezi: se a:ya:.
he fast came
He came fast.

32. हम कठिनाई से स्टेशन पहुँचे।
ham kaṭhina:yi: se sṭešan pahũce.
we difficulty with station reached
We reached the station with difficulty.

3.1.2.4. The Postposition में *mẽ*

The postposition में *mẽ* is used to denote location or presence of something in or within; duration; price; comparison with reference to more than two; or difference.

Location

1. मेरा दफ़्तर दिल्ली में है।
   mera: daftar dilli: mẽ hɛ.
   my office Delhi in is
   My office is in Delhi.

2. मेरा बेटा कालेज में पढ़ता है।
   mera: beṭa: ka:lej mẽ paṛhta: hɛ.
   my son college in study-ptc is
   My son studies in college.

3. इस किताब में तीन सौ पृष्ट हैं।
   is kita:b mẽ ti:n sɔ prašṭh hɛ̃.
   this book in three hundred pages are
   There are three hundred pages in this book.

Duration

4. यह लेख मैंने चार दिन में लिखा।
   yah lekh mɛ̃ne ca:r din mẽ likha:.
   this article I-erg four days in wrote
   I wrote this article in four days.

5. यह इमारत दो साल में बनी।
   yeh ima:rat do sa:l mẽ bani:.
   this building two years in constructed
   This building was constructed in two years.

Price

6. यह मेज़ दो हज़ार रुपयों में मिला।
   yah mez do haza:r rupyõ mẽ mila:.
   this table two thousand rupees-obl in obtained
   This table cost two thousand rupees.

7. मैंने यह कमीज़ तीन सौ रुपयों में ली।
   mɛ̃ne yah kami:z ti:n sɔ rupyõ mẽ li:.

I-erg this shirt three hundred rupees in got
I got this shirt for three hundred rupees.

Comparison

8. इन लड़कों में अमित सबसे चुस्त है।
in laṛkõ mẽ amit sa:bse cust hɛ.
these boys-obl in Amit all from active
Amit is the most active out of all these boys.

3.1.2.5. The Postposition पर *par*

The postposition पर *par* is used to denote location or position, point of time of an action, sequence of actions, cause or reason, and the object of verbs.

Location

1. कागज़ मेज़ पर है।
ka:gaz mez par hɛ.
paper table on is
The paper is on table.

2. मेरे कपड़े छत पर हैं।
mere kapṛe chat par hɛ̃.
my clothes roof on are
My clothes are on the roof.

3. उसका दफ़्तर यहाँ से कुछ दूरी पर है।
uska: daftar yahã: se kuch du:ri: par hɛ.
his office here from some distance at is
His office is some distance from here.

Point of time

4. वह समय पर नहीं पहुँचा।
vah samay par nahĩ: pahũca:.
he time at not reached
He didn't arrive in time.

5. बस चार बजकर दस मिनट पर आएगी।
bas ca:r bajkar das minaṭ par a:yegi:
bus four stuck-cp ten minutes at come-fut-f
The bus will arrive at ten minutes past four.

Sequence of actions

6. वहाँ पहुँचने पर हमने देखा कि कोई नहीं आया।
vahã: pahũcne par hamne dekha: ki koi: nahĩ: a:ya:.
there reach-inf-obl on we-erg saw that no one neg came
On reaching there, we found that no one had come.

7. नेता के आने पर सबने तालियाँ बजाईं।
neta: ke a:ne par sabne ta:liyã: baja:ĩ:.
leader-gen come-inf-obl on all-erg clapped hands
Upon the arrival of the leader, all clapped their hands.

Cause or reason

8. धोखा देने पर उसे सज़ा हुई।
dhokha: dene par use saza: hui:.
deceive give-inf-obl on he-obl punishment given
He was punished for deceiving (someone).

9.झूठ बोलने पर माँ ने बच्चे को डाँटा।
jhu:ṭh bolne par mã:ne bacce ko ḍã:ṭa:.
lie tell-inf-obl on mother-erg child-dat scolded
The mother scolded the child for telling a lie.

Object of verbs

10. गरीबों पर दया करो।
gari:bõ par daya: karo.
poor-obl on mercy do-imp
Be kind to the poor.

11. वह किसी पर क्रोध नहीं करता।
vah kisi: par krodh nahĩ: karta:.
he someone on anger neg do-pr is
He doesn't get angry at anyone.

12. मुझपर विश्वास करो।
mujhpar viśva:s karo.
me on faith do-imp
Have faith in me.

3.1.2.6. The Postposition का *ka*

The postposition का *ka:* is used to denote the relationship between a noun or pronoun and another noun that follows it. It is used to denote possession and relationship, material or composition, worth and measure, source, origin, cause, subject or object of an act, part of a whole, purpose or characteristics or trait. The form of this postposition agrees with the gender and number of the noun as follows.

Masculine				Feminine			
Sg		Pl		Sg		Pl	
का	*ka:*	के	*ke*	की	*ki*	की	*ki*

Possession and relationship

1. अमित का भाई आज आएगा।
   amit ka: bha:i: a:j a:yega:.
   Amit of brother today come-fut
   Amit's brother will come today.

2. अमित की बहिन/ बहिनें कल आएगी/ आएँगे।
   amit ki: bahn/bahnẽ kal a:yegi:/a:yẽgi:.
   Amit of sister/sisters tomorrow come-fut-fs/-fp
   Amit's sister/sisters will come tomorrow.

3. अमित के दो दोस्त परसों आएंगे।
   amit ke do dost parsõ a:ẽge.
   Amit of two friends day after tomorrow come-fut
   Amit's two friends will come day after tomorrow.

Material or composition

4. शीशे की अलमारी टूट गई।
   ši:še ki: alma:ri: ṭu:ṭ gayi:.
   glass-obl of almirah broke went
   The glass almirah broke.

5. मिट्टी के बर्तन अच्छे हैं।
   miṭṭi: ke bartan acche hɛ̃.
   clay of pots good are
   The earthen pots are good.

Measure or worth

6. एक किलो चावल कितने का है?
ek kilo ca:val kitne ka: hɛ?
one kilogram rice how much-obl of is
What is the price of one kilogram of rice?

7. ये दस रुपए के केले हैं।
ye das rupye ke kele hɛ̃.
these ten rupees of bananas are
These bananas cost ten rupees.

Source, origin, or cause

8. प्रेमचंद के उपन्यास यहाँ नहीं हैं।
premcand ke upnya:s yahã: nahĩ: hɛ̃.
Premchand's novels here neg are
The novels of Premchand are not available here.

9. इस पेड़ के फल मीठे हैं।
is peṛ ke phal mi:ṭhe hɛ̃.
this tree gen fruit sweet are
The fruit of this tree is delicious.

Subject (doer of an act)

10. धोबी का काम अच्छा है।
dhobi: ka: ka:m accha: hɛ.
washerman gen work good is
The washerman's work is good.

Object (of an activity)

11. उसके बच्चों की शिक्षा अच्छी है।
uske baccõ ki: šikša: acchi: hɛ.
his children-obl of education good is
The education of the children is good.

12. उसके पास दवाई का खर्चा नहीं है।
uske pa:s dava:i: ka: kharca: nahĩ: hɛ.
he-gen near medicine-gen expenses neg is
He doesn't have money to pay for medicine.

Part of a whole

13. यह कागज़ का टुकड़ा है।
yeh ka:gaz ka: ṭukṛa: hɛ.
this paper gen piece is
This is a piece of paper.

14. यह इस पेड़ की शाख है।
yeh is peṛ ki: ša:kh hɛ.
it this tree-gen branch-fs is
It is the branch of this tree.

Purpose

14. पीने का पानी साफ़ है।
pi:ne ka: pa:ni: sa:f hɛ.
drink-obl gen water clean is
The drinking water is clean.

Characteristics

15. दूध की मिठास अच्छी है।
du:dh ki: miṭha:s acchi: hɛ.
milk gen sweetness good is
The milk is sweet.

3.1.2.7. Compound Postpositions

Compound postpositions are formed by combining the postpositions के *ke,* की *ki:,* and से*se* with other words in certain set phrases as follows.

(i) के *ke*

के अलावा/अतिरिक्त	*ke ala:va:/atirikt*	in addition to
के अनुसार	*ke anusa:r*	according to
के अंदर	*ke andar*	inside
के आगे	*ke a:ge*	in front of
के आरपार	*ke a:rpa:r*	through
के आसपास	*ke a:spa:s*	near about
के बाद/उपरांत/पश्चात	*ke ba:d/uprã:nt/pašca:t*	afterwards
के पार	*ke pa:r*	across
के कारण	*ke ka:raṇ*	because of
के द्वारा/हाथ	*ke dwa:ra:/ha:th*	through

के पास/निकट/नज़दीक/समीप	*ke pa:s/nikaṭ/nazdi:k/sami:p*	near
के ऊपर	*ke upar*	above
के पूर्व	*ke pu:rv*	before
के प्रति	*ke prati*	for, toward
के प्रतिकूल/विरुद्ध/विपरीत	*ke pratiku:l/virudh/vipri:t*	against
के बिना सिवा/बगैर	*ke bina:/siva:/bagɛr*	without
के बदले	*ke badle*	in place of
के बराबर/समान	*ke bara:bar/sama:n*	equal
के बाहर	*ke ba:har*	outside of
के बीच/मध्य	*ke bi:c/madhya*	inside of
के लगभग	*ke lagbhag*	about
के लिए/वास्ते	*ke liye/va:ste*	for
के योग्य/लायक	*ke yogya/la:yak*	appropriate
के समेत/साथ	*ke samet/sa:th*	along with
के सामने	*ke sa:mne*	in front of
के मुकाबले (में)	*ke muka:ble (mẽ)*	comparison to
के यहाँ/हाँ	ke yahã:/hã:	at some place

(ii) की *ki:*

की ओर/तरफ	*ki: or/taraf*	towards
की अपेक्षा	*ki: apekša:*	in comparison with
की तरह/भाँति	*ki: tarah/bhã:ti*	like
की जगह	*ki: jagah*	in place of

(iii) से *se*

से बाहर *se ba:har* out of
से पहले *se pahle* before

The compound postpositions are employed to express various semantic expressions in combination with other elements. There are, however, alternate ways of expression possible where postpositions are not used. Examples of the usage of various semantic expressions are given below.

Cause is expressed either by the (i) postposition से *se*; or by the (ii) compound forms के कारण *ke ka:raṇ* 'for the reason of,' and रकी ओर *ki: or* 'side.'

1. बाढ़ से मकान गिर गया।
ba:ṛh se maka:n gir gaya:.
flood with house fell
The house fell down because of the flood.

2. उसके कारण मुझे नुक्सान हुआ।
uske ka:raṇ mujhe nuksa:n hua:
he-gen-obl reason I-obl loss occurred
I had to suffer loss because of him.

3. उसकी ओर से मुझे कभी सुख नहीं मिला।
uski: or se mujhe kabhi: sukh nahĩ: mila:.
he-gen-obl side I-dat ever comfort neg got
He has never provided comfort to me.

Purpose is expressed by the use of the oblique infinitive verb optionally followed by the postposition के लिए *ke liye* 'for.'

4. वह सब्ज़ी लेने (के लिए) बाज़ार गया।
vah sabzi: lene (ke liye) ba:za:r gaya:.
he vegetables bring-inf-obl for market went
He went to the market to buy vegetables.

Function is expressed by the genitive postpositional phrase - की तरह *ki: tarah* 'like.'

5. वह छाते को सोटी की तरह इस्तिमाल करता है।
vah cha:te ko soṭi: ki: tarah istima:l karta: hɛ.
he is umbrella-obl dat stick-gen like use do-pr is
He uses an umbrella like a stick.

Reference is denoted by the postpositional expression के बारे में *ke ba:re mẽ* 'about.'

6. उसने मुझे अपने बच्चों के बारे में कहा।
usne mujhe apne baccõ ke ba:re mẽ kaha:.
he-erg me self's children-dat about said
He told me about his children.

7. तुम्हे इसके बारे में कोशिश करनी चाहिए।
tumhe iske ba:re mẽ košiš karni: ca:hiye.
you-obl this-gen-obl for effort do-inf-fs should
You should make efforts in this regard.

The compound postposition के रूप/भेस में *ke ru:p/bhes mẽ* expresses the meaning 'in the form of.'

8. राजा एक भिखारी के भेस / रूप में निकला।
ra:ja: ek bhikha:ri: ke bhes/ru:p mẽ nikla:.
king one beggar-gen-obl in set out
The king went out in the disguise of a beggar.

The compound postposition में से *mẽ se* is used to express the sense of 'among/out of'.' Numerals and quantifiers occur after the noun marked में से *mẽ se.*

9. उसके विध्यार्थियों में से चार कश्मीर में हैं।
uske vidya:rthiyõ mẽ se ca:r kašmi:r mẽ hɛ̃.
he-gen-obl students-obl from four Kashmir-abl in are
Among his students, four are in Kashmir.

Value is expressed by the genitive or it can be denoted by the expressions की कीमत *ki: ki:mat,* or का मूल्य *ka: mu:ly* 'the price of X' which precedes the value expression.

10. इस कमीज़ की कीमत तीन सौ रुपए हैं।
is kami:z ki: ki:mat ti:n sɔ rupye hɛ̃.
this shirt-gen price three hundred rupees is
The price of this shirt is three hundred rupees.

The compound postposition के बावजूद *ke ba:vaju:d* is used to express the meaning of 'despite of.'

11. बीमार होने के बावजूद वह कार्यालय आया।
bi:ma:r hone ke ba:vaju:d vah ka:rya:lay a:ya:
sick be-inf-obl despite he office came
He came to the office despite being sick.

Inclusion is expressed by the compound postposition के समेत *ke samet/*साथ *sa:th* 'including.'

12. आपके समेत सारे अनुपस्थित/ गैरहाज़िर थे।
a:pke samet sa:re anupasthit/gɛrha:zir the.
you-gen including all absent were
All, including you, were absent.

13. आपको मिलाकर हम दस सदस्य हैं।
a:pko mila:kar ham das sadasy hɛ̃.
you-dat include-cp we ten members are
We are ten members, including you.

Exclusion is expressed by the dative postpositions के बिना *ke bina:/* बगैर *bagɛr* 'without.'

14. अमर के बिना/ बगैर सारे उपस्थित /हाज़िर थे।
amar ke bina:/bagɛr sa:re upasthit/ha:zir the
Amar-gen without all present were
All, excluding/except Amar, were present.

Addition is expressed either by the use of the comitative compound postposition के साथ *ke sa:th* 'with/ along with,' or by के अतिरिक्त *ke atirikt*/ अलावा *ala:va:* 'in addition to.'

15. मोहन के साथ (साथ)/अलावा उमा भी आई।
mohan ke sa:th (sa:th)/ala:va: uma: bhi: a:yi:
Mohan-gen with /besides Uma too came
In addition to Mohan, Uma came too.

Locational semantic functions are generally marked by the postpositions की ओर *ki: or* 'motion to,' (के बीच *ke bi:c)* में से *mẽ se* 'motion through.'

16. वह गाँव की ओर चला।
vah ga:ũ: ki: or cala:
he village towards set out
He set out towards the village.

17. बस गाँव (के बीच) में से गुज़रती है।
bas ga:ũ: (ke bi:c) mẽ se guzarti: hɛ
bus village-abl through passes-pr is
The bus passes through the village.

The approximate location is expressed by के निकट *ke nikaṭ/* नज़दीक *nazdi:k/* करीब *kari:b* 'near.'

18. मकान के निकट/नज़दीक दुकान है।
maka:n ke nikaṭ /nazdi:k duka:n hɛ.
house near shop is
The shop is near the house.

19. वह दफ़्तर के नज़दीक तक पहुँचा।
vah daphtar ke nazdi:k tak pahũca:.
he office near up to reached
He reached up to/ near the house.

20. बच्चे की आवाज़ घर के करीब से आई।
bacce ki: a:va:z ghar ke kari:b se a:yi:.
child-obl gen voice house-gen near from came
The child's voice came from near the house.

Interior location is expressed by के अंदर *ke andar/* में *mẽ* 'inside of,'or के बीच में से *ke bi:c mẽ se* 'from inside' preceded by the oblique case suffixes.

21. इस मकान में/के अंदर कोई नहीं रहता है।
is maka:n mẽ/ke andar koi: nahĩ: rahta: hɛ.
this house inside anyone neg live-pr is
No one lives inside this house.

22. बच्चा कमरे के बीच में से निकला।
bacca: kamre ke bi:c mẽ se nikla:.
child room-abl from came out
The child came out of the house.

Exterior location is denoted by the postposition के *ke/* से *se* बाहर *ba:har* 'outside of.'

23. वह गाँव के बाहर रहता है।
vah ga:ũ: ke ba:har rahta: hɛ.
he village outside live-pr is
He lives outside the village.

24. वह कमरे से बाहर निकला।
vah kamre se ba:har nikla:.
he room-obl outside set out
He came out of the room.

Anterior location is expressed by the postposition के सामने *ke sa:mne* ‘in front of.’ It may also be followed by other postpositions like से *se* ‘from,’*or* तक *tak* ‘up to.’

25. विध्यालय के सामने एक बाग है।
vidhya:lay ke sa:mne ek ba:g hɛ.
school in front of a garden is
There is a garden in front of the school.’

26. दुकान के सामने से बस निकलती है।
duka:n ke sa:mne se bas nikalti: hɛ.
shop-gen front-obl from bus start-ptc is
A bus starts in front of the shop.

27. दुकान के सामने तक सड़क है।
duka:n ke sa:mne tak saṛak hɛ.
shop-gen in front-obl up to road is
A road is built up to the front of the shop.

Posterior location is denoted by के पीछे *ke pi:che* ‘behind.

28. विध्यालय के पीछे एक दुकान है।
vidhya:lay ke pi:che ek duka:n hɛ.
school-gen behind one shop is
There is a shop behind the school.

29. बस अस्पताल के पीछ से जाती है।
bas aspata:l ke pi:che se ja:ti: hɛ
bus hospital-gen behind-obl from go-ptc is
A bus runs at the back of the hospital.

30. अस्पताल के पीछ तक बस आती है।
aspata:l ke pi:che tak bas a:ti: hɛ
hospital-gen behind-obl up to bus come-ptc is
The bus comes up to the back side of the hospital.

Superior location is denoted by the use of the postpositions ऊपर (से) *u:par* (*se*), 'above,' preceded by the oblique case suffixes added to the nouns.

31. मकान के ऊपर से पक्षी उड़ते हैं।
maka:n ke u:par se pakši: uṛte hɛ̃.
house-gen above from birds fly-ptc are
The birds fly above the (top of the) house.

Interior and interior-contact locations are not distinguished. They are indicated by the postposition नीचे *ni:ce* 'under, below,' नीचे से *ni:ce se* 'from under'and नीचे तक *ni:ce tak* 'up to under' preceded by the case suffixes added to nouns.

32. ज़मीन के नीचे पानी निकला।
zami:n ke ni:ce pa:ni: nikla:.
ground-obl under water came out
Water appeared from under the ground.

33. ज़मीन के नीचे से पानी चलता है।
zami:n ke ni:ce se pa:ni: calta: hɛ.
ground-obl under from water flow-pr is
Water is passing through under the ground.

34. दीवार के नीचे तक पानी है।
di:va:r ke ni:ce tak pa:ni: hɛ.
wall-obl under upto water is
Water is underneath the wall.

Lateral and lateral-contact locations are expressed by the postpositions के पास *ke pa:s*/के साथ *sa:th* 'in the company of/besides.'

35. अमर उमा के पास/साथ बैठा।
amar uma: ke pa:s/sa:th bɛṭha:
Amar Uma near sat
Amar sat near Uma.

Citerior location is expressed by की ओर *ki: or* 'towards' preceded by the proximate demonstrative इस *is* 'this'in the oblique case. It is also denoted by the term इस ओर *is or* 'this side' which does not take a separate proximate demonstrative.

36. उसकी दुकान सड़क के इस ओर है।
uski: duka:n saṛak ke is or hɛ.
his shop road-obl this side
His house is on this side of the road.

37. नदी के इस ओर कितने बच्चे हैं?
nadi: ke is or kitne bacce hɛ?
river this side how many children are
How many children are there on this side of the river?

Ulterior location is expressed by की ओर *ki: or* 'side' preceded by the remote demonstrative उस *us* 'that.' It can also be denoted by the use of उस पार *us pa:r* 'on the other side.'

38. सड़क के उस ओर नए मकान बने हैं।
saṛak ke us or naye maka:n bane hɛ̃.
road-obl that-obl side new houses constructed are
New houses are constructed on that side of the road.

39. सड़क के उस पार काफी आबादी है।
saṛak ke us pa:r kaphi: a:ba:di: hɛ.
road that side abundant population is
There is a large population on the other side of the road.

Medial location is expressed by the terms के बीच में *ke bi:c mẽ* 'in the middle,' के भीतर *ke bhi:tar* 'inside,' or के दरमियान/मध्य में *ke darmia:n/madhy mẽ* 'in the middle,' के बीच से *ke bi:c se* 'through the middle,' के बीच तक *ke bi:c tak* 'up to the middle of.'

40. मेरा घर बाज़ार के बीच में है।
mera: ghar ba:za:r ke bi:c mẽ hɛ.
my house market middle in is
My house is in the middle of the market.

41. यह दुकान दो सड़कों के बीच में है।
yah duka:n do saṛkõ ke bi:c mẽ hɛ.
this shop two roads-obl middle is
This shop is between the two roads.

42. गाँव के दरमियान एक मस्जिद है।
ga:ũ: ke darmiya:n ek masjid hɛ.
village middle is one mosque is
There is a mosque in the middle of the village.

43. गाँव के बीच में से एक नदी बहती है।
ga:ũ: ke bi:c mẽ se ek nadi: bahti: hɛ.
village middle through one stream flow-ptc is
A stream passes through the village.

44. गाँव के बीच तक पानी पहुँचता है।
ga:ũ: ke bi:c tak pa:ni: pahũcta: hɛ.
village center up to water reach-ptc is
Water reaches up to the center of the village.

Circumferential location is denoted by adding के इर्द गिर्द *ke ird gird* 'around,' के चारों ओर *ke ca:rõ or* 'on all sides' preceded by the oblique forms of subject nouns.

45. इस बाग के इर्द गिर्द/चारों ओर एक दीवार है।
is ba:g ke ird gird/ca:rõ or ek di:va:r hɛ.
this-obl garden around/four sides one wall is
There is a wall around this garden.

46. पुलीस बैंक के चारों तरफ खड़ी है।
puli:s bank ke ca:rõ tarph khaṛi: hɛ.
police bank all sides standing is
The police are standing on all the sides of the bank.

Citcrior-anterior location is expressed by सामने *sa:mne* 'in front of'preceded by the subject nouns in oblique case. The expression के सामने से *ke sa:mne se* is used to denote 'in the opposite direction.'

47. अमर चोर के सामने खड़ा है।
amar cor ke sa:mne khaṛa: tha:.
Amar thief-gen front-obl standing was
Amar was standing in front of the thief.

48. वह पुलिसवाला के सामने से गुज़रा।
vah pulisva:la: ke sa:mne se guzra:.
he policeman-gen front-obl from passed
He passed in front of the policeman.

Motion past an object at some distance is expressed by के बीच में से *ke bi:c mẽ se* 'past/through in(side)' preceded by the noun in the oblique case.

49. तेल लंबी पाइप से कारखाने तक पहुँचता है।
tel lambi: payip se ka:rxa:ne tak pahũcta: hɛ.
oil long-fs pipe through factory-obl up to reach-ptc is
Oil reaches the factory through the long pipe.

Motion past an object at right and left angles to it is expressed using phrases such as दाईं ओर *da:ĩ: or* 'on the right-hand side' and बाईं ओर *baĩ: or* 'on the left-hand side.'

50. सड़क के आखिर पर सीधे दाईं ओर निकलो।
saṛak ke a:khir par si:dhe da:ĩ: or niklo.
road-gen end at straight right hand side go-imp
At the end of this road, go straight towards the right.

51. पुल पार करके बाईं ओर जाना।
pul pa:r karke ba:ĩ: or ja:na:.
bridge cross-cp left towards go-imp
After crossing the bridge, go straight towards the left.

Other directional locatives are exemplified as follows.

52. भारत के उत्तर/दक्षिण/पूर्व/पश्चिम में मौसम ठीक है।
bha:rat ke uttar/dakšin/pu:rv/pascim mẽ mɔsim ṭhi:kh hɛ
India-gen north/south/east/west in climate good is
The climate is good in the north/south/east/west of India.

The directional postposition की ओर *ki: or* 'towards' is added to the above terms of directional locatives to indicate the meaning of 'toward north/south/east/west.'

The expression नाक के सीध में *na:k ke si:dh mẽ* 'straight in the direction of nose' is used to denote the directional locative 'straight ahead.'

53. तुम नाक के सीध में चलो।
tum na:k ke si:dh mẽ calo.
you nose-gen straight in walk
Walk straight ahead.

Directional/locational precision is expressed by adding the emphatic particle - ही *hi:* to the locative expression.

54. वह घर में ही रहा।
vah ghar mẽ hi: raha:.
he home inside-emp remained
He stayed right inside the house.

55. उसने मुझे सूचना दरवाज़े पर ही दी।
usne mujhe su:cna: darva:ze par hi: di:
he-erg me message door-at-emp gave
He conveyed the message to me right at the door.

3.1.3. Noun Derivation

A large number of nouns in Hindi are derived from nouns, adjectives, and verbs by using prefixes and suffixes. In this process certain morphophonemic changes take place.

3.1.3.1. Nouns from Nouns

Mostly Persian and Sanskrit prefixes and suffixes are used with the nouns of Persian and Sanskrit origin respectively. Some of these are used with native words. The most common prefixes are: बे *be-*, बद *bad-*, बर *bar-*, ना *na:-* अप *ap-*, कु *ku-*, दुर् *dur-*, and निर *nir-*.

बे be- (Persian) without					
शर्म	šarm	shame	बेशर्म	bešarm	shameless
ईमान	i:ma:n	faith	बेईमान	bei:ma:n	dishonest
मतलब	matlab	meaning	बेमतलब	bematlab	meaningless

बद bad- (Persian) bad					
तमीज़	tami:z	manner	बदतमीज़	badtami:z	mannerless
मिज़ाज	miza:j	temperament	बदमिज़ाज	badmiza:j	bad temperament
ज़ात	za:t	character	बदज़ात	badza:t	bad character

बर bar- (Persian) on				
वक्त	vakt	time	बरवक्त barvakt	on time

ना na:- (Persian) not				
पसंद	pasand	like	नापसंद na:pasand	dislike

अप ap- (Sanskrit) opposite				
मान	ma:n	honor	अपमान apma:n	dishonor
शब्द	šabd	word	अपशब्द apšabd	bad words

दुर dur- (Sanskrit) bad					
दशा	daša:	condition	दुर्दशा	durdaša:	bad condition
गति	gati:	position	दुर्गति	durgati:	bad position

कु ku- (Sanskrit) bad				
कर्म	karm	deed	कुकर्म kukarm	bad deed
पोशन	pošan	nutrition	कुपोशन kupošan	malnutrition

निर nir- (Sanskrit) without				
आदर	a:dar	respect	निरादर nira:dar	disrespect
दोश	doš	fault	निर्दोश nirdoš	innocent

The most common suffixes are -दार *-da:r,* -गर *-gar,* -बंद *-band,* and -दान *-da:n*.

- दार da:r (Persian) owner					
दुकान	duka:n	shop	दुकानदार	duka:nda:r	shopkeeper
ज़मीन	zami:n	land	दज़मीनदार	zami:nda:r	landlord

गर -gar (Persian) with				
सोदा	soda:	items	सोदागर soda:gar	merchant
जादू	ja:du:	magic	जादूगर ja:du:gar	magician

-बंद band (Persian) bound					
कमर	kamar	waist	कमरबंद	kamarband	belt
बिस्तर	bistar	bed	बिस्तरबंद	bistarband	hold-all

-दची ci: (Persian) with				
ख़ज़ाना xaza:na:	treasure	ख़ज़ानची	xaza:anci:	cashier
अफ़ीम afi:m	opium	अफ़ीमची	afi:mci:	opium addict

-दान da:n (Persian) container				
कलम kalam	pen	कलमदान	kalamda:n	penholder
रोशन rošan	light	रोशनदान	rošanda:n	window

-ख़ाना kha:na: (Persian) house			
कार ka:r	work	कारख़ाना ka:rxa:na:	factory
शराब šara:b	liquor	शराबख़ाना šara:bxa:na:	bar

3.1.3.2. Nouns from Adjectives

The most productive suffixes used for deriving abstract nouns from adjectives are -ई *-i:*, -ता *-ta:*, *-pan*, -आई *-a:i:*, -इयत *-iyat*, -आस *-a:s*.

-ई -i:			
कमज़ोर kamzor	weak	कमज़ोरी kamzori:	weakness
ख़ुश xuš	happy	ख़ुशी xuši:	happiness
गरम garam	hot	गरमी garmi:	heat
गरीब gari:b	poor	गरीबी gari:bi:	poverty
सर्द sard	cold	सर्दी sardi:	coldness
मोटा moṭa:	fat	मोटाई moṭa:i:	thickness
ख़राब xara:b	bad	ख़राबी xara:bi:	defect
साफ sa:f	clean	सफाई safa:i:	cleanliness
ऊँचा ũ:ca:	high	ऊँचाई ũ:ca:i:	height
चौड़ा cɔṛa:	wide	चौड़ाई cɔṛa:i:	width
नेक nek	noble	नेकी neki:	nobility
सच्चा sacca:	true	सच्चाई sacca:i:	truth
मीठा mi:ṭha:	sweet	मिठाई miṭha:i:	sweets

-ता -ta:			
मूर्ख mu:rkh	stupid	मूर्खता mu:rkhta:	stupidity
पवित्र pavitr	pure	पवित्रता pavitarta:	purity
विशेष višeš	special	विशेषता višešta:	specialty
विशाल viša:l	large	विशालता viša:lta:	largeness
सुंदर sundar	beauty	सुंदरता sundarta:	beautiful
समान sama:n	equal	समानता sama:nta:	equality
गंभीर gambhi:r	serious	गंभीरता gambhi:rta:	seriousness

-पन -pan			
कच्चा kacca:	raw	कच्चापन kacca:pan	rawness
कमीना kami:na:	mean	कमीनापन kami:na:pan	meanness
पागल pa:gal	mad	पागलपन pa:galpan	madness

-आई -a:i:			
चढ़ caṛh	climb	चढ़ाई caṛha:i:	climbing
पढ़ paṛh	study	पढ़ाई paṛha:i:	studies
कमा kama:	earn	कमाई kama:i:	earning
सुन sun	listen	सुनाई suna:i:	hearing

-इयत -iyat			
असली asli:	real	असलियत asliyat	reality
खास xa:s	special	खासियत xa:siyat	specialty

- आस -a:s			
मीठा mi:ṭha:	sweet	मिठास miṭha:s	sweetness

3.1.3.3. Nouns from Verbs

The suffix -ना -na: is used to derive gerundive nouns from verb stems. The suffixes -अस *-as,* -अन *-an,* -ई *-i:,* -वत *-vat,* and *-2* are also used to derive abstract nouns from verb stems.

-ना -na:			
आ a:	come	आना a:na:	coming
ला la:	bring	लाना la:na:	bringing
लिख likh	write	लिखना likhna:	writing
पढ़ paṛh	read	पढ़ना paṛhna:	reading

- अन -an			
धड़क dhaṛak	throb	धड़कन dhaṛhkan	throbbing
पलग lag	attach	पलगन lagan	devotion

- ई -i:			
जोड़ joṛ	add	जोड़ी joṛi:	a pair
लड़ laṛ	quarrel	लड़ाई laṛa:i:	dispute
लिख likh	write	लिखाई likha:i:	writing
पढ़ paṛh	read	पढाई paṛha:i:	studies

-वट -vaṭ			
बना bana:	make	बनावट bana:vaṭ	shape
सजा saja:	decorate	सजावट saja:vaṭ	decoration
थक thak	be tired	थकावट thaka:vaṭ	tiredness

-2

छाप cha:p	print	छाप cha:p	printing
ठग ṭhag	cheat	ठग ṭhag	cheat
दौड़ dɔṛ	run	दौड़ dɔṛ	race
मार ma:r	beat	मार ma:r	beating
मोड़ moṛ	turn	मोड़ moṛ	turning point
उपज upaj	produce	उपज upaj	product
हार ha:r	be defeated	हार ha:r	defeat
खर्च kharc	spend	खर्च kharc	expenditure
खेल khel	play	खेल khel	play
समझ samajh	understand	समझ samajh	understanding
सोच soc	think	सोच soc	thinking

3.1.4. Noun Compounds

Compounds belonging to the noun category are headed by a noun, which is a final member of the group. The first member may be a noun, an adjective, or a participle and may be declined for number, gender and case. A postposition is attached to the final member of the compound.

3.1.4.1. Noun-Noun Compounds

Noun-noun compounds can be divided into several subgroups based on semantic criteria: copulative compounds, partial duplicated compounds, superordinate compounds, complex compounds, hybrid compounds, genitive-noun compound, and participial compounds.

3.1.4.2. Copulative Compounds

Copulative compounds, also known as co-compounds, are composed of semantically-related nouns. Each noun behaves as an independent constituent in the sense that each may be separately inflected for gender and number, though not for a postposition. Members of some compounds occur in a fixed order.

माता पिता ma:ta: pita:	mother and father	*pita: ma:ta:
भाई बहिन bha:i: bahan	brother and sister	?bahan bha:i:
सुख दुख sukh dukh	happiness and sorrow	dukh sukh
पाप पुन्य pa:p puny	sin and good deeds	*puny pa:p
ऊँच नीच ũ:c ni:c	high and low	*ni:c ũ:c

3.1.4.3. Reduplicated Compounds

Reduplicated compounds express exhaustive meaning.

घर घर ghar ghar	(house-house)	every house
बच्चा बच्चा bacca: bacca:	(child-child)	every child
पैसा पैसा pɛsa: pɛsa:	(penny-penny)	every penny

3.1.4.4. Partially Duplicated Compounds

In a partial duplicated compound, also known as an echo-compound, the second member is formed by changing the initial letter of the first member. An initial व */v/* is changed into श */š/* or पा */p/*; all other initial consonants or vowels are replaced by व */v/* or श */š/*. The meaning of the ompound extends beyond the meaning of their members. The compounds usually represent the meaning of similar or associative things.

वानर शानर va:nar ša:nar	monkey and the like
वादा शादा va:da: ša:da:	promise and the like
वोट शोट voṭ šoṭ	vote and the like
काम शाम/वाम ka:m ša:m/va:m	work and the like
कहानी वानी/शानी kaha:ni: va:ni:/šahni:	story and the like
दूध शूध du:dh šu:dh	milk and the like
पानी वानी/शानी pa:ni: va:ni:/ša:ni:	water and the like

3.1.4.5. Superordinate Compounds

In this type of compound, the meaning projected by the members does not in any way relate to the meaning of the compound as a whole.

हाथ पांव ha:th pa:ũ:	(hand-feet)	body
खाना पीना kha:na: pi:na:	(eating-drinking)	lifestyle
जल वायू jal va:yu	(water-air)	climate
चाय पानी ca:y pa:ni:	(tea-water)	refreshment

3.1.4.6. Complex Compounds

Complex compounds involving three or more nouns are not very common in Hindi.

तन मन धन tan man dhan	(body-mind-money)	devotion

3.1.4.7. Hybrid Compounds

In hybrid compounds, one member is usually borrowed from another language and the second member is a Hindi noun.

डबल रोटी ḍabal roṭi:	(double-bread)	bread
रेल गाड़ी rel ga:ṛi:	(tracks-vehicle)	train

3.1.4.8. Adjective-Noun Compounds

A large number of compounds are composed of an adjective followed by a noun. There are no single terms for them.

काली मिर्च ka:li: mirc	(black-pepper)	pepper
छोटी इलायची choṭi: ila:yci:	(small cardamom)	cardamom

3.1.4.9. Modifier-Noun Compounds

In modifier-noun compounds, the first member acts like a modifier or source and the second member is a noun.

बैल गाड़ी bɛl ga:ṛi:	(bull-vehicle)	bullock cart
गंगा जल gaŋa: jal	(Ganges-water)	water of Ganges

3.2. Pronouns

Pronouns are inflected for number and case. Broadly, there are seven classes of pronouns in Hindi: personal, demonstrative, relative, possessive, reflexive, interrogative, and indefinite. Pronouns in the direct and oblique cases are presented below.

3.2.1. Personal Pronouns

Case	Person	Sg		Pl	
Direct					
	1st	मैं	mẽ	हम	ham
	2nd (sg)	तू	tu	तुम	tum
	(hon sg/pl)	आप	a:p	आप	a:p
	3rd prox	यह	yah	ये	ye
	rem	वह	vah	वे	ve

Note that the personal pronoun आप *a:p* is used as an honorific form of address for both singular and plural subjects. In the polite speech, it is occasionally used for a person spoken about in place of ये *ye*. The term लोग *log* may be attached to a plural pronoun for defining or emphasizing plurality: आप लोग *a:p log*, हम लोग *ham log*, तुम लोग *tum log*, ये लोग *ye log*, वे लोग *ve log*.

Case	Person	Sg	Pl
Dative को ko			
	1st	मुझे mujhe/ मुझको mujhko	हमें hamẽ/ हमको hamko
	2nd	तुम्हे tumhe/तुमको tumko	तुम्हें tumhẽ/तुमको tumko
		आपको a:pko	आपको a:pko
	3rd prox	इसे ise/इसको isko	इन्हें inhẽ/इनको inko
	rem	उसे use/उनको unko	उन्हेंunhẽ/उनको unko
Ergative ने ne			
	1st	मैंने mɛ̃ne	हमने hamne
	2nd	तूने tu:ne	तुमने tumne
		आपने a:pne	आपने a:pne
	3rd prox	इसने isne	इन्होंने inhõne
	rem	उसने usne	उन्होंने unhõne
Locative पर par			
	1st	मुझपर mujhpar	हमपर hampar
	2nd	तुझपर tujhpar	तुमपर tumpar
		आपपर a:ppar	आपपर a:ppar
	3rd prox	इसपर ispar	इनपर inpar
	rem	उसपर uspar	उनपर unpar
Ablative से se			
	1st	मुझसे mujhse	हमसे hamse
	2nd	तुमसे tum se	तुमसे tumse
		आपसे a:pse	आपसे a:pse
	3rd prox	इससे isse	इनसे inse
	rem	उससे usse	उनसे un se
Possessive / Genitive का ka:/ के ke/की ki			
	1st	मेरा mera:	हमारा hama:ra:
	2nd	तेरा tera:	तुम्हारा tumha:ra:
		आपका a:pka:	आपका a:pka:
	3rd prox	इसका iska:	उसका uska:
	rem	उसका uska:	उनका unka:

3.2.2. Demonstrative Pronouns

Direct/Nominative Case		
	Sg	Pl
prox	यह yeh	ये ye
rem	वह vah	वे ve

Oblique Case को ko/में mẽ/पर par/का ka:/के ke/की ki:/ असे se		
	Sg	Pl
prox	इस is	इन in
rem	उस us	उन un

Note that the demonstrative pronouns are also used as personal pronouns of the third person.

There are two additional pronouns which are used in the sense of 'so and so' to refer to third person subjects: अमुक *amuk* and फलां *falã:/* फलाना *fala:na:*.

3.2.3. Relative Pronouns

Hindi has one relative pronoun: **जो** *jo* 'who, which, that, what' in both the singular and plural. It is accompanied with वह *vah* in the main sentence called correlative of **जो** *jo*. The correlative form **सो** *so* 'he, they' is now obsolete, it is used in proverbs and sayings. The term **लोग** *log* may be added to **जो** *jo* to indicate or emphasize plurality: **जो लोग** *jo log*. The oblique forms of the relative pronoun used along with the case-signs are as follows.

Singular	Plural
जिस jis/जिसने jisne	जिन jin/जिंहोंने jinhõne
जिसको jisko/जिसे jise	जिनको jinko/जिंहें jinhẽ
जिससे jis se	जिनसे jin se

3.2.4. Reflexive Pronouns

Reflexive pronouns substitute and refer to a noun or pronoun which is the logical subject of the sentence. Hindi has three reflexive pronouns: आप *a:p*, its oblique forms अपना *apna:* and अपने *apne*, and a compound form of these two, अपने आप *apne-a:p*. The oblique form

आपस *a:pas* means 'each other' or 'one another.' The reflexive pronoun आप *a:p* is also substituted by the Sanskrit borrowed term स्वयं *svayam* or Persian-borrowed term खुद *khud* in Sanskritized and Persianized styles respectively. The reflexive pronoun आप *a:p* optionally followed by the emphatic form ही *hi:* has an adjectival meaning. It can also be used as an adverb in the meaning 'of one's own accord, spontaneously.' Similarly, अपने आप *apne-a:p* can either be used in an emphatic sense or in the adverbial meaning of 'of one's own accord.'

1. वह आप ही/अपने आप घर गया।
   vah a:p hi: / apne-a:p ghar gaya:
   he himself emp home went
   He himself went home.

Note that the oblique forms of अपने *apne* and अपने आप *apne-a:p* (except when adverbial) mean 'oneself' with the case-signs/postpositions को *ko,* से *se,* में *mẽ,* and पर *par*.

3.2.5. Interrogative Pronouns

In both singular and plural, there are two basic interrogative pronouns: कौन *kɔn* 'who'(referring to person) and क्या *kya:* 'what'(referring to things). The interrogative pronoun क्या *kya:* is a neutral form. It is also used for denoting the interrogative nature of the sentence. Note that कौन *kɔn* and क्या *kya:* can be used as relative pronouns too.

2. कौन आया, कोई नहीं जानता।
   kɔn a:ya:, koyi: nahĩ: ja:nta:
   who came no one neg knows
   Nobody knows who came.

The interrogative pronoun क्या *kya:* is also used as an exclamatory adjective.

3. क्या सुंदर बाग है!
   kya: sundar ba:g hɛ!
   what beautiful garden is
   What a beautiful garden!

It is also used as an emphatic negation.

4. लड़की क्या है, नाजुक फूल है।
laṛki: kya: hɛ, na:zuk phu:l hɛ.
girl what is delicate flower is
It is not a girl; it is a delicate flower.
(What a girl! Just like a delicate flower.)

Interrogative adverbial forms related to these pronouns are: कब *kab* 'when,' कैसा *kaisa:* 'how,' कौनसा *kɔnsa:* 'which one,' कितना *kitna:* 'how much.'

3.2.6. Indefinite Pronouns

There are two indefinite pronouns in Hindi: कोई *koi:* 'someone, somebody'and कुछ *kuch* 'something.' कुछ *kuch* is also used as an adjective (numeral and quantitative) and as an adverb meaning 'some, a few, a little, partly.' Similarly, कोई *koi:* can be used as an adverb in the sense of 'some, about.' It can refer to 'something' if used with -सा *-sa:/*-सी *-si:* = कोई सा *koi: sa:/* कोई सी *koi: si:*. कोई *koi:* may also be used as the plural form to indicate 'some people.'

3.2.7. Oblique Forms of Pronouns

Whereas the same case-signs namely ने *ne,* को *ko,* क से *se,* मैं *mẽ,* पर *par* and का *ka:* are attached to pronouns as they are attached to nouns, in some cases the oblique forms of pronouns are formed differently.

Direct		Oblique	
Sg	Pl	Sg	Pl
यह yeh	ये ye	इस is	इन in
वह vah	वे ve	उस us	उन un
जो jo	जो jo	जिस jis	जिन jin
सो so	सो so	तिस tis	तिन tin
कोई koi:	कोई koi:	किसी kisi:	किंहीं kinhĩ:

Note that (i) when the case-signs are added the singular forms यह *yeh,* वह *vah,* जो *jo,* and सो *so* change to इस *is,* उस *us,* जिस *jis* and तिस *tis* respectively; कौन *kɔn* and क्या *kya:* change to किस *kis;* and कुछ *kuch* changes to किसी *kisi:*. (ii) In the plural, except before ने *ne,* these change to इन *in,* उन *un,* जिन *jin,* तिन *tin,* किन *kin,* and किंहीं *kinhĩ:.* (iii) Before ने *ne*, the plural oblique forms are: इन्हूं *inhũ:,* उन्हों *unhũ:,* जिन्हों *jinhũ:,* किन्हों *kinhũ:*, and किन्हीं *kinhĩ:.* (iv) मैं *mɛ̃* and तू *tu:* remain unchanged before ने *ne:* (मैंने *mɛ̃ne,* तूने *tu:ne*). v) Followed by other case-signs, मैं *mɛ̃* and तू *tu:* change to मुझ *mujh* and तूझ *tujh* (मुझको *mujhko,* तुझको *tujhko*). (vi) The pronouns हम *ham* and तुम *tum* remain unchanged before all case-signs: हमको *hamko*, तुम्हें *tumhẽ.* (vii) The postposition का *ka:* is not attached to मैं *mɛ̃,* तू *tu:*, and तुम *tum*. They change to the following forms agreeing with the object noun in gender and number.

Masculine		Feminine
Sg	Pl	Sg/Pl
मेरा mera:	मेरे	मेरी meri:
तेरा tera:	तेरे tere	तेरी teri:
तुम्हारा tumha:ra:	तुम्हारे tumha:re	तुम्हारी tumha:ri:

(viii) As an alternative to को *ko*, all oblique forms attach an ए *e* in singular and हें *hẽ* in plural: इसे *ise/*इसको *isko,* उसे *use/*उनको *unko,* इन्हें *inhẽ* /इनको *inko,* उन्हें *unhẽ/*उनको *unko,* तुम्हें *tumhẽ/*तुझे *tujhe,* हमें *hamẽ/*हमको *hamko.* In the case of *ham,* एं *ẽ* is added, not हें *hẽ*. Note that एं *ẽ* or हें *hẽ* is not attached to the indefinite pronouns कोई *koi:* and कुछ *kuch.*

As pointed out earlier, the reflexive pronoun उआप *a:p* changes to उअपने *apne* before the case signs को *ko,* उसे *se,* में *mẽ,* and पर *par*. ने *ne* is not added to the reflexive आप *a:p* but only to the subject to which आप *a:p* refers. For denoting various senses of का *ka:,* आप *a:p* changes to अपना *apna:,* अपने *apne,* and अपनी *apni:.*

3.2.8. Compound Pronouns

Two, or more than two pronouns may be compounded or the same pronoun may be repeated to convey various shades of meanings. The following are some important compound pronouns.

अपने आप apne a:p	by oneself
आप ही आप a:p hi: a:p	by oneself, to oneself
जो कोई jo koi:	who(so)ever
जो कुछ jo kuch	what(so)ever
जो जो jo jo	whoever/whatever

कोई कोई koi: koi:	some, a few (archaic)
सब कोई sab koi:	all, everybody (archaic)
हर कोई har koi:	all, everybody
कोई koi: na koi:	someone or the other
कोई कोई koi: … koi:	some … others *or* one … another
कुछ न कुछ kuch na kuch	something or the other
कुछ का कुछ kuch ka: kuch	something different from expected
सब कुछ sab kuch	everything
बहुत कुछ bahut kuch	a great deal
कुछ कुछ kuch kuch	somewhat, a little
कोई और koi: ɔr	someone else
और कोई ɔr koi:	someone else
कोई दूसरा koi: du:sra:	someone else
कुछ और kuch ɔr	something else, a little more
और कुछ ɔr kuch	something else
कुछ … कुछ kuch … kuch	some … some (Conjunctive)
कोई सा koi: sa:	anything, something
कोई सा kɔn sa:	which one
कौन कौन kɔn kɔn	which persons, which ones
क्या क्या kya: kya:	which things
क्या से क्या kya: se kya:	something contrary to expectations
क्या क्या kya: … kya:	equally, without difference
आपस में की a:pas mẽ/ki:	each other, one another

All the pronouns can be combined with the emphatic particle ही *hi:* like मैं ही *mɛ̃ hi:* 'I myself,' तू ही *tu: hi:* 'thou thyself,' आप ही *a:p hi:* 'you yourself,' कोई ही *koi: hi:* 'hardly any one,' and कुछ ही *kuch hi:* 'hardly a few.' Note that most of these compounds are affected by Sandhi and are modified: मुझ *mujh* + ही *hi:* = मुझी *mujhi:*, तुझ *tujh* + ही *hi:* = तुझी *tujhi:*, हम *ham* + ही *hi:* = हम्ही *hamhi:* , तुम *tum* + ही *hi:* = तुम्ही ɪ*tumhi:*, वह *vah* +ही *hi:* = वही *vahi:*, यह *yeh* + ही *hi:* = यही *yahi:*, उस *us* + ही *hi:* = उसी *usi:*, इस *is* + ही *hi:* = इसी *isi:*, किस *kis* + ही *hi:* = किसी *kisi:*, इन *in* +ही *hi:* = इन्ही *inhi:*, उन *un* + ही *hi:* = उन्ही *unhi:*, जिन *jin* + ही *hi:* + जिन्ही *jinhi:*, किन *kin* + ही *hi:* = किन्ही *kinhi:*.

3.3. Adjectives

Adjectives in Hindi can be classified into two groups: (i) inflected and (ii) uninflected.

3.3.1. Inflected

These adjectives are inflected for gender and number.

Masculine		Feminine	
Sg	Pl	Sg / Pl	
बड़ा baṛa:	बड़े baṛe	बड़ी baṛi:	big
छोटा choṭa:	छोटे choṭe	छोटी choṭi:	small
लंबा lamba:	लंबे lambe	लंबी lambi:	tall
काला ka:la:	काले kale	काली ka:li:	black
हरा hara:	हरे hare	हरी hari:	green
अच्छा accha:	अच्छे acche	अच्छी acchi:	good

3.3.2. Uninflected

These adjectives are not inflected for number and gender.

सुंदर लड़का/लड़की sundar laṛka: /laṛki:	beautiful boy/girl
दुखी आदमी /औरत dukhi: admi:/ ɔrat	sad man/woman
सफेद कपड़ा /कमीज़ saphed kapṛa: /kami:z	white cloth/shirt

3.3.3. Types of Adjectives

There are two broad types of adjectives: (i) those that describe a quality or quantity, and (ii) those that distinguish one person or thing from another.

(i) Quality is expressed either by a basic adjective or by an adjective derived from a noun.

सुंदर लड़की sundar laṛki:	a beautiful girl
शर्मीला लड़का šarmi:la: laṛka:	a bashful boy

The adjective शर्मीला *šarmi:la:* is derived by adding the suffix - ईला *i:la:* to the noun stem. Negative qualities are expressed by a separate set of adjectives and also by adding negative prefixes.

बदसूरत औरत bad-su:rat ɔrat	an ugly woman
बेशर्म लड़का be-šarm laṛka:	a shameless boy

Quantity may be expressed either by numerals or by the adjectives of quantity like बहुत *bahut* / अधिक *adhik* 'a lot,' काफ़ी *ka:fi:* 'sufficient,' कम *kam* 'less,' थोड़ा *thoṛa:* 'a little.'

छे किताबें che kita:bẽ	six books
बहुत लेग bahut log	many people
थोड़ा दूध thoṛa: du:dh	a little milk

Adjectives of quantity may also be formed by the combination of numeral + unit of measure + (classifier (terms of weight, length))/genitive postposition) (+ the particle वाला *va:la:)* + noun.

दो सौ गज़ लंबी (वाली) रस्सी।
do sɔ gaz lambi: (va:li:) rassi:
two hundred yards long (gen.) rope
the two-hundred-yard long rope

दो किलो वज़न वाला पत्थर।
do kilo vazan va:la: patthar
two kilo weight-gen stone
the stone weighing two kilograms

The postposition से *se* is used in the formation of reduplicated adjectival phrases.

अधिक से अधिक	adhik se adhik	at most
कम से कम	kam se kam	at least
अच्छे से अच्छा	acche se accha:	the best of all
बुरे से बुरा	bure se bura:	worst of all
मीठे से मीठा	mi:ṭhe se mi: ṭha:	very sweet

Almost all pronouns can function as adjectives. The demonstrative adjectives that point out persons or things यह - *yeh* 'this,' *ye* 'these' वह *vah* 'that,' *ve* 'those' - are used in the initial position.

यह घर	yeh ghar	this house
ये किताबें	ye kita:bẽ	these books
वह लड़का	vah laṛka:	that boy
वे बच्चे	ve bacce	those children

Interrogative pronouns are used to ask questions.

कौन लड़का? kɔn lạrka:?	which boy?
क्या काम? kya: ka:m?	what work?

The possessive pronouns particularize or show relation.

मेरा / तेरा दोस्त	mera:/tera: dost	my/your friend
मेरी / आपकी बहिन	meri:/a:pki: bahan	my/your sister
उसका / उनका भाई	uska:/unka: bha:i:	his/their brother

Indefinite and relative pronouns, too, function as adjectives.

कोई अखबार	koi: akhba:r	some newspaper
कुछ सब्ज़ियाँ	kuch sabziyã:	some vegetables
जो बच्चा	jo bacca:	the child who

3.3.4. Degree of Adjectives

There are three varieties of adjectival degrees: superlative, comparative and minimal. Superlative and comparative degrees of qualities are denoted with the help of the postposition से *se* attached to the noun or pronoun (in oblique form) with which the comparison is made. Superlative involves comparison with all. For example,

सब से बड़ी इमारत	sab se bạri: ima:rat	the biggest building
सब से सुंदर लड़की	sab se sundar lạrki:	the most beautiful girl

Comparative involves comparison between two.

अपने दोस्त से लंबा	apne dost se lamba:	taller than his friend

Minimal involves no comparison.

मेरा अच्छा दोस्त	mera: accha: dost	my good friend

The postposition में *mẽ* is also alternately used to denote the superiority of one out of two or more.

दोनों में बड़ा	donõ: mẽ baṛa:	bigger of the two
सब में ऊँचा	sab mẽ ũ:ca:	the tallest

Sometimes, the phrase की अपेक्षा *ki: apekša:* 'in comparison to' is substituted for से *se.*

उमा की अपेक्षा लंबी	uma: ki: apekša: lambi:	taller than Uma

Notice that words अधिक/ज़्यादा *adhik/zya:da:* 'more' and कम *kam* 'less' may be prefixed to adjectives for denoting comparison.

सोने से अधिक चमकीला	sone se adhik camki:la:	brighter than gold
फूल से ज़्यादा कोमल	phu:l se zya:da: komal	more delicate than a flower
बीस से कम	bi:s se kam	less than twenty

3.3.5. Derivation of Adjectives

A large number of adjectives are derived from nouns by adding the suffixes -आ *-a:*, -ई *-i:*, -उ-*u:*, -इला *-i:la:*, -लू *-lu:*, -इक *-ik*, -जनक *-janak*, -दाई-*da:i:*, -मय *-mai:*, -वन *-van*, -आना *-a:na:* , -नाक *-na:k*, -ईन *-i:n*, -मंद *-mand,* and -दार *-da:r.*

-आ -a:			
Noun		Adjective	
सच sac	truth	सच्चा sacca:	truthful
झूठ jhu:ṭh	lie	झूठा jhu:ṭha:	liar
भूख bhu:kh	hunger	भूखा bhu:kha:	hungry

-ई -i:			
कीमत ki:mat	price	कीमती ki:mti:	expensive
सुख sukh	comfort	सुखी sukhi:	happy
नेक nek	good	नेकी neki:	goodness
पहाड़ paha:ṛ	mountain	पहाडी paha:ṛi:	mountainous

-ऊ -u:			
पेट peṭ	stomach	पेटू peṭu:	voracious
बाज़ार ba:za:r	market	बाज़ारू ba:za:ru:	common

-ईला -i:la:			
रस ras	juice	रसीला rasi:la:	juicy
ज़हर zahar	poison	ज़हरीला zahri:la:	poisonous
खर्च kharc	expense	खर्चीला kharci:la:	expensive
पत्थर patthar	stone	पत्थरीला patthri:la:	stony

-लू -lu:			
श्रद्धा šradha:	faith	श्रद्धालू šradha:lu:	devotee
दया daya:	kindness	दयालू daya:lu:	kind

-इक -ik			
समाज sama:j	society	समाजिक sama:jik	social
विज्ञान vigya:n	science	विज्ञानिक vigya:nik	scientific
वर्ष varš	year	वार्षिक va:ršik	yearly

-जनक -janak			
आशा a:ša:	hope	आशाजनक a:ša:janak	hopeful
चिंता cinta:	worry	चिंताजनक cinta:janak	worried

-दाई -da:i:			
सुख sukh	comfort	सुखदाई sukhda:i:	comfortable
दुख dukh	pain	दुखदाई dukhda:i:	painful

-मई -mai:			
आशा a:ša:	hope	आशामई a:ša:mai:	hopeful

-वान -va:n			
धन dhan	wealth	धनवान dhanva:n	wealthy
बल bal	strength	बलवान balva:n	strong

-आना -a:na:			
साल sa:l	year	सालाना sa:la:na:	yearly
रोज़ roz	day	रोज़ाना roza:na:	daily
मर्द mard	man	मर्दाना marda:na:	manly

-नाक -na:k			
दर्द dard	pain	दर्दनाक dardna:k	painful
ख़ौफ xɔf	fear	ख़ौफनाक xɔfna:k	frightful

ख़तरा xatra:	danger	ख़तरनाक xatarna:k	dangerous

-ईन -i:n			
रंग rang	color	रंगीन rangi:n	colorful
नमक namak	salt	नमकीन namki:n	salty
शौक šɔk	liking	शौकीन šɔki:n	fond

-मंद -mand			
अक्ल akl	wisdom	अक्लमंद aklmand	wise
दौलत dɔlat	wealth	दौलतमंद dɔlatmand	wealthy

-दार -da:r	
माल ma:l	property
मालदार ma:lda:r	wealthy
ज़मीन zami:n	land
ज़मीनदार zami:nda:r	landlord
दुकान duka:n	shop
दुकानदार duka:nda:r	shopkeeper

When सा *sa:* 'like' is attached to the oblique forms of nouns or pronouns, they function as adjectives.

फूल सा phu:l sa:	flower-like
मुझसा mujh sa:/ तुमसा tum sa:	me-like/you-like

सा *sa:* is also attached to adjectives to denote 'looking, seeming.' When added to quantitative adjectives, it intensifies the meaning.

लाल सा la:l sa:	red-looking
बड़ा सा baṛa: sa:	big-looking
दुबला सा dubla: sa:	slim-looking
कमज़ोर सा kamzor sa:	weak-looking
ऊँचा सा ũ:ca: sa:	high-looking
बहुत सा bahut sa:	a great deal
थोड़ा सा thoṛa: sa:	just a little

The forms of सा *sa:* (agreeing in number and gender with the noun) are also added to the genitive/possessive forms to denote a similarity of quality, or possession.

गाय का सा मुंह ga:y ka: sa: mũh	a face like that of a cow
उनके से कपड़े unke se kapṛe	clothes similar to his
मेरी meri:/ तेरी सी नाक teteri: si: na:k	a nose like mine/yours

सा *sa:* may be replaced by जैसा *jɛsa:* with nouns and pronouns (other than indefinite or interrogative ones.)

बंदर सा/जैसा bandar sa:/jɛsa:	similar to a monkey
तुम सा/जैसा tum sa:/jɛsa:	like you

The forms of सा *sa:* can be added to कोई *koi:* and कौन *kɔn* to indicate 'any one,' and 'which one' respectively.

कोई सा रंग koi:-sa: raŋ	any color
कोई सी कमीज़ koi:-si: kami:z	any shirt
कौन सा कोट kɔn-sa: koṭ	which coat
कौन सी कमीज़ kɔn-si: kami:z	which shirt

3.3.6. Numerals

Numerals are adjectives indicating number. They may by divided into cardinals, ordinals, or multiplicatives.

3.3.6.1. Cardinals

Cardinal numeral forms in Hindi are given below.

एक	ek	1	दो	do	2
तीन	ti:n	3	चार	ca:r	4
पाँच	pã:c	5	छे	che	6
सात	sa:t	7	आठ	a:ṭh	8
नौ	nav	9	दस	das	10
ग्यारह	gia:rah	11	बारह	ba:rah	12
तेरह	terah	13	चौदह	cɔdah	14
पंद्रह	pandrah	15	सोलह	solah	16
सत्रह	satrah	17	अठारह	aṭha:rah	18
उन्नीस	unni:s	19	बीस	bi:s	20
इक्कीस	ikki:s	21	बाईस	ba:i:s	22

तेईस	tei:s	23	चौबीस	cɔbi:s	24
पच्चीस	pacci:s	25	छब्बीस	chabbi:s	26
सत्ताईस	satta:i:s	27	अट्ठाईस	aṭṭha:i:s	28
उनत्तीस	untti:s	29	तीस	ti:s	30
इकत्तीस	ikatti:s	31	बत्तीस	batti:s	32
तैंतीस	tɛ̃nti:s	33	चौंतीस	cɔnti:s	34
पैंतीस	pɛ̃ti:s	35	छत्तीस	chatti:s	36
सैंतीस	sɛ̃ti:s	37	अड़तीस	aṛti:s	38
उनतालीस	unta:li:s	39	चालीस	ca:li:s	40
इकतालीस	ikta:li:s	41	बयालीस	baya:li:s	42
तैंतालीस	tɛ̃ta:li:s	43	चवालीस	cava:li:s	44
पैंतालीस	pɛ̃ta:li:s	45	छियालीस	chiya:li:s	46
सैंतालीस	sɛ̃ta:li:s	47	अड़तालीस	aṛta:li:s	48
उनचास	unca:s	49	पचास	paca:s	50
इक्यावन	ikya:van	51	बावन	ba:van	52
तिरपन	tirpan	53	चौवन	cɔvan	54
पचपन	pacpan	55	छप्पन	chappan	56
सतावन	sata:van	57	अठावन	aṭha:van	58
उनसठ	unsaṭh	59	साठ	sa:ṭh	60
इकसठ	iksaṭh	61	बासठ	ba:saṭh	62
तिरसठ	tirsaṭh	63	चौंसठ	cɔ̃saṭh	64
पैंसठ	pɛ̃saṭh	65	छियासठ	chiya:saṭh	66
सरसठ	saṛsaṭh	67	अड़सठ	aṛsaṭh	68
उनहत्तर	unahttar	69	सत्तर	sattar	70
इकहत्तर	ikahttar	71	बहत्तर	bahttar	72
तिहत्तर	tehttar	73	चौहत्तर	cɔhttar	74
पचहत्तर	pacahttar	75	छिहत्तर	chihttar	76
सतहत्तर	satahttar	77	अठहत्तर	aṭhahttar	78
उनासी	una:si:	79	अस्सी	assi:	80
इक्यासी	ikya:si:	81	बयासी	baya:si:	82
तिरासी	tira:si:	83	चौरासी	cɔra:si:	84
पचासी	paca:si:	85	छियासी	chiya:si:	86
सतासी	sata:si:	87	अठासी	aṭha:si:	88
नवासी	nava:si:	89	नब्बे	nabbe	90
इक्यानवे	ikya:nave	91	बयानवे	baya:nave	92
तिरानवे	tira:nave	93	चौरानवे	cɔra:nave	94
पचानवे	paca:nave	95	छियानवे	chiya:nave	96
सतानवे	sata:nave	97	अठानवे	aṭha:nave	98

निन्यानवे	ninya:nave	99	सौ	sɔ	100
शून्य	šu:ny	zero	हज़ार	haza:r	1,000

Starting with one hundred, the numerals proceed regularly.

(एक) सौ	(ek) sɔ	100
एक सौ एक	ek sɔ ek	101
एक सौ दो	ek sɔ do	102
दो सौ	do sɔ	200
दो सौ	do sɔ ek	201
एक हज़ार	ek haza:r	1000
दो हज़ार तीन	do haza:r ti:n	2003
दो हज़ार सात	do haza:r sa:t	2007

The numerals one thousand and above are as follows.

(एक) हज़ार	(ek) haza:r	one thousand
दस हज़ार	das haza:r	ten thousand
लाख	la:kh	hundred thousand
दस लाख	das la:kh	million
करोड़	karoṛ	ten million
अरब	arab	thousand million (billion)
खरब	kharab	hundred billion

3.3.6.2. Ordinals

The first six ordinals are पहला *pahla:* 'first,' दूसरा *du:stra:* 'second'; तीसरा *ti:sra:* 'third'; चौथा *cɔtha:* 'fourth'; पांचवा *pã:cva:* 'fifth'; छठा *chaṭha:* 'sixth.' The suffix - आं *-ã* is added to the cardinals from seven onwards to make ordinals: सातवां *sa:tvã:* 'seventh'; आठवां *a:ṭhvã:* 'eighth'; नौवां *navã:* 'ninth'; दसवां *dasvã:* 'tenth'; बीसवां *bi:svã:* 'twentieth'; तीसवां *ti:svã*: 'thirteenth'; सौवां *sɔvã:* 'hundredth'; हज़ारवां *haza:rvã:* 'thousandth' etc.

Adjectives of Quantity

Nouns denoting measure, and weight preceded by a numeral or by an adjective denoting an indefinite number, such as कोई *koi:* or कुछ *kuch,* are used as adjectives of quantity.

तीन किलो चावल	ti:n kilo ca:val	three kilograms of rice
दो प्याले चाय	do pya:le ca:y	two cups of tea
कुछ बोतल शहद	kuch botal šahad	some bottles of honey
कई किलो दूध	kai: kilo du:dh	several kilos of milk

Collective Adjectives

Some regular numerals can be replaced by collective adjectives like जोड़ा *joṛa:* 'pair,' चौकड़ा *cɔkṛa:* 'four,' पंजा *panja:* 'five,' छक्का *chakka:* 'six,' दर्जन *darjan* 'dozen,' बीसी *bi:si:/* कोड़ी *koṛi:* 'score,' सैंकड़ा *sɛ̃kṛa:* 'hundred.' They are treated as nouns and may be qualified by the regular numerals.

दो जोड़े कपड़े	do joṛe kapṛe	two pairs of clothes
तीन दर्जन सेब	ti:n darjan seb	three dozens of apples

The सैंकड़ा *sɛ̃kṛa:* is also used in the sense of 'per hundred.'

बीस रुपए सैंकड़ा	bi:s rupye sɛ̃kṛa:	twenty rupees per hundred

3.3.6.3. Fractions

Fractions are expressed as follows:

एक बटे चार/पाव	ek baṭe ca:r/pa:v	one quarter
(pa:v is used mainly for denoting weights)		
एक बटे तीन/तिहाई	ek baṭe ti:n/tiha:i:	one-third
एक बटे दो/आधा	ek baṭe do/a:dha:	half
तीन बटे चार/पौन	ti:n baṭe ca:r/pɔn	three quarters
एक सही एक बटे चार/सौवा	ek sahi: ek baṭe ca:r/sava:	one and a quarter
एक सही एक बटे दो डेढ़	ek sahi: ek baṭe do/ḍeṛh	one and a half
दो सही एक बटे दो ढ़ाई	do sahi: ek baṭe do/ḍha:i:	two and a half
पौने दो	pɔne do	two less by a quarter
पौने तीन	pɔne ti:n	three less by a quarter
साढ़े तीन	sa:ṛhe ti:n	three and a half

Note that साढ़े *sa:ṛhe* denoting 'half' is attached to the numerals beginning with three: साढ़े चार *sa:ṛhe ca:r* 'four and half,' साढ़े पांच *sa:ṛhe pã:c* 'five and half,' etc. The system of denoting fractions is also used to denote fractions of hundred, thousand, ten thousand, etc.

सवा सौ	*sava: sɔ*	125
डेढ़ सौ	*ḍeṛh sɔ*	150
स्ढ़ाई सौ	*ḍha:i: sɔ*	250
ड़ेढ़ हज़ार	*ḍeṛh haza:r*	1,500
सवा दो लाख	*sava: do la:kh*	2,25,000

3.3.6.4. Multiplicatives

Multiplicatives are formed by attaching गुना *guna:*'multiplied by' to the numerals. The numerals 2 to 8 are slightly modified.

दुगना *dugna:* or दूना *du:na:* 'double,' तिगुना *tiguna:* 'threefold,' चौगना *cɔguna:* 'fourfold,' पंचगुना *pancguna:* 'fivefold,' छगुना *chaguna* 'sixfold,' सतगुना *satguna:* 'sevenfold,' अठगुना *aṭhguna:* 'eightfold.' After this the forms are regular: नवगुना *navguna:* 'ninefold,' दसगुना *dasguna:* 'tenfold,' बीसगुना *bi:sguna:* 'twentyfold,' तीसगुना *ti:sguna:* 'thirtyfold,' सौगुना *sɔguna:* 'hundredfold,' हज़ारगुना *haza:rguna:* 'thousandfold. The गुना *guna:* can be attached to fractions too: सवा गुना *sava: guna:* 1¼ times as much, ड़ेढ गुना *ḍeṛh guna:* 1½ times as much, ढ़ाई गुना *ḍha:i: guna:* 2 ½ times as much.

3.3.6.5. Approximation

Approximation is expressed by placing कोई *koi:,* लगभग *lagbhag,* or प्रायः *pra:ya*: before the numeral.

कोई बीस आदमी	koi: bi:s a:dmi:	about twenty persons
लगभग पाँच सौ लोग	lagbhag pã:c sɔ log	about five hundred people
प्रायः दो सौ वर्ष पहिले	pra:ya: do sɔ varš pahle	about two hundred years ago

It is also expressed by certain pairs of numerals.

दो-एक	do-ek	one or two
दो-तीन	do-ti:n	about two or three
दस-पांच	das-pã:c	about ten
सौ-सवा सौ	sɔ- sava: sɔ	about 125

Reduplication of a numeral denotes '... at a time,' or '...per piece.'

दो-दो लड़के	do-do laṛke	two boys at a time
एक-एक लड़के को तीन-तीन किताबें दो।	ek-ek laṛke ko ti:n-ti:n kita:bẽ do	Give three books to each boy.

3.3.6.6. Aggregation

Aggregation is expressed by adding - ओं *-õ* to a numeral. In the case of दो *do*, -नों *-nõ* is added. (e.g., दोनों *donõ* 'both,' तीनों *ti:nõ* 'all the three,' चारों *ca:rõ* 'all the four,' दसों *dasõ* 'all the ten,' बीसों *bi:sõ* 'all the twenty,' etc.). Notice that -इयों *-iyõ* is added to numerals दस *das* or बीस *bi:s* to indicate an indefinite large number (e.g., दसियों *dasiyõ* 'several tens,' बीसियों *bi:siyõ* 'several scores,' etc.)

The suffix -ओं *-õ* is also added to the nouns signifying duration, measures, weight to indicate large and indefinite number or quantity. (e.g., महीनों *mahi:nõ* 'a number of months,' बरसों *barsõ* 'a number of years,' बोरियों अनाज *boriyõ ana:j* 'sackfulls of grains,' etc.

3.4. Verbs

There are two types of verbs: main and auxiliary.

3.4.1. The Verb *hona:*

The verb होना *hona:* 'to be' is used as a copula in simple predicative sentences, as well as an auxiliary in different types of verbal constructions. The verb होना *hona:* has four sets of verbal forms: present, past, presumptive, and subjunctive.

(a) The present tense forms of होना *hona:* agree with their subjects in number and person.

Person	Singular	Plural
1st	हूँ hũ:	हैं hɛ̃
2nd (intimate)	है hɛ	हो ho
2nd (polite)	हैं hɛ̃	हैं hɛ̃
3rd	है hɛ	हैं hɛ̃

मैं हूँ	mɛ̃ hũ:	I am	हम हैं	ham hɛ̃	we are
तू है	tu: hɛ	you are	तुम हो	tum ho	you are
आप हैं	a:p hɛ̃	you are	वह है	vah hɛ	he/she is
वे हैं	ve hɛ̃	(s)he is/ they are			

(b) The past tense forms of होना *hona:* agree with their subjects in gender and number.

Masculine		Feminine	
Sg	Pl	Sg	Pl
था tha:	थे the	थी thi:	थीं thĩ:

मैं था/थी	mɛ̃ tha:/thi:	I was
वह था/थी	vah tha:/thi:	he/she was
तू था/थी	tu: tha:/thi:	you were
हम/ तुम/ आप/ ये/ वे थे।	ham/tum/a:p/ye/ve the.	we/you/she/they were
हम/ तुम/ आप/ ये/ वे थीं।	ham/tum/a:p/ye/ve thĩ:	we/you/she/they were

(c) The presumptive forms of the verb होना *hona:* agree with their subjects in person, gender, and number.

Person	Masculine		Feminine	
	Sg	Pl	Sg	Pl
1st	हूँगा hũ:ga:	होंगे hõge	हूँगी hũ:gi:	होंगी hõgi:
2nd (intimate)	होगा hoga:	होगे hoge	होगी hogi:	होगी hogi:
2nd (hon sg/pl)	होंगे hõge	होंगे hõge	होंगी hõgi:	होंगी hõgi:
3rd	होगा hoga:	होंगे hõge	होगी hogi:	होंगी hõgi:

(d) The subjunctive forms of होना *hona:* are used to indicate the situations of speculative, hypothetical, contingent, or desired nature. They agree with their subjects in person and number.

Person	Singular	Plural
1st	होऊँ hoũ:	हों hõ
2nd (intimate)	हो ho	हो ho
2nd (hon sg/pl)	हों hõ	हों hõ
3rd	हो ho	हों hõ

मैं होऊँ	mɛ̃ hoũ:	हम हों	ham hõ
तू हो	tu: ho	तुम हो	tum ho/ho
आप हों	a:p hõ	यह/वह हो	yeh/vah ho
ये/वे हों	ye/ve hõ		

3.4.2. Main Verbs

There are three types of main verbs: simple verbs, conjunct verbs, and compound verbs. A simple verb may consist of one main verb and person, gender, number, tense, and aspect markers. In the compound verb construction, the person, gender, number, and aspect markers are taken by the explicators/operators, and in the conjunct verbal construction they are taken by the verb element. We will classify the verbal constructions as intransitive, transitive, ditransitive, causative, dative, conjunct, and compound.

3.4.2.1. Intransitive Verbs

Intransitive verbs like आ *a:* 'come,' जा *ja:* 'go' उठ *uṭh* 'get up,' and बैठ *bɛṭh* 'sit.' do not take a direct object and are not marked by any postposition in the present or future tense. Subjects in such cases are controlled by the verb agreement.

1. वह जाता है।
   vah ja:ta: hɛ.
   he go-ptc is
   He goes.

2. अमित घर जाएगा।
   amit ghar ja:ega:.
   Amit home go-fut
   Amit will go home.

Besides verb agreement, subjects demonstrate a number of other properties which are explained below. Intransitive verbs in the past tense take their subjects in the direct case.

3. वह बहुत थक गई।
vah bahut thak gai:.
she very tired aux
She was dead tired.

4. अमित समय पर आया।
amit samay par a:ya:.
Amit time at came
Amit came on time.

Some intransitive verbs, such as खेल *khel* 'play' and लड़ *laṛ* 'fight,' may sometimes be used as transitives when they take abstract nouns as objects.

Intransitive		Transitive	
खेलना khelna:	to play	खेल खेलना khel khelna:	to play a game
लड़ाई laṛa:i:	fight	लड़ाई लड़ना laṛa:i: laṛna:	fight a battle

5. मोहन खेला।
mohan khela:.
Mohan played.

5a. मोहन खेल खेला।
mohan ne khel khela:.
Mohan played a game.

3.4.2.2. Transitive Verbs

Transitive verbs, such as पढ़ *paṛh* 'read,' लिख *likh* 'write,' ला *la:* 'bring,' दे *de* 'give,' ले *le* 'take,' and कर *kar* 'do,' take direct objects, and in the past tense they require their subjects must be marked with the ergative case markers agreeing with the object in gender and number.

6. उमा ने किताब पढ़ी।
uma: ne kita:b paṛhi:.
Uma-erg book-fs read-fs
Uma read a book.

7. अमर ने अख़बार ख़रीदा।
amar ne axba:r xari:da:.
Amar-erg newspaper-ms bought-ms
Amar bought a newspaper.

Some transitive verbs are derived from intransitives by certain vocalic changes to the verb roots.

Intransitive		Transitive	
मर mar	die	मार ma:r	kill
छप chap	be printed	छाप cha:p	print
कट kaṭ	be cut	काट ka:ṭ	cut
गिर gir	fall	गिरा gira:	fell
पिस pis	be ground	पीस pi:s	grind
बंद bandh	be tied	बांद ba:ndh	tie
खुल khul	be open	खोल khol	open
उठ uṭh	rise	उठा uṭha:	raise
जग jag	wake up	जगा jaga:	awaken
फैल phɛl	stretch	फैला phɛla:	spread
दिख dikh	be able to see	देख dekh	see
बन ban	be made	बना bana:	make
घूम ghu:m	go round	घूमना ghuma:	turn round
दौड़ dɔṛ	run	दौड़ा dɔṛa:	make x race

In certain cases besides vocalic changes, some consonantal changes also take place.

Intransitive		Transitive	
टूट ṭu:ṭ	break	तोड़ toṛ	break
बिक bik	be sold	बेच bec	sell
फट phaṭ	be torn	फाड़ pha:ṛ	tear
सो so:	be asleep	सुला sula:	to make x to sleep
बन ban	be made	बना bana:	to make

A few transitive verbs like बोल *bol* 'to speak,' समझ *samjh* 'to understand' and भूल *bhu:l* 'to forget' are sometimes used as intransitives and do not take an ergative case marker.

8. मैं बोला/ समझा/ भूला।
mɛ̃ bola: / samjha: / bhu:la:.
I said/ understood/ forgot.

3.4.2.3. Ditransitive Verbs

Some verbs like देना *dena:* 'to give,' सुना *suna:* 'to tell,' बेचना *becna:* 'to sell' are called ditransitives. Ditransitives take three arguments, namely, subject, object, and indirect objects. Indirect objects are always marked in the dative. Other arguments follow the transitive pattern noted above.

9. अमर ने उमा को किताब दी।
amar ne uma: ko kita:b di:.
Amar-erg Uma-dat book-fs gave-fs
Amar gave a book to Uma.

10. उमा ने बच्चे को कहानी सुनाई।
uma: ne bacce ko kaha:ni: suna:i:.
Uma-erg child-dat story-fs told-fs
Uma told a story to the child.

3.4.2.4. Causative Verbs

Casuative verbs may be derived from transitive verbs by adding causative suffixes. They include the transitive verbs derived from intransitives. Causative verbs are, therefore, invariably transitive and take the same forms as other transitive verbs. There are two types of causative forms: causal I and causal II.

Causal I forms

Causal I verbs are formed by adding the causal suffix *-a:* to the transitive verb form. As a result of adding this suffix, certain morphophonemic changes take place.

(a) Consonant ending roots with short vowels remain unchanged.

Transitive		Causal I	
कर kar	do	करा kara:	make x do
सुन sun	listen	सुना suna:	make x tell
पढ़ paṛh	study	पढ़ा paṛha:	teach x

(b) The long vowels of the verb roots are shortened. The vowels ए /e/ and ई /i:/ change to इ /i/.

Transitive		Causal I	
देख dekh	see	दिखा dikha:	show
सीख si:kh	learn	सिखा sikha:	make x learn

(c) The long vowel ending verb roots are shortened and the suffix -ला *-la:* instead of -आ-*a:*, is added to derive the first causal forms. As a result of adding the causative suffix to the verb root, the vowels ए /e/ and आ /a:/ change to इ/i/, and ओ /o/ changes to /u/.

Transitive		Causal I	
पी pi:	drink	पिला pila:	make x drink
सी si:	stitch	सिला sila:	make x stitch
खा kha:	eat	खिला khila:	feed x
दे de	give	दिला dila:	make x give
धो dho	wash	धुला dhula:	make x wash

Causal II

Causal II or extended causatives are formed by adding the causal II suffix -वा *-va:* to the verb roots.

Causal I		Causal II	
सुना suna:	tell	सुनवा sunva:	cause x to tell
पढ़ा paṛha:	teach	पढ़वा paṛhva:	cause x to teach y
उठा uṭha:	lift	उठवा uṭhva:	make x to lift
पिला pila:	make x drink	पिलवा pilva:	cause x to drink
जगा jaga:	awaken	जगवा jagva:	cause to awaken
घुमा ghuma:	move	घुमवा ghumva:	cause x to move
दौड़ा dɔṛa:	make x run	दौड़वा dɔṛva:	cause x to run
दिला dila:	cause x give	दिलवा dilva:	cause x to give y

खिला khila:	feed	खिलवा khilva:	cause x to feed y
बना bana:	make	बनवाना banva:na	cause x to make
कर kar	get done	करवा karva:	cause x to do
धुला dhula:	make x wash	धुलवा dhulva:	cause x to wash

(a) As a result of adding the causal II suffix to the transitive verb root, the vowel ओ /o/ changes to उ /u/.

तोड़ toṛ	break	तुड़वा tuṛva:	cause x to break

(b) There are few irregular forms. In the following example, the causal suffix -वा *-va* is added to the intransitive verb root बिक *bik* 'sell' instead of its transitive verb form बेच *be:c*:

बेच bec	sell	बिकवा bikva:	cause x to sell

(c) In certain cases, the meanings of the first and second causals are the same as in कराना *kara:na:/* करवाना *karva:na:* 'to get done' or धुलाना *dhula:na:/* धुलवाना *dhulva:na:* 'to get washed.'

11. माँ ने बच्चे को दूध पिलाया।
mã: ne bacce ko du:dh pila:ya:.
mother-erg child to milk drink-caus-past
The mother made the child drink milk.

11a. माँ ने बच्चे को नर्स से दूध पिलवाया।
mã: ne bacce ko nars se du:dh pilva:ya:.
mother-er child to nurse by milk drink-cause
The mother caused the child to drink milk from the nurse.

3.4.2.5. Dative Verbs

Most dative verbs fall into the stative-inchoative category of verbs. They represent a small class of verbs but are very frequently used. They can be derived by substituting the intransitive verbs होना *hona:* 'to be,' and आना *a:na:* 'to come' in place of करना *karna:* 'to do' in active/conjunct verbs as given below.

Stative	Inchoative	Active	
पसंद होना	पसंद आना	पसंद करना	
pasand hona:	pasand a:na:	pasand karna:	to like

याद होना	याद आना	याद करना	
ya:d hona:	ya:d a:na:	ya:d karna:	to remember
पता होना		पता करना	
pata: hona:	…	pata: karna:	to find out

12. उसको यह किताब पसंद है।
usko yeh kita:b pasand hɛ.
he-dat this book like is
He likes this book.

12a. उसको यह किताब पसंद आई।
usko yeh kita:b pasand a:i:.
he-dat this book like came
He liked this book.

12b. उसने यह किताब पसंद की।
usne yeh kita:b pasand ki:.
he-erg this book like did
He liked this book.

13. उसको सारी बात याद है।
usko sa:ri: ba:t ya:d hɛ.
he-dat all matter remember is
He remembers the whole matter.

13a. उसको सारी बात याद आई।
usko sa:ri: ba:t ya:d a:i:.
he-dat all matter remember came
He remembered the whole matter.

13b. उसने सारी बात याद की।
usne sa:ri: ba:t ya:d ki:.
he-erg all matter remember did
He remembered the whole matter.

14. उसको यह बात पता है।
usko yah ba:t pata: hɛ.
he-dat this matter know be
He knows this matter.

14a. उसने यह बात पता की।
usne yah ba:t pata: ki:.
he-dat this matter find did
He found out this thing.

3.4.2.6. Conjunct Verbs

A conjunct verb consists of a noun or an adjective and a verb, which takes all the verbal inflections. The verbs may be transitive or intransitive. The most frequent verbs used in conjunct verbal const+ructions are करना *karna:* 'to do' and होना *hona:* 'to be.' Other verbs used are देना *dena:* 'to give,' आना *a:na:* 'to come,' and लगना *lagna:* 'to feel.'

15. मैंने अपना काम समाप्त किया।
mɛ̃ne apna: ka:m sama:pt kiya:.
I-erg self's work finish did
I finished my work.

15a. यह काम समाप्त हुआ।
yeh ka:m sama:pt hua:.
this work finish be-past
This work is done.

16. दरवाज़ा बंद करो।
darva:za: band karo.
door close do-imp
Close the door.

16a. दरवाज़ा बंद हुआ।
darva:za: band hua:.
door close be-past
The door was closed.

One class of conjunct verbs is formed by the combination of a noun and an intransitive verb, which requires the subject to be marked in the oblique case. This class includes psychological predicates such as गुस्सा आना *gussa: a:na:* 'to be angry,' भूख लगना *bhu:kh lagna:*'to be hungry,' प्यास लगना *pya:s lagna:,* 'to be thirsty,' तरस आना *taras a:na:* 'to have pity.' It also includes non-volitional verbs such as दिखाई देना *dikha:i: dena:* 'to be seen.'

17. अमर को गुस्सा आया।
amar ko gussa: a:ya:.
Amar-dat anger came
Amar was angry.

18. सुनीता को भूख/ प्यास लगी।
suni:ta ko bhu:kh/pya:s lagi:.
Sunita-dat hunger/thirst struck
Sunita was hungry/thirsty.

19. मोहन को गरीब पर तरस आया।
mohan ko gari:b par taras a:ya:.
Mohan-dat poor on pity came
Mohan took pity on the poor.

20. उसको अंतर दिखता नहीं।
usko antar dikhta: nahĩ:.
he-dat difference see-ptc neg
He is not able to see the difference.

3.4.2.7. Compound Verbs

Compound verbs in Hindi are combination of Verb 1 + Verb 2 (+ inflections). Whereas Verb 1 (also called main verb) expresses general meaning and occurs in its stem form, verb 2, which is called an explicator/operator, takes all the inflections. The explicators belong to a small group of verbs. The original meaning of the explicator is lost. They add certain aspectual values, such as completion of an action, benefaction, or intensification, to the main verb. The most frequent explicators are listed below with their actual meaning and the aspectual meanings they add to main verbs.

Explicators		Aspectual Values
आ a:	come	change of state from within
जा ja:	go	change of state
ले le	take	action for or toward others
पड़ paṛ	fall	action for or towards self
दे de	give	change of state, suddenness
जा ja:	go	direction away, simple completion
डाल ḍa:l	throw	speed, recklessness, relief, completion
छोड़ choṛ	release	psychological separation, relief

रख rakh	put/keep	proactiveness, future use in view
बैठ bɛṭh	sit	action for or towards self
उठ uṭh	rise	action for or towards self
पहुंच pahũc	reach	action for completion, direction
चल cal	walk	direction away, completion
मर mar	die	completion, lack of control
मार ma:r	kill	change of state, suddenness

Thus, a compound verb is made of two verbs, the first, the main verb which expresses its general meaning and, the second, an explicator/operator which is conjugated for different inflections. A large number of compound verbs are formed by the combination of verbs in which the first verb represents the meaning and the explicator takes all the grammatical inflections. Examples of such verbs are: आ जाना *a: ja:na:* 'to come,' मिल जाना *mil ja:na:* 'to get,' खा लेना *kha: lena:* 'to eat,' पी लेना *pi: lena:* 'to drink,' ले आना *le a:na:* 'to bring,' खरीद लेना *xari:d lena:* 'to buy,' चल देना *cal dena:* 'to leave,' कर बैठना *kar bɛṭhna:* 'to do,' कर डालना *kar ḍa:lna:* 'to do,' कर छोड़ना *kar choṛna:* 'to do,' दे देना *de dena:* 'to give.'

21. सभी बच्चे समय पर आ गए।
sabhi: bacce samay par a: gaye.
all children time on came went
All the children came on time.

22. बच्चे ने सेब खा लिया।
bacce ne seb kha: liya:.
child-erg apple eat took
The child ate an apple.

23. वह सारे पैसे ले गया।
vah sa:re pɛse le gaya:.
he all money take went
He took all the money.

24. उसने नई कार ख़रीद ली।
usne nai: ka:r xari:d li:.
he-erg new car buy took-fs
He bought a new car.

25. मैंने अपना काम कर डाला।
mɛ̃ne apna: ka:m kar ḍa:la:.
I-erg self's work do threw
I completed my work.

There are verbal phrases in which there are two or more inflexible verbs, such as पीता गया *pi:ta gaya:* 'went on drinking,' सुनता रहा *sunta: raha:* 'kept on listing,' सोया पड़ा रहा *soya: paṛa: raha:* 'remained sleeping,' चला गया *cala: gaya:* 'gone.'

26. वह सारी रात चाय पीता गया।
vah sa:ri: ra:t ca:y pi:ta: gaya:.
he all night tea drink-ptc went-ms
He kept on drinking tea throughout the night.

27. वह मेरी बात ध्यान से सुनता रहा।
vah meri: ba:t dhya:n se sunta: raha:.
he my talk attention with listened-ptc remained-ms
He kept on listening to my story with attention.

28. वह सारा दिन सोया पड़ा रहा।
vah sa:ra: din soya: paṛa: raha:.
he whole day slept fell remained-ms
He kept on sleeping for the whole day.

3.4.3. Tense

Tense and aspect are major grammatical categories of the verbal system in Hindi. There are three grammatical aspects: habitual, progressive, and perfective. Each of them is expressed by marking the verbal stems.

Hindi has six tenses: present, past, future, present perfect, habitual past, and past perfect. The present tense represents an ongoing action, a habitual, repeated or characteristic action, or simply expresses a fact.

1. अमर घर जा रहा है।
amar ghar ja: raha: hɛ.
Amar home go-prog is
Amar is going home.

2. वह कालिज में पढ़ता है।
vah ka:lej mẽ paṛhta: hɛ.
he college in study-pre-hab. be
He studies in college.

The verb in (1) is in the progressive aspect and in (2) in the habitual aspect.

The past tense represents an ongoing action or an action completed in the past.

3. अमर दिल्ली जा रहा था।
amar dilli: ja: raha: tha:.
Amar Delhi-obl go-prog was
Amar was going to Delhi.

4. उसने अख़बार पढ़ा।
usne axba:r paṛha:.
he-erg newspaper read-perf
He read the newspaper.

The verb in (3) is in the progressive aspect and in (4) is in the perfect aspect.

The future tense represents an action yet to take place or a state yet to come into being.

5. उमा कल दिल्ली जाएगी।
uma: kal dilli: ja:egi:.
Uma tomorrow Delhi-obl go-fut
Uma will go to Delhi tomorrow.

The present perfect tense represents a completed act the effect of which is still present.

6. उसने यह जगह देखी है।
usne yah jagah dekhi: hɛ.
he-erg this place see-perf be
He has seen this place.

The habitual past tense represents an act habitually done in the past.

7. वह हमेशा मेहनत करताा था।
vah hameša: mehnat karta: tha:.
he always hard work do-hab be-past
He always used to work hard.

The past perfect tense represents an action completed in the past or before a certain past time.

8. अमर परसों सवेरे आया था।
amar parsõ savere a:ya: tha:.
Amar day before yesterday morning-obl came be-past
Amar had come the day before yesterday in the morning.

3.4.4. Aspect

Verbal forms indicating one of these aspects are specified for one of the four tenses: present, past, presumptive, and subjunctive. The combination of one of the three aspects with the four different tenses results in the production of various aspectual-tenses: present-habitual, past-habitual, presumptive-habitual, subjunctive-habitual, present-progressive, past-progressive, presumptive-progressive, subjunctive-progressive, present-perfective, past-perfective, presumptive-perfective, and subjunctive-perfective. It also permits the simple-perfective form. Besides these aspectual verb forms, some non-aspectual verb forms of Hindi are the future, root subjunctive, and the imperative and infinitive forms. They will be discussed separately.

3.4.4.1. Habitual Aspect

The habitual aspectual-tenses are formed by adding the following suffixes to the verb stems agreeing with the subject in gender and number:

Masculine		Feminine
Sg	Pl	Sg / Pl
-ता -ta:	-ते -te	-ती -ti:

They are followed by appropriate forms of the auxiliary verb होना *hona:*. Present and past habitual forms are used to express habitual actions or the state of affairs viewed from the perspective of the present and the past respectively.

Present-habitual

1. मैं घर रोज़ आता/ आती हूँ ।
   mɛ̃ ghar roz a:ta:/a:ti: hũ:.
   I home daily come-ptc-ms/-fs be
   I come home daily.

2. हम घर रोज़ आते / आती हैं ।
   ham ghar roz a:te/a:ti: hɛ̃.
   we home daily come-ptc-mp/-fp be
   We come home daily.

3. तू घर रोज़ जाता/ जाती है ।
   tu: ghar roz ja:ta:/ja:ti: hɛ.
   you home daily go-ptc-ms/go-fs be
   You go home daily.

4. तुम घर रोज़ जाते/ जाती हो ।
   tum ghar roz ja:te/ja:ti: ho.
   you home daily go-ptc-mp/go-fs be
   You go home daily.

5. आप घर रोज़ जाते/ जाती हैं ।
   a:p ghar roz ja:te/ja:ti: hɛ̃.
   you home daily go-m/go-f be
   You go home daily.

6. यह/ वह शहर जाता/ जाती है ।
   yah/vah šahar ja:ta:/ja:ti: hɛ.
   (s)he city go-ptc-ms/go-fs be
   He/she goes to the city.

7. वे शहर जाते/ जाती हैं ।
   ve šahar ja:te/ja:ti: hɛ̃.
   they city go-ptc-mp/go-f be
   He/she/they goes/goes/go to the city.

Past-habitual

8. मैं रोज़ बाज़ार जाता था /जाती थी।
mɛ̃ roz ba:za:r ja:ta: tha:/ja:ti: thi:.
I daily market go-ptc-ms was /go-fs was
I used to go to the market daily.

9. तू रोज़ बाज़ार जाता था/ जाती थी।
tu: roz ba:za:r ja:ta: tha:/ja:ti: thi:.
you daily market go-ptc-ms was/go-ptc-fs was
You used to go to the market daily.

10. तुम/ आप रोज़ दफ़्तर जाते थे/जाती थीं।
tum/a:p roz daftar ja:te the/ja:ti: thĩ:.
you-fam/you-hon daily office go-ptc-ms were/go-ptc-fs were
You used to go to the office daily.

11. वह सवेरे गाँव जाता था/ जाती थी।
vah savere ga:ũ: ja:ta: tha:/ja:ti: thi:.
he/she morning-abl village go-ptc-ms was/go-ptc-fs was
He/She used to go to the village in the morning.

12. वे शाम को गाँव जाते थे / जाती थीं।
ve ša:m ko ga:ũ: ja:te the/ja:ti: thĩ:.
they evening-dat at village go-ptc-ms was/go-ptc-fs was
They used to go to the village in the evening.

Present-habitual in conjunction with the adverb अभी *abhi:* 'right away'indicates that an action is to be carried out in the near future.

13. मैं अभी जाता हूँ।
mɛ̃ abhi: ja:ta: hũ:.
I right away go-ptc.ms am
I'll go right away.

In the negative construction of the present-habitual form, the present form of the verb होना *hona:* is usually deleted.

14. वह सुबह चाय नहीं पीता।
vah subah ca:y nahĩ: pi:ta:.
he morning-abl tea neg drink-ptc.ms
He doesn't drink tea in the morning.

Past-habitual also indicates that an action has taken place in remote past.

15. उमा होटल में गाना गाती थी।
uma: hoṭal mẽ ga:na: ga:ti: thi:.
Uma hotel in song sing-ptc was
Uma used to sing at the hotel.

Presumptive-habitual
Presumptive-habitual forms are used to indicate that an action or state of affairs is both habitual and presumed, but not known definitely.

16. मैं आता होऊँगा/ आती होऊँगी।
mɛ̃ a:ta: hoũ:ga: /a:ti: hoũ:gi:.
I come-ms be-pre.hab/ go-fs be-pre.hab.
I would be coming.

17. हम आते होंगे/ आती होंगीं।
ham a:te hõge/a:ti: hõgĩ:.
We would be coming.

18. तू/ वह आता होगा/ आती होगी।
tu:/vah a:ta: hoga:/a:ti: hogi:.
You/he would be coming.

19. तुम/ आप/ वे आते होंगे / आती होंगी।
tum/a:p/ve a:te hõge/ a:ti: hõgi:.
You/they would be coming.

Subjunctive-habitual
Subjunctive-habitual forms are used to indicate actions that are both habitual and hypothetical, contingent, or speculative, but not directly guaranteed to take place.

20. मैं चाहता हूँ वह आएँ।
mɛ̃ ca:hta: hũ: vah a:yẽ.
I want him/her to come.

21. मेरी इच्छा है आप यह किताब पढ़ें।
meri: iccha: hɛ a:p yeh kita:b paṛhẽ.
I want you to read this book.

22. वह घर पर काम करता था/ करती थी।
vah ghar par ka:m karta: tha: /karti: thi:.
he/she home at work do-ms/do-fs was
He/she used to work at home.

3.4.4.2. Progressive Aspect

Progressive aspect verbs are formed by adding the following auxiliary forms immediately after the verb stems and appropriate forms of the verb *hona:* 'to be' and they agree with the person, gender, and number of the subject of the verb:

Masculine		Feminine
Sg	Pl	Sg / Pl
रहा raha:	रहे rahe	रही rahi:

The progressive aspect is used to indicate actions or states of affairs of a continuous nature or extended through time. There are two primary categories: present-progressive and past-progressive.

Present-progressive

23. मैं घर जा रहा/ जा रही हूँ।
mɛ̃ ghar ja: raha:/ja: rahi: hũ:.
I home go-prog-ms/ go-prog-fs am
I am going home.

24. मैं/ हम/ वे घर जा रहे/ जा रही हैं।
ham/ve ghar ja: rahe/ ja rahi: hɛ̃.
we/they home go-prog-mpl/-prog-fpl be-pl
We/they are going home.

25. तू कालिज से आ रहा है/ रही है।
tu: ka:lej se a: raha: hɛ / rahi: hɛ.
you-fam/he/she college from come-prog-ms /-prog-fs be-sg
You are coming from the college.

26. तुम खाना खा रहे/ रही हो।
tum kha:na: kha: rahe/rahi: ho.
you-non.hon pl food eat-prog-mpl/-fpl be
You are eating food.

27. आप/ वे चाय पी रहे हैं।
a:p/ve ca:y pi: rahe hɛ̃.
you/they tea drink-prog are
You /they are drinking tea.

Past-progressive

28. मैं गा रहा था/ रही थी।
mɛ̃ ga: raha: tha:/ rahi: thi:.
I sing-prog was-ms/sing-prog was-fs
I was singing.

29. तू सेब खा रहा था/ रही थी।
tu: seb kha: raha: tha:/ rahi: thi:.
you-fam. apple eat-prog-ms was/ -prog-fs was
You were eating an apple.

30. तुम किताब पढ़ रहे थे / रही थी।
tum kita:b paṛh rahe/rahi: ho.
you book read-prog-mp/ -fp be
You are reading a book.

31. आप पत्र लिख रहे थे।
a:p patr likh rahe the.
you-hon letter write-prog be
You were writing a letter.

Presumptive-progressive

Presumptive-progressive forms are used to indicate that an action or state of affairs is extended in time and presumed to be occuring.

32. उमा दिल्ली से आ रही होगी।
uma: dilli: se a: rahi: hogi:.
Uma Delhi from come-prog be-presumptive
Uma must be coming from Delhi.

Subjunctive-progressive

33. सम्भव है वह जा रहा हो।
sambhav hɛ vah ja: raha: ho.
possible is he go-prog be-subj
It is possible he would be going.

34. मुमकिन है वे आ रहे हों।
mumkin hɛ ve a: rahe hõ.
possible is they come-prog be-subj
It is possible they would be coming.

3.4.4.3. Perfective Aspect

Perfective aspect indicates an action or state of affairs that has been completed. There are five sets of perfective forms in Hindi: simple-perfective, present-perfective, past-perfective, presumptive-perfective and subjunctive-perfective. The following perfect participle suffixes are added to the main verb stems. In constructions with intransitive verbs, they agree with the subject in gender and number. In constructions with transitive verbs, they agree with the object's gender and number.

Masculine		Feminine	
Sg	Pl	Sg	Pl
-आ -a:	-ए -e	-ई -i:	-ईं -ĩ:

These suffixes are added to both intransitive and transitive verbs.

Verb		Masculine		Feminine	
		Sg	Pl	Sg	Pl
गिर gir	fall	गिरा gira:	गिरे gire	गिरी giri:	गिरीं girĩ:
चल cal	walk	चला cala:	चले cale	चली cali:	चलीं calĩ:
पढ़ paṛh	read	पढ़ा paṛha:	पढ़े paṛhe	पढ़ी paṛhi:	पढ़ीं paṛhĩ:
लिख likh	write	लिखा likha:	लिखे likhe	लिखी likhi:	लिखीं likhĩ:

In vowel-ending verb stems, the glide -य *-y* is inserted before the masculine singular ending -आ *-a:* is added to the verb stem.

Verb		Masculine		Feminine	
		Sg	Pl	Sg	Pl
आ a:	come	आया a:ya:	आए a:e	आई a:i:	आईं a:ĩ:
सो so	sleep	सोया soya:	सोए soe	सोई soi:	सोईं soĩ:
सी si:	sew	सिया siya:	सिए sie	सी si:	सीं sĩ:
खे khe	row	खेया kheya:	खेये kheye	खेई khei:	खेईं kheĩ:
जा ja:	go	गया gaya:	गए gae	गई gai:	गईं gaĩ:
खा kha:	eat	खाया kha:ya:	खाए kha:e	खाई kha:i:	खाईं kha:ĩ:

Notice that the verbs सो *so* 'sleep' and सी *si:* 'sew' have alternate feminine plural forms; the verb खे *khe* 'row' has the feminine plural form with inserted य *y* glide; the verb जा *ja:* 'go' has an irregular past perfective form.

Some transitive verbs have irregular perfective participle forms.

Verb		Masculine		Feminine	
		Sg	Pl	Sg	Pl
कर kar	do	किया kiya:	किए kiye	की ki:	कीं kĩ:
ले le	take	लिया liya:	लिए liye	ली li:	लीं lĩ:
पी pi:	drink	पिया piya:	पिये piye	पी pi:	पीं pĩ:
दे de	give	दिया diya:	दिये diye	दी di:	दीं dĩ:

Simple-perfective

The simple-perfective form appears without verbal auxiliaries.

35. लड़का/लड़की घर गया/ गई।
laṛka:/laṛki: ghar ga:ya:/ ga:yi:.
boy/girl home went-ms/went-fs
The boy/girl went home.

36. मैंने /उसने/ उन्होंने तस्वीर देखी।
mɛnẽ /hamne/usne/unhõne tasvi:r dekhi:.
I-erg/we-erg/(s)he-erg/they-erg picture-fs saw-fs
I/we/(s)he/they saw the picture.

Present-perfective

37. मैं कोलकता गया हूँ।
mɛ̃ kolkata: gaya: hũ:.

I Kolkata went be-pre
I have gone to Kolkata.

38. मैंने/ हमने /उन्होंने कोलकता देखा है।
mɛ̃ne/hamne/unhõne kolkata: dekha: hɛ.
I-erg/we-erg/thy-erg Kolkata see-perf be-pre
I/we/they have seen Kolkata.

Past-perfective

39. मैं/ तू /वह बाज़ार गया था।
mɛ̃/tu:/vah ba:za:r gaya: tha:
I/you/(s)he market went-perf be-past
I/you/(s)he had gone to the market.

40. मैंने/ तुमने /उन्होंने/ खाना खाया था।
mɛ̃ne/tumne/unhõne kha:na: kha:ya: tha:
I-erg/you-erg/(s)he-erg/they-erg food eat-perf be-past
I/ you/(s)he/they had eaten the food.

Presumptive-perfective

41. वह कल दिल्ली गया होगा।
vah kal dilli: gaya: hoga:.
he tomorrow Delhi went be-pre.perf
He would have gone to Delhi tomorrow.

42. उसने कल यह किताब पढ़ी होगी।
usne kal yah kita:b paṛhi: hogi:.
he-erg tomorrow this book read-fs be-pre.perf
He would have read this book tomorrow.

Subjunctive-perfective

43. वह आया हो।
vah a:ya: ho.
he came be-subj.perf
He might have come.

44. पत्ते पेड़ से गिरे हों।
patte peṛ se gire hõ.
leaves tree from fell be-subj.perf
The leaves may have fallen from the tree.

3.4.5. Mood

In Hindi there are three moods: indicative, imperative, and optative.

3.4.5.1. Indicative Mood

The indicative represents the action as a fact or makes a query about it. The verb can be used in habitual (hab), progressive (prog), or perfective (perf) aspects. The present and past participle forms of these verbs have been explained above. The following aspectual marks are added to the verb stem *bol* 'say' in the indicative mood.

	Masculine		Feminine	
	Sg	Pl	Sg	Pl
Habitual	बोलता	बोलते	बोलती	बोलतीं
	bolta:	bolte	bolti:	boltĩ:
Progressive	बोल रहा	बोल रहे	बोल रही	बोल रहीं
	bol raha:	bol rahe	bol rahi:	bol rahĩ:
Perfective	बोला	बोले	बोली	बोलीं
	bola:	bole	boli:	bolĩ:

The above paradigm shows the agreement of indicative mood with gender and number.

3.4.5.2. Imperative Mood

The imperative expresses an action as a command, a request, a warning, a prohibition, etc. The imperative is restricted to the future and cannot refer to the present or past tenses. Since the imperative denotes a command, request, etc., its proper domain is the second person. Indirect commands or requests made to a third person are expressed by the subjunctive form. In imperative constructions, the subject is omitted and can be guessed from both the context and the form of the verb. The verb agrees with the second person subject which has three second person pronominal forms: (i) intimate, (ii) familiar, and (iii) polite.

The intimate imperative forms are used in issuing orders/commands for those who are usually addressed with the intimate second person pronoun तू *tu:* 'you.' The familiar imperatives are used in issuing commands to all those who are normally addressed by the familiar second-person pronoun तुम *tum* 'you.' Polite imperatives are used for making requests to those who are normally addressed by the second person pronoun आप *a:p* 'you.'

Second Person				
Verb		Intimate	Familiar	Polite
आ a:	come	आ a:	आओ a:o	आइए a:iye
जा ja:	go	जा ja:	जाओ ja:o	जाइए ja:iye
खा kha:	eat	खा kha:	खाओ kha:o	खाइए kha:iye
पढ़ paṛh	read	पढ़ paṛh	पढ़ो paṛho	पढ़िए paṛhiye
लिख् likh	write	लिख likh	लिखो likho	लिखिए likhiye
ख़रीद xari:d	buy	ख़रीद xari:d	ख़रीदो xari:do	ख़रीदिए xari:diye

In the above, the intimate forms are the same as the verb stem forms; in familiar forms, -ओ *-o* is added to the verb stem form and in polite forms -इए *-iye* is added.

1. (तू) आ /जा /खा /पढ़ /लिख /ख़रीद।
   (tu:) a:/ ja:/kha: / paṛh /likh/xari:d
   you-intimate come/go/eat/read/write/buy
   Come/go/eat/read/write/buy.

1a. (तुम) आओ /जाओ /खाओ /पढ़ो / लिखो /ख़रीदो।
   (tum) a:o/ja:o/kha:o/ paṛho/likho/xari:do
   you-familiar come/go/eat/read/write/buy

1b. (आप) आइए/ जाइए/ खाइए /पढिए /लिखिए /ख़रीदिए।
   (a:p) a:iye/ja:iye/ kha:iye/pṛhiye/likhiye/khari:diye.
   (you-polite) come/go/read/write/ buy
   Please come/go/eat/read/write/buy

A few verbs have irregular familiar and polite forms.

दे de	give	दे de	दो do	दीजिए di:jiye
ले le	take	ले le	लो lo	लीजिए li:jiye
कर kar	do	कर kar	करो karo	करिए kariye/कीजिए ki:jiye

In the above forms, - ओ *-o* is added to the vowel-ending verb stems in the intimate form and the stem vowel is elided. The suffix -ईजिए *-i:jiye* is added in the polite form and the stem vowel is elided. The verb कर *kar* 'do' has an alternate form करिए *kariye* 'do' in its polite form, as well.

2. (तू) दे / ले / कर
(tu:) de/le/kar
(you-familiar.sg) give/take/do

2a. (तुम) दो / लो / करो
(tum) do/lo/karo
(you-familiar.pl) give/take/do

2b. (आप) दीजिए / लीजिए / कीजिए
(a:p) di:jiye/li:jiye/ki:jiye
(polite) give/take/do

The operators take the same imperative forms in the compound verb constructions.

3. यह किताब ले लो।
yah kita:b le lo.
this book take-explicator
Take this book.

3a. यह किताब ले लीजिए।
yah kita:b le li:jiye.
this book take explicator-polite
Please take this book.

4. दरवाज़ा बंद कर लो।
darva:za: band kar lo.
door close do take-explicator-familiar
Close the door.

4a. दरवाज़ा बंद कर लीजिए।
darva:za: band kar li:jiye.
door close do take-explicator-polite
Please close the door.

In negative or prohibitive imperative constructions, the negative markers *na /nahĩĩ* 'no' may precede the verb in the infinitive form.

However, it is optional with the use of prohibitive morpheme *mat* 'don't.'

5. दवाई मत / न / नहीं खाना / खा लेना।
dava:i: mat/na/nahĩ: kha:na:/kha: lena:.
medicine neg eat-inf./eat take-inf
Don't take medicine.

5a. दवाई मत खा लीजिए।
dava:i: mat kha: li:jiye.
medicine neg eat take-inf.
Don't take medicine.

3.4.5.3. Subjunctive Mood

The subjunctive forms are formed by adding certain suffixes to the verb stems that agree with the subjects in person and number, e.g.,

	Sg	Pl
1st person	-ऊँ -ũ:	-एँ -ẽ
2nd person (familiar)	-ए -e	-ओ -o
2nd person (polite)	-एँ -ẽ	-एँ -ẽ
3rd person	-ए -e	-एँ -ẽ

The subjunctive forms of the verb होना *hona:* 'to be' have been given in 3.4.1.(d). Here we will illustrate the subjunctive forms of a few other verbs.

6. मैं जाऊँ / करूँ / पढ़ूँ।
mɛ̃ ja:ũ:/karũ:/ paṛhũ:
I go-subj /do-subj /read-subj

6a. हम जाएँ / करें / पढ़ें।
ham ja:ẽ/karẽ/ paṛhẽ
we go-subj /do-subj /read-subj

6b. तू जाए / करे / पढ़े।
tu: ja:e/kare/ paṛhe
you go-subj /do-subj /read-subj

6c. तुम जाओ / करो /पढ़ो।
tum ja:o/karo/ paṛho
you go-subj /do-subj /read-subj

6d. आप जाएँ / करें / पढ़ें।
a:p ja:ẽ/karẽ/ paṛhẽ
you go-subj /do-subj /read-subj

6e. वह आए / करे / पढ़े।
vah a:e/kare/ paṛhe
he come-subj /do-subj /read-subj

6f. वे आएँ /करें/ पढ़ें।
ve a:ẽ/karẽ/ paṛhẽ
they come-subj/do-subj /read-subj

The stem final vowels -ई *-i:* and -ऊ *-u:,* as in पी *pi:* 'drink,' and छू *chu:* 'touch', are shortened in length as -इ *-i* and -उ *-u* before the subjunctive verb suffixes are added to them.

7. मैं पिऊँ /छुऊँ।
mɛ̃ piũ:/chuũ:
I drink-subj /touch-subj

7a. हम पिएँ /छुएँ।
ham piẽ/chuẽ
we drink-subj/touch-subj

7b. तू पिए /छुए।
tu: pie/chue
you drink-subj/touch-subj

7c. तुम पिओ /छुओ।
tum pio/chuo
you drink-subj/touch-subj

7d. आप पिएँ / छुएँ।
a:p piẽ/chuẽ
yiu drink-subj/touch-subj

7e. वह पिए / छुए।
vah pie/chue
he drink-subj/touch-subj

7f. वे पिएँ /छुएँ।
ve piẽ/chuẽ
they drink-subj/touch-subj

3.4.6. Voice

The verbal stem can also be used to indicate the passive voice. It indicates the subject of a verb in the passive voice and it has agreement of number, person, and gender.

1. उमा से पत्र न लिखा गया।
uma: se patr na likha: gaya:.
Uma by letter neg write-pass
Uma couldn't write a letter.

2. उससे चला न गया।
us-se cala: na gaya:.
she-by walk neg be able
She couldn't walk.

3. उससे यह काम नहीं हो सकता।
us-se yah ka:m nahĩ: ho sakta:
she-by this work neg be able-model
She would not be able to do this work.

4. मुझसे किताब गिर गई।
mujh-se kita:b gir gayi:.
me-by book fell down
The book fell from my hands.

5. उससे आईना टूट गया।
us-se a:yi:na: ṭu:ṭ gaya:.
she-by mirror break explicator
The mirror was broken by her.

6. पुराने अखबारों को फेंका गया।
pura:ne akhba:rõ ko phẽka: gaya:.
old newspapers-obl dat thrown explicator
The old newspapers were thrown away.

It can also be used to express 'from'or 'through'

7. मुझसे अंग्रेज़ी पढ़ लो।
mujh-se ãgrezi: paṛh lo.
me-from English learn explicator
Learn English from me.

It is used with the indirect objects of verbs meaning 'to tell, say, ask, ask for, beg, demand, claim, request,'

8. उसने उमा से कहा कि …
usne uma: se kaha: ki …
he-erg Uma said that
He told Uma that …

9. उमा ने मुझसे पूछा कि …
uma: ne mujh se pu:cha: ...
Uma er me-obl from asked
Uma asked me …

10. अमित ने उससे प्रार्थना की
amit ne us-se pra:rthana: ki:.
Amit-erg him/her request made
Amit requested him/her.

3.4.7. Non-finite Verb Forms

We have discussed various finite verbal forms under tense, aspect, mood, and voice above. We will now discuss the non-finite forms of verbs which include infinitives and participles.

3.4.7.1. Infinitives

Infinitives are formed by adding the suffix -ना *-na:* to the verb stems: आना *a:na:* 'to come,' जाना *ja:na:* 'to go,' करना *karna:* 'to do,' लिखना *likhna:* 'to write,' etc. Infinitives are used both as nouns and as adjectives. An infinitive is usually an abstract noun and, being an abstract noun, it is not used in the plural.

1. जल्दी सोना ठीक है।
   jaldi: sona: ṭhi:kh hɛ.
   early sleep-inf good is
   It is good to go to sleep early.

2. उसके आने में देर हुई।
   uske a:ne mẽ der hui:.
   he-gen-obl come-inf-obl in late be-fsg
   He/she arrived late.

3. मैंने उसे जाने से रोका।
   mɛ̃ne use ja:ne se roka:.
   I-erg he-dat go-inf-obl from stop-pst
   I stopped him from going.

Despite being a noun, the infinite can take an object.

4. वह काम करने में तेज़ है।
   vah ka:m karne mẽ tez hɛ.
   he work do-inf-obl in fast is
   He is prompt in (his) work.

The postposition को *ko* 'to' is not added when the infinitive is used as an object.

5. वह किताब लाना भूल गया।
   vah kita:b la:na: bhu:l gaya:.
   he book bring-inf forget go-operator-pst
   He forgot to bring the book.

6. मैं उसे मिलने जाऊँगा।
   mɛ̃ use milne ja:ũ:ga:.
   I him-obl meet-inf-obl go-fut
   I will go to see him.

Infinitives are frequently used as adjectives in combination with verbs denoting obligation, necessity, requirement, or compulsion like चाह *ca:h* 'want,' हो *ho* 'be,' and पड़ *paṛ* 'compulsion. The compounds made are passive in meaning.

7. मैं चाय पीना चाहता हूँ।
mɛ̃ ca:y pi:na: cahta: hũ:
I tea drink-inf want-ptc am
I want to drink tea.

8. मुझे दिल्ली जाना पड़ा।
mujhe dilli: ja:na: paṛa:.
I-dat Delhi go-inf fell(explicator)
I had to go to Delhi.

9. उसे काम शाम तक समाप्त करना था।
use ka:m ša:m tak sama:pt karna: tha:
he-obl work evening up to finish do-inf be-past-obligatory
He had to finish the work by evening.

When an infinitive is transitive, it is used as an adjective for its object and changes its ending -ना *-na:* to -नी *-ni:* or -ने *-ne.*

10. उसे पैसे लाने हैं।
use pɛse la:ne hɛ̃.
he-obl money bring-inf-obl-pl be-obligatory
He has to bring money.

11. उसे / उसको दवाई पीनी पड़ेगी।
use/usko dava:i: pi:ni: paṛegi:.
he-obl tea medicine drink-inf-fs necessary-fut
He has to drink medicine.

12. मैंने उसकी मदद करनी चाही।
umɛ̃ne uski: madad karni: ca:hi:.
I-erg his/her help-f. do-inf.fs want-fs
I wanted to help him/her.

3.4.7.2. Participles

Participles in Hindi are largely verbal in nature and function as adjectives and adverbs. They are of two types: imperfective and perfective. Whereas imperfective participles represent incomplete or unfinished activities, perfective participles designate completed verbal activities.

3.4.7.2.1. Imperfective Participles

When used adjectivally, imperfective participles are formed by adding the suffixes -ता *-ta:* (ms), -ते *-te* (mp), -ती *-ti* (fs), and -तीं *-tĩ:* (fp) that are made to agree with the noun in gender and number. Adjectival imperfective participles are expanded with one of the simple perfective forms of होना *hona:* 'to be,' like हुआ *hua:* (ms), and हुए *hue* (p), and हुई *hui:* (fs).

1. दौड़ता हुआ आदमी रुक गया।
   dɔṛta: hua: a:dmi: ruk gaya:.
   run-imp.ptc be-ms man stop went
   The running man stopped.

2. दौड़ते हुए बच्चे शोर कर रहे हैं।
   dɔṛte hue bacce šor kar rahe hɛ̃.
   run-imp.ptc be-mp children noise do-prog.asp are
   The running children are making noise.

3. चलती हुई बस रुक गई।
   calti: hui: bas ruk gai:.
   move-imp.ptc-fs bus stop went
   The moving bus stopped.

When used adverbially, the suffix -ते *-te* is added to the verb stem and is followed by हुए *hue.*

4. दफ़्तर से लौटते हुए मैंने फल खरीदे।
   daftar se lɔṭte hue mɛ̃ne phal khari:de.
   office from return-while I-erg fruit bought
   I bought fruit while returning from the office.

5. बच्चे स्कूल जाते हुए गा रहे थे।
   bacce sku:l ja:tee hue ga: rahe the.
   children school go-while sing-prog.asp were
   The children were singing songs while going to school.

Adverbial imperfective participles may be reduplicated.

6. वह पैदल चलते - चलते थक गया।
vah pɛdal calte-calte thak gaya:.
he on foot walk-ptc walk-ptc tired went
He was tired of walking on foot.

7. वह छत से गिरते - गिरते बच गया।
vah chat se girte-girte bac gaya:
he roof from fall-ptc-fall-ptc save went
He almost fell from the roof.

Adverbial imperfective participles are used with different time expressions.

8. वह घर जाते समय मायूस था।
vah ghar ja:te samay ma:yu:s tha:
he home go-ptc time sad was
He was sad when it was time to go home.

3.4.7.2.2. Perfective Participles

Perfective participles are formed by adding the adjectival suffixes -आ *-a:*, -ए *-e*, and -ई *-i:* to verb stems agreeing with the noun in person, gender, and number. A few perfective stems are irregular. Perfective participles represent a verbal activity carried through to completion. Perfective participles may be employed either adjectivally or adverbially. The adjectival participles are expanded with the forms of हुआ *hua:*, हुए *hue,* and हुई *hui:* that agree with the modified noun in person, gender, and number.

9. बैठा (हुआ) लड़का
bɛṭha: (hua:) laṛka:
the sitting (i.e., seated) boy

9a. बैठे (हुए) लड़के
bɛṭhe (hue) laṛke
the sitting boys

9b. बैठी (हुई) लड़की लड़कियाँ
bɛṭhi (hui:) laṛki:/laṛkiyã:
the sitting girl/girls

The adjectival participles may precede or follow the noun they qualify.

10a. कमीज़ धुली (हुई) है।
kami:z dhuli: (hui:) hɛ.
shirt washed (perf-ptc) is
The shirt is washed.

10b. धुली (हुई) कमीज़ अलमारी में है।
dhuli: (hui:) kami:z alma:ri: mẽ hɛ.
washed (ptc) shirt almirah in is
The washed shirt is in almirah.

There are two types of adverbial participles. In one type, the invariable suffix –ए *-e* is employed.

11. छत पर बैठे हुए वह गा रहा था।
chat par bɛṭhe hue vah ga: raha: tha:.
roof at siting-perf.ptc he sing-prog was
He was singing while sitting on the roof.

In the other type, the adverbial participle uses the adjectival suffixes –आ *-a:*,- ए *-e*, and –ई *-i:*.

12. नई कमीज़ पहनी हुई रमा बाज़ार जा रही थी।
nai: kami:z pahni: hui: rama: baza:r ja: rahi: thi:.
new shirt wear-perf.ptc Rama market go-prog was
Wearing a new shirt, Rama was going to market.

The perfective adverbial participles are frequently reduplicated.

13. वह घर पर बैठे - बैठे थक गया।
vah ghar par bɛṭhe-bɛṭhe thak gaya:
he home at sitting-perf.ptc tired went(explicator)
He was tired of sitting at home.

The perfective participles are used to indicate the passing of time.

14. अमर को अमरीका से आए हुए दो साल हो गए हैं।
amar ko amri:ka: se a:ye hue do sa:l ho gaye hɛ̃.
Amar-dat America from came-perf.ptc two years elapsed are
It has been two years since Amar came from America.

3.4.7.2.3. Conjunctive Participles

Conjunctive participles are used to form sentences in which two verbal activities share the same subject and one of the activities is a temporal antecedent of the other. In this construction, the verb of the first clause is used in the verb stem form and is immediately followed by *kar,* while the verb of the subsequent clause takes all the conjugation markers.

15. वह घर पहुँचकर बाज़ार गया।
vah ghar pahũckar ba:za:r gaya:.
he home reach after-cp market went
He went to the market after coming home.

16. उसने अख़बार पढ़कर चिट्ठी लिखी।
usne axba:r paṛh kar ciṭṭhi: likhi:.
he-erg neewspaper read after-cp letter-fs wrote-fs
He wrote a letter after reading the newspaper.

If the verb करना *karna:* 'to do' appears in the main clause either independently or as a part of a compound, the form *ke* is used in place of कर *kar.*

17. दफ़्तर का काम समाप्त करके वह घर गया।
daftar ka: ka:m sama:pt karke vah ghar gaya:
office of work finish do-cp he home went
He went home after finishing the office work.
Sometimes the conjunctive clauses are used in the adverbial sense.

18. अमर दौड़कर आया।
amar dɔṛ kar a:ya:.
Amar run do-cp came
Amar came running.

19. उमा मुस्कराकर बोली ...
uma: muskara kar boli: ...
Uma smile do-cp said
Uma said smilingly ...

The conjunctive participle marker *kar* is also used in certain fixed expressions.

20. मैं विशेष/ ख़ास करके अमर से मिला।
mɛ̃ višeš/xa:s karke amar se mila:.
I especially do-cp Amar with met
I especially met Amar.

21. वह दिल्ली होकर आया।
vah dilli: ho kar a:ya:.
he Delhi be do-cp came
He came via Delhi.

22. एक - एक करके सभी विध्यार्थी आए।
ek - ek karke sabhhi: vidhya:rthi: a:ye.
one one do-cp all students came
All the students came one by one.

3.5. Adverbs

An adverb may precede an adjective, a verb, and sometimes another adverb as a qualifier or modifier.

Preceding an adjective

1. वह मेरा बहुत अच्छा दोस्त है।
vah mera: bahut accha: dost hɛ.
He my very good friend is
He is my very good friend.

Preceding a verb

2. मेरा दोस्त रोज़ आता है।
mera: dost roz a:ta: hɛ.
my friend daily come-ptc is
My friend comes daily.

Preceding another adverb

3. वह कल बहुत तेज़ दौड़ा।
vah kal bahut tez dɔṛha:.
he yesterday very fast ran
He ran very fast yesterday.

3.5.1. Types of Adverbs

Adverbs can be classified by form or function. By function, adverbs can be grouped into the following subclasses.

(a) Adverbs of time/duration: आज *a:j* 'today,' कल *kal* 'yesterday,' सुबह *subah* 'morning.'

(b) Adverbs of place or direction: अंदर *andar* 'in/inside,' बाहर *ba:har* 'out/outside.'

(c) Adverbs of manner: आसानी से *a:sa:ni: se* 'easily,' धीरे-धीरे *dhi:re-dhi:re* 'slowly.'

(d) Adverbs of reason: गरीबी के कारण *gari:bi: ke ka:raṇ* 'for the reason of poverty,' कमज़ोरी के कारण *kamzori: ke ka:raṇ* 'for the reason of weakness.'

(e) Adverbs of instrument: कलम से *kalam se* 'with pen,' चाकू से *ca:ku: se* 'with knife.'

(f) Adverbs of purpose: पढ़ने के लिए *paṛhne ke liye* 'for reading,' काम के लिए *ka:m ke liye* 'for work.'

(g) Comitative: X -के साथ *-ke sa:th* 'with/ in the company of X,' and

(h) Adverbs of degree/intensity: बहुत *bahut* 'very,' काफी *ka:phi:* 'enough,' विरला ही कोई *virla: hi: koyi:* 'hardly any,' लगभग *lagbhag* 'approximately.'

By form, adverbs can be classified into the following subgroups: (a) basic or non-derived adverbs, (b) derived adverbs, (c) phrasal adverbs, (d) reduplicated adverbs, and (e) particles.

(a) The basic or non-derived adverbs may be either pure adverbs like आज *a:j* 'today,' सदा *sada:/* हमेशा *hameša:* 'always,' or may be formed by adding the postposition *se* to nouns, adjectives, or adverbs.

4. वह हमेशा अच्छी मेहनत करता है।
vah hameša: acchi: mehnat karta: hɛ.
he always good hard work do-ptc is
He always works very hard.

5. उसने अपना काम ख़ुशी से किया।
usne apna: ka:m khuši: se kiya:.
she-erg own work happiness with did
She did her work very happily.

6. नीचे से ऊपर अच्छा दिखता है।
ni:ce se u:par accha: dikhta: hɛ.
below from top good appear is
It looks better at the top than at the bottom.

7. बाहर से अंदर अधिक ठंड़ा है।
ba:har se andar adhik ṭhãḍa: hɛ.
outside from inside more cold is
It is colder inside than outside.

8. उसने एकदम से मेरा हाथ पकड़ा।
usne ekdam se mera: ha:th pakṛa:
he-erg at once my hand caught
He caught hold of my hand at once.

9. मैंने झट से उसकी बात मान ली।
mɛ̃ne jhaṭ se uski: ba:t ma:n li:.
I-erg at once his talk agreed
I agreed with what he said immediately.

(b) Derived adverbs are formed by adding adverbial suffixes to the base form of demonstrative, relative, correlative, and interrogative pronouns. Locative adverbs are formed by adding the -ई *-ĩ:/* -आं पर *-ã: par* suffixes: यहाँ *yahã:/* यहीं पर *yahĩ:(par)* 'here,' वहाँ *vah-ã:/* वहीं *vahĩ:/* वहाँ ही *vahã: hi:* 'there,' कहाँ *kahã:/* कहीं *kahĩ:* 'where.' Directional adverbs are formed by adding the suffix -से *-se/*-की *-ki: or* as in यहाँ से *yahā̃: se*/इधर से *idhar se* 'in this direction,' वहाँ से *vahā̃: se*/ वहाँ की ओर *vahā̃: ki: or*/ उधर से *udhar se* 'in that direction', कहाँ से *kahā̃: se*/ कहाँ की ओर *kahā̃: ki: or* 'in which direction.' Manner adverbs are formed by adding the suffixes -तरह *tarah*/प्रकार *praka:r* as in इस तरह *is tarah*/ इस प्रकार *is praka:r* 'in this manner,' उस तरह *us tarah*/ उस प्रकार *us praka:r* 'in that manner,' किस तरह *kis tarah* 'in which manner.'

(c) Phrasal adverbs are formed by adding a simple or a compound postposition to a noun.

10. वह तीन दिन के बाद/पश्चात आया।
vah ti:n din ke ba:d/pašca:t a:ya:.
he three days post. after came
He came after three days.

11. उसने पढ़ने से पहले अपनी ऐनक साफ़ की।
usne patr paṛhne se pahle apnii ɛnak sa:f ki:.
he-erg letter read-inf-obl post before self's glasses clean did
He cleaned his glasses before reading the letter.

12. हमारे घर के पीछे एक बड़ा पार्क है।
hama:re ghar ke pi:che ek baṛa: pa:rk hɛ.
our house post. behind a big park is
There is a big park behind our house.

(d) Adverbs can be reduplicated to show intensity and distribution: धीरे- धीरे *dhi:re-dhi:re* 'slowly,' तेज़ - तेज़ *tez- tez* 'fast', कहाँ- कहाँ *kahā̃: - kahā̃:* 'where', कभी- कभी *kabhi: - kabhi:* 'sometimes.'

13. वह धीरे- धीरे/ तेज़ - तेज़ चलता है।
vah dhi:re- dhi:re/tez- tez calta: hɛ.
he slowly/fast walk-ptc is
He walks slowly/quickly.'

14. पता नहीं वह कहाँ- कहाँ गया।
pata: nahī̃: vah kahā̃: - kahā̃: gaya:.
aware neg he where where went
One doesn't know which places did he go to?

Reduplicated adverbs may be separated by the negative particle *na* to express indefiniteness: कभी न कभी *kabhi: na kabhi:* 'sometime or other.'

15. कभी न कभी वह अपनी गल्ती मानेगी।
kabhi: na kabhi: vah apni: galti: ma:nega:.
sometime neg sometime he self's mistake accept-fut
He will realize his mistake some day.

3.5.2. Expressions of Time

3.5.2.1. General Time Expressions

General time expressions employ nouns in the direct and oblique cases. The dative sufix को *ko* is added to adverbs of time, such as दुपहर *duphar* 'noon,' शाम *ša:m* 'evening,' रात *ra:t* 'night,' दिन *din* 'day,' कल *kal* 'tomorrow/yesterday.'

1. आप दुपहर को आइए।
a:p duphar ko a:yiye.
you noon dat come-pol
Please come at noon.

2. रात को अधिक गर्मी नहीं रहती।
ra:t ko adhik garmi: nahĩ: rahti:.
night dat more hot neg remain-ptc
It is not very hot during the night.

3.5.2.2. Time of Day

Time of day is expressed by बजे *baje*. It is used in reporting time and not in expressions such as एक घंटे के बाद *ek ghanṭe ke ba:d* 'after one hour.' In such cases, घंटा *ghanṭa:* 'hour' is used in the oblique case with a postposition.

3. वह दफ़्तर से दस बजे आई।
vah daftar se das baje a:yi:.
she office from ten o'clock came-fs
She came from the office at ten o'clock.

4. वह दो घंटे के बाद आई।
vah do ghanṭe ke ba:d a:yi:.
she two hour-obl post came-fs
She came after two hours.'

The expressions 'quarter,' 'three-quarters,' and 'half an hour' precede the numerals.

5. वह सवा/ पौने/ साढ़े चार बजे गया।
vah sɔa:/pɔne/sa:ṛe ca:r baje: gaya:.
he quarter past/quarter to/half past four o'clock went
He went at quarter past/quarter to/half past four.

Expressons indicating minutes before the hour add the dative suffix to the infinitive of the verb followed by the postposition में *mẽ* 'in'. The expression कम *kam* 'less' also is used.

6. वह छे बजने में दस मिनट पर आया।
vah che bajne mẽ das minaṭ par a:ya:.
he six o'clock-inf-obl in ten minute at came
He came at ten minutes to six.

6a. वह दस मिनट कम छे बजे आया।
vah das minaṭ kam che baje a:ya:.
he ten minutes less six o'clock came
He came at ten minutes to six.

Two types of expressions are used to ask for the time.

7. सनय क्या हुआ/ है?
samay k'a: hua:/hɛ?
time what happened/is
What time is it?

7a. कितने बज गए?
kitne baj gaye?
how much strike went
What time is it?

3.5.2.3. Period of Day

Periods of day are usually expressed by various nouns in the direct or oblique case with or without postpositions: सवेरे- सवेरे *savere (savere)* 'early in the morning,' रात को *ra:t ko* 'during the night', दिन में *din mẽ* 'during the day,' देर से *der se* 'late.' Other frequent expressions are: प्रातः काल *pra:ta: ka:l* 'eary in the morning,' संध्या *sandhya:* 'dusk/evening,' दोपहर *dophar* 'noon', दोपहर के बाद *dophar ke ba:d* 'afternoon.'

3.5.2.4. Days of the Week

The days of the week are:

सोमवार *somva:r*	Monday
मंगलवार *mangalva:r*	Tuesday
बुधवार *budhva:r*	Wednesday
गुरुवार *guruva:r*	Thursday
शुक्रवार *šukrva:r*	Friday
शनिवार *šaniva:r/šani:car va:r*	Saturday
रविवार/इतवार *raviva:r/itva:r*	Sunday

3.5.2.5. Months of the Year

Months are expressed in both indigenous and English forms.

1. Hindi months

बैसाख *vaiša:kh*	April-May
ज्येष्ठ *jyešṭh*	May-June
अषाढ़ *aša:ṛh*	June-July
श्रावन *šra:vaṇ*	July-August
भाद्र *bha:dr*	August-September
आश्विन *a:švin*	September-October
कार्तिक *ka:rtik*	October-November
मार्ग *ma:rg*	November-December
पौष *pɔš*	December-January
माघ *ma:gh*	January-February
फाल्गुन *pha:lgun*	February-March
चैत्र *caitra*	March-April

2. English nativized versions: जनवरी *janvari:,* फरवरी *pharvari:,* मार्च *ma:rc,* अप्रिल *april,* मई *mai:,* जून *ju:n,* जुलई *julay,* अगस्त *agast,* सितम्बर *sitambar,* अक्तोबर *akto:bar,* नवंबर *navambar,* दिसंबर *disambar.*

3.5.2.6. Year

In Hindi, a reference to a year is usually to the year AD called ईस्वी *i:svi:*. Hindus refer to their indigenous calendar as बिक्रमी *bikrami* or शाक *ša:k* and Muslims as हिजरी *hijiri:*. The term सन् *san* used before the Christian year, is optionally followed by ईस्वी *i:svi:*. Similarly, an indigenous year starts with संवत् *samvat* before the year and ends with बिक्रमी *bikrami.*

8. सन् उनीस सौ साठ ईस्वी में
   san uni:s sɔ sa:ṭh i:svi: mẽ
   year nineteen hundred sixty Christian era in
   in the year 1960 AD

9. संवत् दो हज़ार साठ बिक्रमी में
   samvat do haza:r sa:ṭh bikrami: mẽ
   year two thousand sixty Bikrami in
   in the year 2060 Bikrami

The terms ईसा पूर्व *i:sa: pu:rv* 'before Christ' are used to denote BC.

10. ईसा पूर्व छे सौ वर्ष
    i:sa: pu:rv che sɔ varš
    Christ before six hundred years
    six hundred years before Christ

3.5.2.7. Seasons

There are five major seasons: वसंत *vasant* 'spring,' ग्रीश्म *gri:šm* 'summer,' बरसात *barsa:t* 'rainy season', शरद *sharad* 'autumn,' and शीतकाल *ši:tka:l* 'winter.' These terms can be followed by?तु *ritu*/ मौसम *mɔsim* 'season' in both the direct and oblique cases with or without a postposition.

11. वसंत (ऋतु)में फूल खिलते हैं।
vasant (ritu) mẽ phu:l khilte hɛ̃.
spring (season) in flowers bloom-ptc are
Flowers bloom during spring.

3.5.3. Frequentative

Frequentative expressions employ reduplication, an emphatic particle, or प्रति *prati/* हर *har* 'every' before a time expression.

रोज़ रोज़	*roz roz*	every day
प्रति दिन	*prati din*	every day
हर घंटे	*har ganṭe*	every hour
रात भर	*ra:t bhar*	whole night
वहर पल	*har pal*	every moment

12. वह रोज़ रोज़ / प्रति दिन पैसे माँगता है।
vah roz roz/ prati din pɛse mã:gta: hɛ.
he daily/every day money demand-ptc is
He asks for money daily.

3.6. Particles

Particles are generally attached to a particular word in a sentences to mark emphasis, or contrast. The main particles used in Hindi are*:* भी *bhi:,* ही *hi:,* तो *to,* तक *tak,* भर *bhar*, and मात्र *ma:tra*. The use of these particles with different word classes covers a wide range of shades of meaning and semantic interpretations. Here we will illustrate the use of these particles with detailed reference to the prominent particles भी *bhi:* and ही *hi:*.

3.6.1. The Particle भर *bhi:* 'also'

The particle भी *bhi:* is used with different types of nouns in the direct or oblique case. It immediately follows a noun in the direct case and the postposition in the oblique case.

1. अमर भी गया।
amar bhi: gaya:.
Amar part went
Amar also went.

2. लड़का भी आया।
laṛka: bhi: a:ya:.
boy part came
The boy also came.

3. गर्मी भी है।
garmi: bhi: hɛ.
hot part is
It is hot, too.

In the oblique case, भी *bhi:* is placed immediately after the postposition following the noun.

4. अमर को भी जाना है।
amar ko bhi: ja:na: hɛ.
Amar-dat part go-inf is
Amar, too, will have to go.

5. मोहन ने भी रोटी खाई।
mohan ne bhi: roṭi: kha:yi:.
Mohan-erg part bread ate-fem
Mohan, too, ate his meals.'

6. राधा से भी गल्ती हुई।
radha: se bhi: galti: hui:.
Radha-abl part mistake happened
Radha, too, committed a mistake.

It is to be noted that भी *bhi:* cannot be used between a noun and a postposition.

7. घर में भी गर्मी है।
ghar mẽ bhi: garmi: hɛ.
house in part hot is
It is hot in the house as well.

But not
7a. *घर भी में गर्मी है।
**ghar bhi: mẽ garmi: hɛ.*

It is also not used in vocative constructions.

8. *सोहन भी आओ!
sohan bhi: ao!
Sohan part come-voc

9. *हे लड़के भी
he! laṛke bhi:
oh! boy-voc part

The particle भी *bhi:* can be used with all types of direct and oblique personal, demonstrative, indefinite, relative, and reflexive pronouns.

10. मैं/ तू/ वह भी आया।
mɛ̃/tu:/vah bhi: a:ya:.
I/you/he part came
I/you/he came too.

11. हम/ तुम / वे भी आए।
ham/tum/ve bhi: a:ye.
we/you/they part came
We/you/they came too.

12. मुझे / तुझे भी जाना है।
mujhe/tujhe bhi: ja:na: hɛ.
I/you/he-obl part go-inf aux
I/you, too, have to go.

13. हमें/ आपको / उन्हें भी जाना है।
hamẽ/a:pko/unhẽ bhi: ja:na: hɛ.
we/you/they-obl part go-inf aux
We/you/they, too, have to go.'

14. मुझको / तुझको / उसको भी वापस आना है।
mujhko/tujhko/usko bhi: va:pas a:na: hɛ.
I/you/he-obl part go-inf aux
I/you/he, too, will have to return.

15. वह मेरा /तुम्हारा/ आपका/ उसका/ उनका भी दोस्त है।
vah mera:/tumha:ra:/a:pka:/uska:/unka: bhi: dost hɛ.
he my/your/his/their friend is part friend is
He is my/your/his/their friend, too.

16. वह मुझसे /तुम्हारे से/ आपसे/उससे/ उनसे भी बड़ा है।
vah mujhse/tuma:hre se/a:pse/usse/unse bhi: baṛa: hɛ.
he me/you/him/they also elder is
He is older than me/you/him/her.

17. उसे/उसको/ उन्हें/उनको भी बुला लाइए।
use/usko/unhẽ/unko bhi: bula: la:yie.
he/they part call bring.
Please call him/her/them also.

18. आप इसके बारे में भी कुछ कीजिए।
a:p iske ba:re mẽ bhi: kuch ki:jiye.
you this-gen about part something do-pl
Please do something for it.

19. आप कितनी भी कोशिश कीजिए सफल नहीं होंगे।
a:p kitni: bhi: košiš ki:jiye, saphal nahĩ: hõge.
you how much part try do success neg be
No matter how much you try, you won't succeed.

20. आप मुझे कोई भी किताब दे दीजिए।
a:p mujhe koyi: bhi: kita:b de di:jiye.
you me-dat any part book give-pl
Please give me any book.

In the oblique form of the indefinite pronouns, the particle भी *bhi:* is placed after the postpositions.

21. आप किसी को भी बुलाइए।
a:p kisi: ko bhi: bula:iye.
you any-dat part call-pl
Please call anyone.

Not
21a. *आप किसी भी को बुलाइए।
a:p kisi: bhi: ko bula:yie.

The use of the particle भी *bhi:* with the indefinite pronouns कोई *koyi:* and कुछ *kuch,* represent different meanings: कोई भी *koyi: bhi:* 'anyone,' कुछ भी *kuch bhi:* 'anything.'

22. आप जो भी काम करना चाहते हैं, कर लीजिए।
a:p jo bhi: ka:m karna: cahte hɛ̃, kar li:jiye.
you any part work want is do take
Whatever work you want to do, go ahead.

23. जब भी आप आते हैं, किताब साथ ले आते हैं।
jab bhi: a:p a:te hɛ̃, kita:b sa:th le a:te hɛ̃.
when part you come are book with bring past aux
Whenever you come, bring your book with you.

24. वह आाप जैसा भी नहीं है।
vah a:p jɛsa: bhi: nahĩ: hɛ̃.
he you like part neg is
'He is not even like you.'

25. आप जितना भी पैसा दे सकते हैं, दे दीजिए।
a:p jitna: bhi: pɛsa: de sakte hɛ̃, de di:jiye.
you as much part money give can give-pl
Whatever money you can give, please give it.

In the oblique case, the particle भी *bhi:* is placed after the postpositions.

26. जिसको/जिनको भी जाना है, जाओ/ चले जाएँ।
jisko/jinko bhi: ja:na hɛ, ja:o/cale ja:yẽ.
who-dat part go-inf. is go go-subj
Whosoever has to go may leave.

The use of the particle भी *bhi:* with relative pronouns represents different meanings: जो भी *jo bhi:* 'whosoever' or 'whatsoever,' जब भी *jab bhi:* 'whenever,' जितना भी *jitna: bhi:* 'whatever.'

27. वह आप भी मेहनत करता है, दूसरों को भी करवाता है।
vah a:p bhi: mehnat karta: hɛ, du:srõko bhi: karva:ta: hɛ.
he self part hard work do is others-obl dat part do-caus is
He works hard himself and makes others work hard too.

28. आप अपने आप/ स्वयं / स्वत: भी यह काम कर सकते हैं।
a:p apne a:p/svayam/ svatah bhi: yah ka:m kar sakte hɛ̃.
you self part this work do-abl are
You can do this work yourself.

In the case of oblique forms, the particle भी *bhi:* is placed after the postposition, not between the pronoun and the postposition.

The particle भी *bhi:* is used with different types of adjectives. It always follows the adjectives.

29. वह लड़की सुंदर भी है और बुद्धिमान भी।
vah laṛki: sundar bhi: hɛ ɔr buddhima:n bhi:.
that girl beautiful part is and intelligent part
That girl is beautiful as well as intelligent.

30. कितने भी मज़दूर क्यों न आएँ, यह काम आज नहीं हो सकता।
kitne bhi: mazdu:r kyõ na a:yẽ, yah ka:m a:j nahĩ: ho sakta:.
how much part laborers neg come-subj this work today neg possible
No matter how many laborers come, this work cannot be finished today.

31. इस दुकान पर किलो भर भी चीनी नहीं है।
is duka:n par kilo bhar bhi: ci:ni: nahĩ: hɛ.
this shop at kilogram about part sugar neg is
There is not even a kilogram of sugar in this shop.

32. कैसा भी काम हो, वह कर लेगा।
kɛsa: bhi: ka:m ho, vah kar lega:.
what type part work be he do explicator-fut
No matter what type of work it is, he would be able to do it.

In (29), (30), and (31), the particle भी *bhi:* is merely an emphatic marker. In (32), however, the expression कैसा भी *kɛsa: bhi:* is a combined phrase meaning 'any type of.' If भी *bhi:* is deleted, the sentence will be ungrammatical.

The particle भी *bhi:* is used with different forms of the verb हो *ho* 'be' and the auxiliary verb.

33. मोहन है (भी) कि नहीं?
mohan hɛ (bhi:) ki nahĩ:?
Mohan be (part) or neg
Is Mohan there or not?

34. वह होगा भी कि नहीं?
vah hoga: bhi: ki nahĩ:?
he be-fut part or neg
Will he be there or not?

35. आप आएँगे भी कि नहीं?
a:p a:yẽge bhi: ki nahĩ:?
you come-fut part or neg
Will you come or not?

In the above examples, the particle भी *bhi:* is used for emphasis only. Barring the progressive forms, the particle भी *bhi:* is used with different types of verbs.

36. उसका घर जाना भी ठीक नहीं था।
uska: ghar ja:na: bhi: ṭhi:k nahĩ: tha:.
his home go-ing part right neg was
His going home was not good.

37. वह करने वाला भी है और करवाने वाला भी।
vah karne va:la: bhi: hɛ ɔr karva:ne va:la: bhi:.
he do-ing-obl part is and do-caus part
He can do it himself and get it done, too.

38. वह दुकान पर जाता भी है कि नहीं।
vah duka:n par ja:ta: bhi: hɛ ki nahĩ:.
he shop at go part is or neg
Does he go to the shop or not?

39. आप आए भी और चले भी गए।
a:p a:ye bhi: ɔr cale bhi: gaye.
you came part and go-obl part went
You came and have left, too.

40. आपको वहाँ गए भी बहुत दिन हो गए।
a:p ko vahã: gaye bhi: bahut din ho gaye.
you-dat there went-obl part many days passed
It is a long time since you have gone over there.

41. वह खा भी रहा है और बातें भी कर रहा है।
vah kha: bhi: raha: hɛ ɔr ba:tẽ bhi: kar raha: hɛ.
he eat part prog is and talk part do-prog is
He is eating as well as talking.

It is to be noted that the particle भी *bhi:* cannot follow the progressive aspect marker रहा *raha:.*

42. वह खा भी रहा है।
vah kha: bhi: raha: hɛ.
he eat part prog is
He has been eating.

Not
42a. *वह खा रहा भी है।
**vah kha: raha: bhi: hɛ.*

The particle भी *bhi:* can be used with conjunct verbs. It is used either between the main verb and the operator (auxiliary verb) or following the main verb and the operator as follows.

43. उसने देखा भी था।
usne dekha: bhi: tha:.
he-erg saw part was
He had seen it.

44. उसे लाने भी दो।
use la:ne bhi: do.
he-abl being-inf-obl part let
Let him bring (it).

45. अब जाने भी दो।
ab ja:ne bhi: do.
now go-inf-obl part let
Now let it go.

46. मैंने चिट्ठी लिख भी दी है।
mɛ̃ne ciṭṭhi: likh bhi: di: hɛ.
I-erg letter write part gave (explicator) is
I have written a letter, too.

The particle भी *bhi:* is also used between the main verb and the negative marker.

47. वह आया भी नहीं।
vah a:ya: bhi: nahĩ:.
he came part neg
He did not even come.

48. रमेश भी आया नहीं।
rameš bhi: a:ya: nahĩ:.
Ramesh part came neg
Even Ramesh did not come.

Notice the change of meaning in the use of the particle भी *bhi:* different from the lexical meaning 'also' in the following examples.

49. वह उसके घर गया भी मगर उसे मिल भी न सका।
vah uske ghar gaya: bhi:, magar use mil bhi: na saka:.
he his home went part but he-dat met part neg able
He did go to his house, but could not meet him.

50. वह जाएगा भी या बैठा ही रहेगा।
vah ja:yega: bhi: ya: bɛṭha: hi: rahega:.
he go-fut part or sit part remain-fut
Will he go or keep on sitting?

51. वह वहाँ गया भी नहीं।
vah vahã: gaya: bhi: nahĩ:.
he came part neg
He did not even go there.

52. जाने भी दो।
ja:ne bhi: do.
go-inf-obl part let-imp
Let it go.

53. रहने भी दो।
rahne bhi: do.
remain-inf-obl part let-imp
Let it be.

The particle भी *bhi:* can be used with different types of adverbs.

54. यहाँ भी ठंड़ है।
yahã: bhi: ṭhãḍ hɛ.
here part cold is
It is cold over here, too.

55. वहाँ भी देखो।
vahã: bhi: dekho.
there part See-imp
Please look over there, too.

56. दिन भर भी यहाँ काम न हुआ।
din bhar bhi: yahã: ka:m na hua:.
day part here work neg be-part
The work could not be done for the whole day over here.

57. पाँच भी बज गए, वह आया नहीं।
pã:c bhi: baj gaye, vah a:ya: nahĩ:.
five part struck went he came neg
It is now five o'clock and he has not come.

58. बार बार भी जाना ठीक नहीं है।
ba:r ba:r bhi: ja:na ṭhi:k nahĩ: hɛ.
again part go-inf right neg is
It is not good to go time and again.

59. जैसे भी हो वह आ जाएगा।
jɛse bhi: ho vah a: ja:yega:.
somehow part be he com-fut
He will come somehow.

60. वह इसलिए गया शायद पैसे मिले।
vah isliye bhi: gaya: ša:yad pɛse milẽ.
he for this part went perhaps money get-subj
He went in the hope of getting money.

61. मैं न भी जाऊँ तुम ज़रूर जाना।
mɛ̃ na bhi: ja:ũ: tum zaru:r ja:na:.
I neg part go-subj you definitely go-inf-imp
You should go, even if I don't.

62. कभी हाँ भी करोगे?
kabhi: hã: bhi: karoge?
sometime yes part do-fut
Will you ever say yes?

63. यह भी नहीं करोगे तो क्या करोगे?
yeh bhi: nahĩ: karoge to kya: karoge?
this part neg do-fut part what do-fut
If you are not able to do this much, what else will you do?

The use of the particle भी *bhi:* with different adverbs represents different meanings: अब भी *ab bhi:* 'even now' तब भी *tab bhi:* 'even then,' 'even so,' जब भी *jab bhi:* 'whenever,' जहाँ भी *jahã: bhi:* 'where ever' कहीं भी *kahĩ: bhi:* 'anywhere,' जहाँ कहीं भी *jahã: kahĩ: bhi:* 'in any place whatsoever,' फिर भी *phir bhi:* 'yet' 'even so.'

The particle भी *bhi:* is used after certain case markers and /or postpositions as well.

64. उसके पास भी काम नहीं है।
uske pa:s bhi: ka:m nahĩ: hɛ.
he-gen-abl near part work neg is
He, too, doesn't have work.

65. इसके बिना भी काम होगा।
iske bina: bhi: ka:m hoga:.
this-gen-obl without part work be-fut
The work can be done even without it.

66. उसके बदले भी कोई नहीं आया।
uske badle bhi: koyi: nahĩ: a:ya:.
he-gen-obl place part someone neg came
No one came in his place.

The particle भी *bhi:* used with और *ɔr* 'and' indicates the meaning of 'more.'

67. नीली साड़ी में वह और भी सुंदर लगती है।
ni:li: sa:ṛi: mẽ vah ɔr bhi: sundar lagti: hɛ.
blue saree in she more beautiful appear-ptc-is
She appears more beautiful in a blue *sari*.

68. और भी अच्छा हुआ।
ɔr bhi: accha: hua:.
more good happened
It is better still.

From the semantic point of view, भी *bhi:* represents different meanings depending on its use in different contexts. The meanings are represented in the following examples.

69. काम आसान भी है और दिलचस्प भी।
ka:m a:sa:n bhi: hɛ ɔr dilcasp bhi:.
work easy part is and interesting part
The work is easy and interesting, too.

70. वह मेरे साथ बोलता भी नहीं।
vah mere sa:th bolta: bhi: nahĩ:.
he I-poss-obl with speak-ptc part neg
He doesn't even talk with me.

71. जाने भी दो।
ja:ne bhi: do.
go-inf-obl part let-imp
Let it go.

72. सेब छोटा है फिर भी मीठा है।
seb choṭa: hɛ phir bhi: mi:ṭha: hɛ.
apple small is even then part sweet is
Despite of being small, the apple is sweet.

73. माँ को देखकर बच्चा और भी ज़ोर से रोया।
mã: ko dekh kar bacca: ɔr bhi: zor se cila:ya:.
mother-dat see-cp child more part loudly cried
On seeing the mother, the child cried more loudly.

74. उसे कुछ भी समझ में नहीं आया।
use kuch bhi: samajh mẽ nahĩ: a:ya:.
he-dat anything understand in neg came
He was not able to understand anything.

In the above sentences, भी *bhi:* represents the general meaning of 'too,' 'even' and 'let' in the sentences (69), (70), and (71) respectively. In (72), फिर भी *phir bhi:* represents the meaning of 'even then.' In (73), और भी *ɔr bhi:* represents the meaning of 'more,' and in (74), कुछ भी *kuch bhi:* represents the meaning of 'anything.'

The particle भी *bhi:* can be used interchangeably with ही *hi:* in certain examples with no change in the meaning.

75. उसे मेरा सुझाव बिल्कुल भी / ही पसंद न आया।
use mera: sujha:v bilkul bhi:/hi: pasand na a:ya:.
he-dat my suggestion exact part like neg came
He did not like my suggestion at all.

In such cases, the use of the particle भी *bhi:* or ही *hi:* is meant to emphasize only. Wherever भी *bhi:* adds meaning to the sentence, it cannot be interchanged with ही *hi:*.

76. नीली साड़ी में वह और भी सुंदर लगती है।
ni:li: sa:ṛi: mẽ vah ɔr bhi: sundar lagti: hɛ.
blue sari in she more part beautiful appear is
She looks more beautiful in the blue *sari*.

76a. *नीली साड़ी में वह और ही सुंदर लगती है।
**ni:li: sa:ṛi: mẽ vah ɔr hi: sundar lagti: hɛ.*

3.6.2. The particle ही *hi:*

The particle ही *hi:* is generally used for emphasis and also in the sense of 'exclusiveness' or 'alone.' As indicated above, the particle ही *hi:* can be used as an emphatic marker with nouns. It can also be used with different types of pronouns in both the direct and the oblique cases: मैं ही *mɛ̃ hi:* 'I myself,' तू ही *tu: hi:* 'thou thyself,' आप ही *a:p hi:* 'you yourself,' कोई ही *koi: hi:* 'hardly anyone,' कुछ ही *kuch hi:* 'hardly anything,' 'hardly a few.'

1. मैं ही आऊँगा।
mɛ̃ hi: a:ũ:ga:.
I past come-fut
I will come myself.

2. आप ही बताइए।
a:p hi: bata:yiye.
you part say
You say (it) yourself.

3. कोई ही यह काम कर सकता है।
koyi: hi: yah ka:m kar sakta: hɛ.
any part this work do able-ptc aux
Hardly anyone can do this work.

4. कुछ ही लोग आए थे।
kuch hi: log a:ye the.
some part people came aux
Hardly a few people had come.

Adding the emphatic particle ही *hi:* to certain words results in certain phonological changes.

(a) अब *ab* + ही *hi:* = अभी *abhi:* just now
तब *tab* + ही *hi:* = तभी *tabhi:* just then
सब *sab* + ही *hi:* = सभी *sabhi:* all, everybody

When ही *hi:* is preceded by pronouns in the oblique case, such as इस *is*, उस *us*, किस *kis*, and जिस *jis,* the ह *h* is elided.

(b)	इस *is*	+ ही *hi:*	= इसी *isi:*	this very
	उस *us*	+ ही *hi:*	= उसी *usi:*	that same
	किस *kis*	+ ही *hi:*	= किसी *kisi:*	someone
	ही *jis*	+ ही *hi:*	= जिसी *jisi:*	the very one which

The ह *h* is dropped when preceded by मुझ *mujh*, तुझ *tujh*, यह *yah*, वह *vah*, or हम *ham*.

(c)	मुझ *mujh*	+ ही *hi:*	= मुझी *mujhi:*	me myself
	तुझ *tujh*	+ ही *hi:*	= तुझी *tujhi:*	you yourself
	यह *yah*	+ ही *hi:*	= यही *yahi:*	this itself
	वह *vah*	+ ही *hi:*	= वही *vahi:*	he himself
	हम *ham*	+ ही *hi:*	= हमीं *hamĩ:*	we ourselves

In certain cases, exclusiveness is dropped in the preceding word and the final vowel is nasalized.

यहाँ *yahã:* + ही *hi:* = यहीं *yahĩ:*	at this very place
जहाँ *jahã:* + ही *hi:* = ही जहीं *jahĩ:*	wherever
वहाँ *vahã:* + ही *hi:* = वहीं *vahĩ:*	at that very place
कहाँ *kahã:* + ही *hi:* = कहीं *kahĩ:*	somewhere

The emphatic particle ही *hi:* is frequently used with different types of pronouns. Its use with reflexive pronouns is quite interesting. Hindi has only four reflexive pronouns: आप *a:p*, its oblique forms अपना *apna:* and अपने *apne*, and a compound of these two अपने आप *apne-a:p* 'by oneself'*;* आपस *a:pas* meaning 'each other,' or 'one another.' When आप *a:p* is followed by ही *hi:,* it has an adjectival intensifying force and qualifies a noun or a pronoun which, as a rule, is the logical subject of the sentences.

5. मोहन आप ही वहाँ गया।
mohan a:p hi: vahã: gaya:.
Mohan self part there went
Mohan went there on his own.

6. मुझे आप ही जाना पड़ेगा।
mujhe a:p hi: ja:na: paṛega:.
me-dat self part go-inf fall-fut
I shall have to go myself.

7. वे आप ही आएँगे।
ve a:p hi: a:yẽge.
they self part come-fut
They themselves will come.

8. श्याम ने आप ही यह चिट्ठी लिखी है।
šya:m ne a:p hi: yah ciṭṭhi: likhi: hɛ.
Shyam-erg self part this letter wrote is
Shyam has himself written this letter.

आप ही *a:p hi:* sometimes qualifies nouns or pronouns which are not the logical subjects of the sentences.

9. उसमें आप ही साहस नहीं है।
usmẽ a:p hi: sa:has nahĩ: hɛ.
he in self part courage neg is
He himself has no courage.

10. उसका आप ही दिवाला निकल जाएगा।
uska: a:p hi: diva:la: nikal ja:yega:
he -gen self part bankrupt come go-fut
He will himself become bankrupt.

आप ही *a:p hi:* can be used as an adverb to mean 'of one's own accord.'

11. वह आप ही अस्पताल गया।
vah a:p hi: aspata:l gaya:.
he self part hospital went
He went to the hospital on his own.

It is interesting to note the different shades of the meanings of the particle ही *hi:* in the following sentences.

12. अमर के आते ही मोहन चला गया।
amar ke a:te hi: mohan cala: gaya:.
Amar-gen-come-ptc part mohan went
As soon as Amar came, Mohan left.

13a. राधा आ रही थी।
ra:dha: a: rahi: thi:.
Radha come-prog was-f
Radha was coming.

13b. राधा आ ही रही थी।
ra:dha: a: hi: rahi: thi:.
Radha was come-part-prog was-f
Radha was just coming.

14a. मोहन जाएगा।
mohan ja:yega:.
Mohan go-fut
Mohan will go.

14b. मोहन जाएगा ही।
mohan ja:yega: hi:.
Mohan go-fut part
Mohan will certainly go.

15a. मैं गया नहीं।
mɛ̃ gaya: nahĩ:.
I went part neg
I did not go.

15b. मैं गया ही नहीं।
mɛ̃ gaya: hi: nahĩ:.
I went part neg
I did not go at all.

16a. वह आज गया होगा।
vah a:j gaya: hoga:.
he today went be-presumptive
He might have gone today.

16b. वह आज ही गया होगा।
vah a:j hi: gaya: hoga:.
he today part went be-presumptive
He might have gone just today.

17a. यह अच्छा हुआ।
yeh accha: hua:.
this good happened
It is good.

17b. यह अच्छा ही हुआ।
yeh accha: hi: hua:.
this good part happened
It is good (emphatic).

18a. अच्छा हूँ।
accha: hũ:
good am
I am fine.

18b. अच्छा ही हूँ।
accha: hi: hũ:.
good part am
I am fine (emphatic).

19a. कुछ और मज़ा आया।
kuch ɔr maza: a:ya:.
some more enjoyment came
It was an extra enjoyment.

19b. कुछ और ही मज़ा आया।
kuch ɔr hi: maza: a:ya:
some more part enjoyment came
It was quite a different kind of enjoyment.

20. बच्चे ने तस्वीर क्या देखी, तस्वीर ही फाड़ डाली।
bacce ne tasvi:r kya: dekhi:, tasvi:r (hi:) pha:ṛ ḍa:li:
child-erg picture what saw picture (emp) tear explicator-past
Instead of seeing it, the child has torn off the picture.

In sentence (12), the particle ही *hi:* becomes part of the verb adding the meaning 'as soon as.' In (13b), the particle ही *hi:* adds the meaning of 'just.' In (14b), the particle ही *hi:* adds the meaning 'certainly.' In (15b), it adds the meaning 'at all.' In (16b) and (17b), it makes the adjectives emphatic. By adding the particle ही *hi:* to कुछ और *kuch ɔr* in sentence (19b), it gives the meaning 'different kind of.' Thus, besides its use for emphasis, the particle ही *hi:* adds different shades of meaning depending on its use.

3.6.3. The Particle तो *to*

The particle तो *to* is mostly used as an emphatic marker and also denotes contrast.

1. वह आया तो है।
   vah a:ya: to hɛ.
   he came part is
   He has come indeed.

2. उसे अंदर आने तो दो।
   use andar a:ne to do.
   he-dat inside come-inf+obl part let
   Let him come inside.

3. मोमबती तो मिली, दियासलाई नहीं।
   mombati: to mili:, diya:sala:yi: nahĩ:.
   candle part found match-box neg
   The candle was found, (but) not the matchbox.

4. वह उसके पास तो गया, पर बोला नहीं।
   vah uske pa:s to gaya:, par bola: nahĩ:.
   he he-gen+obl near part went but said neg
   He did go near him, but did not speak.

The particle *to* is also added to the negative marker नहीं *nahĩ:*. The phrase नहीं तो *nahĩ: to* has several uses including as an emphatic negative reply denoting 'surprise' or 'disapproval.'

5. आप आगरा गए थे?
a:p a:gra: gaye the?
you Agra went were
Did you go to Agra?

5a. नहीं तो।
nahĩ: to.
neg part
Not really/Not at all.

As a coordinate conjunction, नहीं तो *nahĩ: to* means 'otherwise.'

6. तेज़ चलो, नहीं तो गाड़ी छूट जाएगी।
tez calo, nahĩ: to ga:ṛi: chu:ṭ ja:yegi:.
Fast walk neg part train miss-fut
Walk fast, otherwise you will miss the train.

Another use in combination with the particle भी *bhi:* indicates 'yet, even so.'

7. अगर वह कहेगा भी, तो भी मैं उसके साथ नहीं जाऊँगा।
agar vah kahega: bhi:, to bhi: mɛ̃ uske sa:th nahĩ: ja:ũ:ga:.
If he say-fut part part ĩ he-gen-obl with neg go-fut
Even if he says so, I will not go with him.

In sentence (7), तो भी *to bhi:* can be replaced by फिर भी *phir bhi:* 'even so, yet.' In its adverbial use, तो *to* is a correlative of जब *jab* 'when' or of यदि *yadi* 'if' and it signifies 'then.'

8. जब उसे मालूम हुआ, तो वह रोने लगा।
jab use ma:lu:m hua, to vah rone laga:.
when he-dat know be-past part he cry-inf-obl starts
When he came to know, (then) he began to cry.

8a. यदि तुम घर गए तो पछताओगे।
yadi tum ghar gaye to pachta:oge.
if you home went part repent-fut
If you go to your home, (then) you will repent.

3.6.4. The Particle तक *tak* 'up to'

The particle तक *tak* has two primary meanings: as the limited particle 'even' and as the postposition 'up to.'

1. उसने तार तक नहीं भेजा।
   usne ta:r tak nahĩ: bheja:.
   he-erg wire part neg sent
   He did not even send a telegram.

2. उसने मेरी बात तक नहीं सुनी।
   usne meri: ba:t tak nahĩ: suni:.
   he-erg my talk part neg listened
   He did not even listen to what I said.

As a postposition, तक *tak* is used in the sense of 'up to' or 'until.'

3. वह कल तक ज़रूर आएगा।
   vah kal tak zaru:r a:yega:.
   he tomorrow part definitely come-fut
   He will come by tomorrow definitely.

4. वह कल तक पैसा लौटाएगा।
   vah kal tak pɛsa: lɔṭa:yega:.
   he tomorrow part money return-fut
   He will return the money by tomorrow.

5. वहाँ पहुँचने तक दो दिन लगेंगे।
   vahã: pahũcne tak do din lagẽge.
   there reach-inf-obl part two days take-fut
   It will take two days to reach there.

6. जब तक आप आज्ञा नहीं देंगे मैं नहीं जाऊँगा।
   jab tak a:p a:gya: nahĩ: dẽge, mɛ̃ nahĩ: ja:ũ:ga:.
   when part you permission neg give-fut I neg go-fut
   Until you permit me, I will not go.

3.6.5. The Particle भर *bhar*

The particle भर *bhar* denotes the meaning of 'measuring a …,' 'weighing a…,' 'a…ful,' etc. In this meaning, it acts like a suffix, forming the adjectives from nouns. Unlike the English suffix *-full,* it is a separate word which can be attached to nouns, adjectives, verbs, and other parts of speech.

1. मीटर भर कपड़ा दे दीजिए।
   mi:ṭar bhar kapṛa: de di:jiye.
   meter part cloth give-fut
   Please give (a piece of) cloth measuring a meter.

2. वह किलो भर दूध एक बार पी सकता है।
   vah kilo bhar du:dh ek ba:r pi: sakta: hɛ.
   he kilogram part milk one time drink able-ptc aux
   He can drink a kilogram of milk at a time.

3. घर में मुट्ठी भर चावल नहीं है।
   ghar mẽ muṭṭhi: bhar ca:val nahĩ: hɛ.
   home in handful part rice neg is
   There is not even a handful of rice in the house.

As a particle, भर *bhar* denotes the meanings 'the entire…,' 'the whole…, 'only,' and 'just.'

4. देश भर में चुनाव हो रहे हैं।
   deš bhar mẽ cuna:v ho rahe hɛ̃.
   country part in election be prog are
   The elections are being held throughout the entire country.

5. वह दिन भर सोया रहा।
   vah din bhar soya: raha:.
   he day part slept remained
   He slept for the whole day.

6. उसने पल भर भी आराम नहीं किया।
   usne pal bhar bhi: a:ra:m nahɛ̃ kiya:.
   he-erg moment part rest neg did
   He did not rest even for a moment.

7. घर भर में बच्चे शोर करते रहे।
ghar bhar mẽ bacce šor karte rahe.
home part in children noise do-pr remained
The children made noise throughout the entire house.'

8. आप देखते भर हो, खरीदते नहीं।
a:p dekhte bhar ho, khari:dte nahĩ:.
you see-pr part be purchase-pr neg
You only look but do not purchase.

Notice that in sentence (8), भर *bhar* can be replaced by the particle ही *hi:*.

3.6.6. The Particle मात्र *ma:tr*

The particle मात्र *ma:tr* is borrowed from Sanskrit and means 'only' or 'whole.' In Sanskrit, it is used as a suffix and is attached to nouns.

विध्या *vidhya:* + मात्र *ma:tr* = विध्यामात्र *vidhya:ma:tr*	only learning
पल *pal* + मात्र *ma:tr* = पलमात्र *palma:tr*	only a moment
मानव *ma:nav* + मात्र *ma:tr* = मानवमात्र *ma:navma:tr*	all of humanity

In Hindi, the particle मात्र *ma:tr* is an equivalent of केवल *keval* or ही *hi:* 'only,' 'alone.' It is also used as a separate word.

1. आप किताब मात्र दीजिए।
a:p kita:b ma:tr di:jiye.
You book part give-fut
Please give only the book.

1a. आप केवल किताब दीजिए।
a:p keval kita:b di:jiye.
Please give only the book.

1b. आप किताब ही दीजिए।
a:p kita:b hi: di:jiye.
Please give just the book.

2. मुझे सौ रुपए मात्र दीजिए।
mujhe sɔ rupaye ma:tr di:jiye.
me hundred rupees part give-fut
Please give me a hundred rupees only.

2a. मुझे मात्र सौ रुपए दीजिए।
mujhe ma:tr sɔ rupaye di:jiye.

2b. मुझे केवल सौ रुपए दीजिए।
mujhe keval sɔ rupaye di:jiye.

The particle भर *ma:tr* can also be used in the initial position in sentences. It can be replaced by भर *keval* as in (3a).

3. मात्र उसने यह काम नहीं किया।
ma:tra usne yah ka:m nahĩ: kiya:.
part he-erg this work neg did
He was the only one not to do this work.

3a. केवल उसने यह काम नहीं किया।
keval usne yah ka:m nahĩ: kiya:.

To sum up, the use of various particles in Hindi is important from a semantic point of view. Besides their use as emphatic markers, they cover a wide range of meanings and further shades of meanings when used in combination with various word classes. They are frequently used in different dialects and styles of speech in Hindi.

3.7. Connectives

Connectives are words that join two elements.

और ɔr	and	या	ya:	or
लेकिन lekin	but	कि	ki	that
मगर magar	but	बल्कि	balki	rather
वर्ना varna:	otherwise	इस लिए	isi: liye	that is why, therefore
क्योंकि kyõki	because	ताकि	ta:ki	so that
अगर agar	'if'	हालांकि	ha:lã:ki	'though'

Structurally, connectives are divided into three classes: (i) mono-morphemic, (ii) poly-morphemic, and (iii) phrasal.

3.7.1. Mono-morphemic

Mono-morphemic is composed of only one morpheme.

1. मैं घर गया और अमर बाज़ार गया।
   mɛ̃ ghar gaya: ɔr amar ba:za:r gaya:.
   I house went and Amar market went
   I went home and Amar went to the market.

2. तुम इधर आओगे या मैं उधर आऊँगा।
   tum idhar a:oge ya: mɛ̃ udhar a:ũ:ga:.
   you here come-fut or I there come-fut
   You will come here or I will come there.

3.7.2. Poly-morphemic

Poly-morphemics are composed of two or more morphemes.

3. मैं आज कालेज नहीं गया, क्योंकि मेरी तबीयत ठीक नहीं है।
   mɛ̃ a:j ka:lej nahĩ: gaya: kyũki meri: tabiyat ṭhi:k nahĩ:hɛ.
   I today college neg went because my health right neg be
   Today I didn't go to college because I am not well.

4. उसने खाना नहीं खाया, इसलिए मैंने भी नहीं खाया।
   usne kha:na: nahĩ: kha:ya:, is liye mɛ̃ne bhi: nahĩ: kha:ya:.
   He food neg ate for that I part neg eat
   He did't eat the food, therefore I also didn't eat.

3.7.3. Phrasal

Phrasals consist of two elements interrupted by intervening words, such as अगर *agar* ... तो *to* 'if ... then.'

5. अगर तुम कहो तो मैं आऊँगा।
   agar tum kaho to mɛ̃ a:ũga:.
   If you say-fut then I come-fut
   If you say so then I will come.

3.8. Interjections

Interjections express some emotions such as pain, pleasure, anger, surprise, and disgust. An interjection is in the vocative case and has no grammatical relation with any other word in the sentence. In Hindi, interjections are used as independent words or they can be prefixed to nouns.

हे भगवान!	*he bhagva:n!*	O God!
ओ लड़के!	*o larke!*	O boy!

Surprise is expressed by: ओह *oh!* अरे *are!* ओहो *oho!* क्या *kya:!*

1. ओह / अरे / ओहो / क्या तुम आ गए!
oh/are/oho/kya: tum a: gaye!
o/what you came
O you came!

Applause is expressed by: वाह *va:h!* खूब *khu:b!* शाबाश *ša:ba:š!*

2. वाह / खूब / शाबाश बेटे तुमने अच्छा काम किया!
va:h/khu:b/ša:ba:š beṭe tumne accha: ka:m kiya:!
oh son-voc you-erg good work did
Oh (my) son, you have done good work!

Sorrow or grief is expressed by: हाय *ha:y!* हा *ha:!* अहा *a:h!* उफ *uph!* अफसोस *afsos!*

3. हाय / हा / आह /उफ /अफसोस यह क्या हुआ!
ha:y/ha:/a:h/uph/afsos yah kya: hua:!
alas this what happened
Alas what happened!

Joy is expressed by: आहा *a:ha:!* अहा *aha:!* वाह वाह *va:h - va:h!*

4. आहा / अहा / वाह - वाह क्या सुंदर जगह है!
a:ha:/aha:/va:h-va:h kya: sundar jaga:h hɛ!
oh what beautiful place is
Oh what a beautiful place!

Disgust or disapproval is expressed by: छी *chi: (छी chi:)!* थू *thu:!* धिक्कार *dhikka:r!*

5. छी (छी)/ थू / धिक्कार कितना गंदा है!
   chi: (chi:)/thu:/dikka:r kitna: ganda: hɛ!
   shame, how dirty is
   Shame, how dirty it is!

Distress is expressed by: हाय रे *ha:y re!*

6. हाय रे मैं लुट गया!
   ha:y re mɛ̃ luṭ gaya:
   oh I rob went(explicator)
   Oh I am robbed (of everything)!

Certain nouns, pronouns, adjectives and verbs are used as interjections.

7. राम राम ra:m ra:m! (expresses sympathy or disapproval)
8. बाप रे बाप ba:p re ba:p! (expresses surprise or distress)
9. अच्छा accha:! (expresses surprise)
10. क्या kya:! (expresses surprise)
11. जा मर ja: mar! (expresses rebuke)

Some interjections can be used as nouns.

12. क्यों हाय हाय कर रहे हो?
    kyõ ha:y ha:y kar rahe ho?
    why expression of ditress do-prp be
    Why are you raising the hue and cry?

4. Syntax

4.1. Structure of Phrases

4.1.1. Noun Phrase

A noun phrase is defined as a nominal head preceded by one or more modifiers. It also serves as a nucleus of a postpositional phrase. It may function as a subject or object (indirect or direct) predicative complement or as a direct object of a postposition. A noun or a pronoun can be the minimum constituent of a noun phrase. A nominal may be modified by a variety of modifiers such as adjectives, quantifiers, numerals, emphatic markers, limiters and comparative, equative, and superlative markers.

Attributive adjectives immediately precede a nominal head as a modifier, e.g., नया कोट *naya: koṭ* 'new coat' and सुंदर लड़की *sundar laṛki:* 'beautiful girl.' Possessive adjectives precede the head noun as modifiers in noun phrases. They may or may not also be preceded by an appropriate form of the genitive postposition का *ka:/* के *ke/* की *ki:* agreeing in gender and number with the object noun.

1. अजीत का बड़ा बेटा आया।
   aji:t ka: baṛa: beṭa: a:ya:.
   Ajit-gen-ms elder son came
   Ajit's elder son came.

2. अजीत के दो मित्र आए।
   aji:t ke do mitr a:ye
   Ajit-gen-mpl two friends came
   Ajit's two friends came.

3. मोहन की छोटी बेटी सुंदर है।
   mohan ki: choṭi: beṭi: sundar hɛ..
   Mohan-gen-f younger daughter beautiful is
   Mohan's younger daughter is beautiful.

4. मोहन की छोटी बेटियाँ जा रही हैं।
   mohan ki: choṭi: beṭiyã: ja rahi: hɛ̃.
   Mohan-gen-fpl small daughters go-prog are
   Mohan's younger daughters are going.

There is no distinct category of articles used in Hindi. The concept of definiteness and indefiniteness is expressed indirectly by means of pronouns, and the numeral एक *ek* 'one.'

5. कोई एक लड़का
   koi:/ek laṛka:
   some /a/one boy

6. यह/वह बच्चा
   yah/vah bacca:
   this/that child

The numeral एक *ek* and the indefinite pronoun कोई *koi:* 'some(one)' are used in place of an indefinite article. A definite determiner involves either a demonstrative/personal pronoun or a zero marking as given in (6). It is only the context which disambiguates the potential ambiguity present in the above two sentences.

Besides determiners, a noun may be preceded by quantifiers and numerals in the form of (i) approximate/ordinal (e.g., लगभग *lagbhag* 'about,' करीब *kari:b* 'almost,' केवल *keval* 'only,' पहला *pahla:* 'first', दूसरा *du:sra:* 'second', तीसरा *ti:sra:* 'third', चौथा *cautha:* 'fourth'), (ii) cardinal/ multiplicative/fraction (e.g., एक *ek* 'one,' दो *do* 'two,' दुगना *dugna:* 'twice,' तिगना *tigna:* 'three-fold,' आधा *a:dha:* 'half', तीसरा भाग *ti:sra: bha:g/* हिसा *hisa:* 'one-third', चौथा भाग *cɔtha: bha:g/*हिसा *hisa:* 'one-fourth,'), and (iii) collective/measure (e.g., जोड़ी *joṛi:* 'pair', दर्जन *darjan* 'dozen,' किलो *kilo* 'kilogram,' आधा किलो *a:dha: kilo* 'half a kilogram').

Definite + Cardinal + Noun

7. ये चार कमीज़ें अच्छी हैं।
   ye ca:r kami:zẽ acchi: hɛ̃
   these four shirts good are
   These four shirts are good.

Definite + Ordinal + Noun

8. पहला बच्चा हमेशा लजीला होता है।
   pahla: bacca: hameša: lajji:la: hota: hɛ.

first child always shy be-ptc
The first child is always shy.

Definite + Ordinal + Cardinal + Noun

9. ये पहले दो लेख छपने योग्य हैं।
ye pahle do lekh chapne yogya hɛ̃.
these first two essays print-inf-obl suitable are
These first two essays are worth publishing.

Definite + Cardinal + Collective

10. ये तीन दर्जन अंडे ताज़े हैं।
ye ti:n darjan ãḍe ta:ze hɛ̃.
these three dozen eggs fresh are
These three dozen eggs are fresh.

Definite + Cardinal + Measure

11. वे पाँच बोरियाँ चावल पिछले साल की हैं।
ve pã:c boriyã: ca:val pichle sa:l ki: hɛ̃.
those five sacks rice last year gen-fp are
Those five sacks of rice are last year's.

Definite + Ordinal + Fractional + Measure

12. यह दूसरा वाला आधा किलो चावल ठीक नहीं है।
yah du:sra:(va:la:) a:dha: kilo ca:val ṭhi:k nahĩ: hɛ.
this second half kilogram rice good not is
This second half kilogram of rice is not good.

Notice that quantifiers such as सारे *sa:re/* तमाम *tama:m* 'all' follow a head noun when the head noun is a pronoun.

13. ये सभी किताबें मैंने पढ़ी हैं।
ye sabhi: kita:bẽ mɛ̃ne paṛhi: hɛ̃.
these all books I-erg read-past-fp are
I have read all these books.

14. हम सारे निशात बाग सैर करने जाएँगे।
ham sa:re niša:t ba:g sɛr karne ja:yẽge.
we all Nishat Bagh walk do-inf-abl go-fut
All of us will go for a walk to Nishat Bagh.

Limiters such as सिर्फ *sirf/* केवल *keval/* 'only' precede the head noun, whereas emphatic particles -ही *-hi:* 'only' and भी *bhi:* 'also' follow the head noun.

15. केवल ये पहले दो बच्चे इम्तिहान में बैठे।
keval ye pahle do bacce imtiha:n mẽ bɛṭhe.
only these first two children exam in sat
Only these two children appeared in the examination.

16. केवल बच्चा ही बाज़ार आया।
keval bacca: hi: ba:za:r a:ya:.
only child-limiter market came
Only the child came to the market.

17. माँ भी आई और बच्चा भी।
mã: bhi: a:yi: ɔr bacca: bhi:.
mother also came and child too
The mother came and so did the child.

Comparative, superlative and equative structures are formed by adding certain morphological forms after the head noun. The comparatives are formed by adding *se* after adding the ablative case markers to the genitive forms of the head noun.

18. नीरज सुनील से बुद्धिमान है।
neeraj suni:l se buddhima:n hɛ.
Neeraj Sunil than intelligent is
Neeraj is more intelligent than Sunil.

19. वह मेरे से मोटा है।
vah mere se moṭa: hɛ.
he is me-gen-abl than fat is
He is fatter than me.

Superlatives are formed by adding सबसे *sab se* before the head noun.

20. सबसे लंबा लड़का कौन है?
sabse lamba: laṛka: kɔn hɛ?
superlative tall boy who is
Who is the tallest boy?

21. अजीत क्लास में सबसे छोटा है।
aji:t kala:s mẽ sab se choṭa: hɛ.
Ajit class in superlative young is
Ajit is the youngest of all in the class.

Equative structures are formed by adding a form of जैसा *jɛsa:/* जैसे *jɛse/*जैसी *jɛsi:* 'like' that agrees with the head noun in gender and number.

22. अजीत अमर जैसा चालाक है।
aji:t amar jɛsa: ca:la:k hɛ.
Ajit Amar like clever is
Ajit is as clever as Amar.

23. हम उन जैसे चालाक नहीं हैं।
ham un jɛse ca:la:k nahĩ: hɛ̃.
we they like clever not are
We are not as clever as they are.

24. शीला उमा जैसी गोरी नहीं है।
ši:la: uma: jɛsi: gori: nahĩ: hɛ.
Shiela Uma like fair complexioned neg is
Shiela is not as fair-complexioned as Uma.

25. ये सेब उन सेबों जैसे मीठे हैं।
ye seb un sebõ jɛse mi:ṭhe hɛ̃.
these apples those apples like delicious are
These apples are as delicious as those ones are.

The terms एक जैसे *ek jɛse/* जैसी *jɛsi:* 'as good as/alike' are also used in equative expressions.

26. ये दो भाई एक जैसे हैं।
ye do bha:i: ek jɛse hɛ̃.
these two brothers alike are
These two brothers are alike.

27. ये बहनें एक जैसी हैं।
ye bahnẽ ek jɛsi: hɛ̃.
these sisters alike are
These sisters are alike.

There are certain co-occurrence restrictions. Indefinite determiners do not co-occur with ordinals. Similarly, the multiplicatives do not co-occur with collective or measure quantifiers. There are other usage constraints on modifiers. For example, the combination of indefinite determiners and cardinal quantifiers is possible; the combination of an indefinite determiner and a demonstrative pronoun in not allowed.

28. कोई बच्चा यह काम नहीं कर सकता।
koi: bacca: yah ka:m nahĩ: kar sakta:.
some/any(one) child this work neg do can-ptc
No child can do this work.

28a. *कोई वह बच्चा यह काम नहीं कर सकता।
**koi: vah bacca: yah ka:m nahĩ: kar sakta:.*

Similarly, the combination of multiplicative and collective quantifiers do not yield well-formed sentences.

29. *दुगना जोड़ा दस्ताना
**dugna: joṛi: dasta:na:*
twice pair gloves

As mentioned above, emphatic particles and limiters follow head nouns. All other constituents precede the head noun they modify. There is a flexibility in the word order of the preceding modifiers as illustrated below.

Demonstrative - possessive - quantifier - adjective - head noun

30. ये मेरे सारे अच्छे मित्र
ye mere sa:re acche mitr
these my all good friends
all these good friends of mine

Possessive - demonstrative - quantifier - adverbial - adjective - noun

30a. मेरे ये सारे बहुत अच्छे मित्र
mere ye sa:re bahut acche mitr
my these all very good friends
all these very good friends of mine

Demonstrative - quantifier - possessive - adverbial -adjective - noun

30b. ये सारे मेरे बहुत अच्छे मित्र
ye sa:re mere bahut acche mitr
these all my very good friends

Possessive - quantifier - demonstrative - adverbial -adjective - noun

30c. मेरे सारे ये बहुत अच्छे मित्र
mere sa:re ye bahut acche mitr
my all these very good friends

Quantifier - demonstrative - possessive - adverbial -adjective - noun

30d. सारे ये मेरे बहुत अच्छे मित्र
sa:re ye mere bahut acche mitr

The word order constraint for adverbs and adjective is quite strict. The word order of the constituents of demonstrative, possessive and quantifier appear quite flexible.

4.1.2. Postpositional Phrases

A postpositional phrase is defined as a noun phrase followed by an oblique case marker and a postposition. Time adverbials take case markers as well as postpositions.

1. वह सवेरे घर से आया।
vah savere ghar se a:ya:.
he morning-obl home from came
He came in the morning from home.

1a. *वह सवेरा आया (घर से)
**vah savera: a:ya: (ghar se).*

2. अजीत शाम को काम करता है।
aji:t ša:m ko ka:m karta: hɛ.
Ajit is evening-obl work do-ptc is
Ajit works in the evening.

2a. *अजीत शाम काम करता है।
**aji:t ša:m ka:m karta: hɛ.*

3. उसने दिन को कुछ नहीं खाया।
usne din ko kuch nahĩ: kha:ya:.
he-erg day-obl for nothing neg ate
He didn't eat anything during the day.

4. उसने दिन भर कुछ नहीं खाया।
usne din bhar kuch nahĩ: kha:ya:.
he-erg day for nothing neg ate
He didn't eat anything for the whole day.

5. वह सवेरे से शाम तक काम करता है।
vah savere se ša:m tak ka:m karta: hɛ.
he morning-obl from evening up to work do-ptc is
He works from morning till evening.

The use of the direct forms of the time adverbials सवेरा *savera:* and शाम *ša:m* in sentences (1a) and (2a) make them ungrammatical.

A postposition may be added to simple or compound noun phrases that consist of more than one element.

6. हमारे दफ़्तर से
hama:re daftar se
our-obl office from
from our office

7. मकान के दरवाज़े से
maka:n ke darva:ze se
house of door-obl from
from the door of the house

Notice that the presence of a postposition changes all the elements of the compound noun phrase from direct to oblique by adding the oblique case markers.

There are a limited number of compound postpositions used in Hindi such as आगे *a:ge/* पीछे की ओर *pi:che ki: or* 'in front/back of', and दाईं *da:ĩ:/* बाईं ओर *ba:ĩ: or* 'towards right/left'. All these are directional. The first element indicates the direction, and is followed by the postpositional form की ओर *ki: or* 'toward'. They are always used after the oblique noun. Notice that a free postposition without an argument functions as an adverb.

It is possible to modify postpositions by using a limiter तक *tak* 'up to/till,' or a particle ही *hi:* 'only.'

8. वह शाम तक पहुँचेगा।
vah ša:m tak pahũcega:.
he evening up to reach-m
He will reach by evening.

9. तुम किताब मेज़ पर ही रखो।
tum kita:b mez par hi: rakho.
you book table on emp keep
You just keep the book on the table.

4.1.3. Adjectival Phrases

Adjective phrases are of two types: simple and complex. Simple adjectives may also be divided into basic and derived adjectives. The derived adjectives are derived from other word classes such as nouns. The examples of basic adjectives are: अच्छा *accha:* 'good,' लंबा *lamba:* 'long,' साफ़ *sa:f* 'clean,' etc. Derived adjectives are derived from nouns:

मेहनत *mehnat* hard work	+ ई *i:*	= मेहनती *mehnati:* hard worker
हिम्मत *himmat* courage	+ ई *i:*	= हिम्मती *himmati:* courageous
दाढ़ी *da:ṛhi:* beard	+ वाला *va:la:*	= दाढ़ी वाला *da:ṛhi: va:la:* bearded

Adjectives may also be derived from adverbs:

पीछे *pi:che* behind	+ ला *la:*	= पिछला *pichla:* last
नज़दीक *nazdi:k* near	+ ई *i*	= नज़दीकी *nazdi:ki:* close one

The use of the forms of वाला *va:la:* and genitive markers का *ka:/* के *ke/* की *ki:* are frequently employed in the derivation of adjectives. Their forms agree with the following noun in number and and gender as follows:

Masculine		Feminine	
Sg	Pl	Sg	Pl
वाला va:la:	वाले va:le	वाली va:li:	वाली va:li:
-का ka:	-के ke	-की ki:	-की ki:

1. दिल्ली वाला दुकानदार
   dilli: va:la: duka:nda:r
   Delhi of shopkeeper
   the shopkeeper from Delhi

2. दूर का रिश्तेदार
   du:r ka: rišteda:r
   distance of relative
   a distant relative

Complex adjectives are finite (full relative clauses) as well as non-finite (participle used as adjectives). Adjectives usually precede the nouns they modify.

It is difficult to define adjective phrases because adjectives are not distinguished morphologically from nouns. However, it is possible to distinguish an adjectival phrase from a noun phrase because: (1) the semantics of adjectives is quite distinct from that of nouns; (2) an adjective phrase functions as a modifier for a substantive; (3)

some adjectives are bound forms and their surface form is determined by the number and gender of a following noun. In nouns the gender is marked inherently; (4) adjectives usually precede a head noun and occur in the attributive position. The word order of adjectives with respect to other constituents of an adjective phrase is as follows: determiner - quantifier - adjective - noun.

3. ये दो लंबी कमीज़ें
ye do lambi: kami:zẽ
these-f two long-fp shirts
these two long shirts

There are two types of adjectives: those which do not take a complement, and those which do take a complement. Adjectives like मैला *mɛla:* dirty do not take a complement, whereas adjectives like तैयार *taya:r* ready do take it. The latter type of adjectives with their complements occurs attributively.

4. कपड़े धोने के लिए तैयार लड़का
kapṛe dhone ke liye tɛya:r laṛka:
clothes wash-inf-obl for ready boy
the boy who is ready to wash clothes

4a. *तैयार लड़का
*tɛya:r laṛka:

4b. लड़का तैयार है।
laṛka: tɛya:r hɛ.
The boy is ready.

Adjectives can be either stative (अच्छा *accha:* good, सुंदर *sundar* beautiful) or non-stative (प्रसन्न *prasann* 'happy', नाराज़ *na:ra:z* 'angry').

The adverbs of degree in their basic form can serve as modifiers of adjectives.

5a. यह बहुत बड़ा/छोटा पेड़ है।
yeh bahut baṛa:/choṭa: peṛ hɛ.
this very big/ small tree is
This is a very big/small tree.

The marker –ही *-hi:* can be added to adverbs of degree for intensification of meaning.

5b. यह बहुत ही बड़ा/छोटा पेड़ है।
yeh bahut hi: baṛa:/choṭa: peṛ hɛ
This is a very big/small tree.

4.1.4. Adverbial Phrases

Phrasal adverbs are formed by adding a simple or a compound postposition to a noun.

1. तीन महीने के बाद
ti:n mahi:ne ke ba:d
three month-obl after
after three months

2. पढ़ने से पहले
paṛhne se pahle
read-inf-obl before
before reading

3. दुकान के पीछे
duka:n ke pi:che
shop-obl back side
in the back of the shop

Adverbs are reduplicated to show intensity and distribution.

4. आप कहाँ कहाँ गए?
a:p kahã: kahã: gaye?
you-p where where went
Which places did you visit?

5. वह कब कब अनुपस्थित रही?
vah kab kab anupasthit rahi:?
she when absent remained-fs
On which dates did she remain absent?

6. वह कभी कभी यहाँ आता है।
vah kabhi: kabhi: yahã: a:ta: hɛ.
he sometimes here come-ptc is
He comes here sometimes.

Reduplicated adverbs may be separated by the negative particle न *na* as in the phrases कभी न कभी *kabhi: na kabhi:* 'sometime or other'. This category of adverbials expresses indefiniteness.

7. वह कभी न कभी ज़रूर आएगा।
vah kabhi: na kabhi: zaru:r a:yega:.
he sometime neg sometime definitely come-fut
He will come sometime or other.

The emphatic particle ही *hi:* can occur with an adverb or a noun to render an adverbial reading.

8. वह केवल समय ही नष्ट करता है।
vah keval samay hi: našṭ karta: hɛ.
he is only time-emp waste do-ptc is
He merely wastes time.

9. अमर ही आएगा मोहन नहीं आएगा।
amar hi: a:yega: mohan nahĩ: a:yega:.
Amar-emp come-fut Mohan neg come-fut
Only Amar will come, not Mohan.

Various case markers and postpositions are employed with a noun to render an adverbial reading, for example, सवेरे *savere* 'in the morning', दीवार पर *di:va:r par* 'on the wall', घर से *ghar se* 'from the house', and चाकू से *ca:ku: se* 'with the knife'.

10. वह सवेरे जल्दी दफ़्तर जाता है।
vah savere jaldi: daftar ja:ta: hɛ
he morning-obl early office go-ptc is
He goes to his office early in the morning.

11. यह तस्वीर दीवार पर टाँगो।
yeh tasvi:r di:va:r par tã:go.
this picture wall on hang
Hang this picture on the wall.

12. मैं कल घर से आऊँगा।
mɛ̃ kal ghar se a:ũ:ga:.
I tomorrow home from come-fut
I'll come from home tomorrow.

13. सेब चाकू से काटो।
seb ca:ku: se ka:ṭo.
apple knife with cut
Cut the apple with the knife.

Adverbials may precede or follow the direct object depending on the emphasis given to it in the sentence. Compare the examples (10-13) with (10a-13a).

10a. सवेरे वह जल्दी दफ़्तर जाता है।
savere vah jaldi: daftar ja:ta: hɛ.

11a. दीवार पर यह तस्वीर टाँगो।
di:va:r par yeh tasvi:r tã:go.

12a. घर से मैं कल आऊँगा।
ghar se mɛ̃ kal aũ:ga:.

13a. चाकू से सेब काटो।
ca:ku: se seb ka:ṭo.

Certain adverbs of degree and derived adverbs with *jɛsa:* like can sometimes serve as adverbial modifiers of an adverb.

14. तेज़ दौड़।
tez dɔṛ
fast run
Run fast.

14a. बच्चों जैसी तेज़ दौड़
baccõ jɛsi: tez dɔṛ
children-obl like fast run
as fast as children run

Adverbials are always optional and not obligatory in any construction.

4.2. Structure of Clauses

In this section major constituents of a sentence namely subordinate clauses, main clauses (or noun clauses), relative clauses, adverbial clauses are discussed.

4.2.1. Subordinate Clauses

Subordinate clauses are of two types: finite and non-finite. Finite clauses normally have the same sentence structure as main clauses. Sometimes they may precede the main clause due to the consideration of focus. Consider the following examples:

Main clause

1. वह आएगा।
   vah a:yega:.
   he come-fu
   He'll come.

Subordinate clause

1a. मुझे आशा है कि वह आएगा।
   mujhe a:ša: hɛ ki vah a:yega:.
   I-obl hope that he come-fut
   I hope that he will come.

1b. *कि वह आएगा मुझे आशा है
   **ki vah a:yega: mujhe a:ša: hɛ*

In case non-finite clause precedes the main clause due to the consideration of focus, the complimentizer is dropped and the element यह *yeh* this is added in the initial position of the main clause.

1c. वह आएगा यह मेरी आशा है।
   vah a:yega:, yeh meri: a:ša: hɛ.
   he come-fut, this my hope is
   I hope that he will come.

Non-finite subordinate clauses are structurally quite distinct from the main clauses. They are marked by (i) verb modification, (ii) lack of agreement, and (iii) word order. The subordinate verb undergoes a process of verbal participation or infinitivization/gerundivization. The subordinate verb does not agree with subject and/or object in number and gender and is not marked for tense.

Participle subordinate verb

2. वह चिल्लाते हुए निकला।
vah cilla:te hue nikla:.
he shriek-ptc left
He left shrieking.

The infinitive subordinate clause with an adverbial phrase can be put in the initial position.

3. मेरा वापिस आना मुमकिन नहीं।
mera: va:pas a:na: mumkin nahĩ:.
my return come-inf possible neg
It is not possible for me to come back.

4. मशीन चल रही थी।
maši:n cal rahi: thi:.
machine move prog was
The machine was working.

4a. वह चलती मशीन को देख रहा था।
vah calti: maši:n (ko) dekh raha: tha:.
he running machine-dat see-prog was
He was watching the running machine.

4b. *वह मशीन चल रही थी देख रहा था
**vah maši:n cal rahi: thi: dekh raha: tha:.*

4.2.2. Noun Clauses

Noun clauses are of two types: finite and non-finite.

4.2.2.1. Finite Noun Clauses

Finite noun clauses are introduced by the subordinator / complementizer *ki* that and follow the main clause verb. They function as subjects, direct objects, or complements of the main predicate. Finite subject clauses usually occur as subjects of adjectival predicates such as सच *sac* 'true', साफ़ *sa:f*/ स्पष्ट *spašṭ* 'clear', and मुमकिन *mumkin*/ संभव *sambhav* 'possible'.

1. यह सच है कि मोहन बीमार है।
   yeh sac hɛ ki mohan bi:ma:r hɛ.
   it true is that Mohan sick is
   It is true that Mohan is sick.

1a. यह साफ़ / स्पष्ट था कि मोहन बीमार था।
   yeh sa:f/spašṭ tha: ki mohan bi:ma:r tha:.
   it clear was that Mohan sick was
   It was clear that Mohan was sick.

4.2.2.1.1. The कि *ki* Complement Clauses

ki that complement clauses are usually governed by verbs like जानना *ja:nna:* 'to know', पता होना *pata: hona:* 'to know', कहना *kahna:* 'to say', देखना *dekhna:* 'to see', and लगना *lagna:* 'to appear/seem'. Consider the following examples.

2. मैं जानता था कि बर्फ़ गिरेगी।
   mɛ̃ ja:nta: tha: ki barf giregi:.
   I know-ptc was that snow fall-fut
   I knew that it would snow.

3. मुझे लगा कि वह बीमार है।
   mujhe laga: ki vah bi:ma:r hɛ.
   I-obl felt that he sick is
   It seemed to me that he was sick.

The verb चाहना *cahna:* 'to wish, desire' in the matrix clause selects a conditional verb form in its complement clause.

4. मैं चाहता हूँ कि वह इम्तिहान दे।
mɛ̃ ca:hta: hũ: ki vah imtiha:n de.
I desire-ptc am that he exam give
I wish that he appears in examination.

4.2.2.1.2. Direct and Indirect Speech

Direct and indirect speech are not distinguished by the use of any syntactic device, such as a quotative marker or particle. However, both quoted and reported material may be preceded by the complementizer कि *ki* that which is subordinate to the higher verb of communication in the matrix sentence, such as कह *kah-* 'say', पूछ *pu:ch-* 'ask', लिख *likh-* 'write', सुन *sun-* 'hear', सोच *soc* 'think', चाह *ca:h* 'desire/want'.

5. उसने कहा कि दवा ख़रीदो।
usne kaha: ki dava: xari:do.
he-erg said that medicine buy
He said, buy medicine.

6. ऊषा ने पूछा कि मैं क्यों गाँव जाऊँगा?
u:ša: ne pu:cha: ki mɛ̃ kyõ ga:ũ: ja:ũ:ga:?
Usha-erg asked that I why village go-fut
Usha asked, why should I go to the village?

7. मोहन ने लिखा कि तुम यह किताब पढ़ो।
mohan ne likha: ki tum yah kita:b paṛho.
Mohan-erg wrote that you this book read
Mohan wrote, Read this book.

8. हमने सुना कि वह डॉक्टर है। ।
hamne suna: ki vah ḍa:kṭar hɛ.
we-erg heard that he doctor is
We heard that he is a doctor.

9. मैंने सोचा कि वह नहीं आएगा।
mɛ̃ne soca: ki vah nahĩ: a:yega:.
I-erg thought that he neg come-fut
I thought that he would not come.

Verbs like सुन *sun-*, सोच *soc-* are 'hear/say' type verbs, and they usually occur as higher verbs in reported speech. In sentences (7-9), the complementizer कि *ki* precedes quoted material and in sentences (10-11), it precedes the reported material. The complementizer is frequently omitted. In Hindi, direct speech is preferred to indirect speech. Sentence (12) may appear ambiguous.

10. राम ने कहा (कि) वह किताब पढ़ेगा।
ra:mne kaha: (ki) vah kita:b paṛhega:.
Ram-erg said (that) he bookread-3s-fut
(a) Ram(i) said, he(j) will read the book.
(b) Ram(i) said that he(i) will read the book.

In (a) Ram and the noun and pronoun are not co-referential, and in (b) they are. In this sentence, the first or direct speech reading is preferred to the second or indirect speech reading. Instead of using indirect speech, it would be more natural to use direct speech in the second meaning as in (11).

11. राम ने कहा (कि) मैं किताब पढ़ूँगा।
ra:m ne kaha: (ki) mɛ̃ kita:b paṛũ:ga:
Ram-erg said (that) I book read-1s-fut
Ram said, I'll read a book.

Sometimes direct and indirect speech can be differentiated with the help of number and gender markers. For instance, the gender discrepancy between the matrix verb and the embedded verb may indicate an indirect quotation.

12. राम ने कहा (कि) मैं पत्र लिख रहा हूँ।
ra:mne kaha: (ki) mɛ̃ patr likh raha: hũ:
Ram-erg said (that) I letter write-prog am
Ram (i) said, I(i)m writing a letter.
Ram (i) said that I (j) am writing a letter.

12a. राम ने कहा (कि) मैं पत्र लिख रही हूँ।
ra:mne kaha: (ki) mɛ̃ patr likh rahi: hũ:
Ram-erg said (that) I letter write-prog.fs am
Ram(i) said that I(j) am writing a letter.
*Ram(i) said that I(i) am writing a letter.

In (12a) the auxiliary verb of the embedded sentence is feminine, therefore it cannot be co-referential with Ram. Whereas in (12), the verb of the embedded sentence is co-referential with the verb of the matrix sentence. Sentence (12) can be disambiguated by adding a reflexive pronoun स्वयं *svayam/* अपने आप *apne a:p* 'self'.

12b. राम ने कहा (कि) मैं स्वयं अपने आप पत्र लिख रहा हूँ।
ra:m ne kaha: (ki) mɛ̃ svayam/apne a:p patrlikh raha: hũ:.
Ram-erg said (that) I self letter write-prog.ms am
Ram (i) said, Im (i) writing a letter myself.

Similarly, the nominalization of an embedded sentence may also result in a reported speech interpretation.

13. राम ने मेरे/अपने आप पत्र लिखने के बारे में कहा।
ra:m ne mere/apne a:p patr likhne ke ba:re mẽ kaha:.
Ram-erg my/he-refl letter write-inf-obl about said
Ram told about my/his writing the letter.

Thus, there are no quotative markers to distinguish between direct and indirect speech. Direct speech is preferred over indirect speech.

4.2.2.1.3. Non-finite Noun Clause

A non-finite noun clause may consist of an infinitive (or gerundive) verb form. Infinitive gerundive forms can precede or follow the matrix clause and are inflected for case like other types of noun clauses. Non-finite noun clauses change the embedded verb into its infinitival form (stem + ना *na:*) which lacks subject - verb agreement and tense information. The infinitival form is like a derived noun which can take case markers and postpositions. The oblique form of the infinitival ends in -ना *-na:*. When changing finite noun clauses into nonfinite clauses, certain morphological markers like person, number, tense, aspectual suffixes are lost.

Finite verb		Infinitival form	
पढ़ paṛh	read	पढ़ना paṛhna:	to read

14a. मैं पढ़ूँगा।
(mɛ̃) paṛhũ:ga:.
(I)read-1s-fut
I'll read.

14b. हम पढ़ेंगे।
(ham) paṛhẽge.
(we) read-1p-fut
We'll read.

14c. कभी देखा नहीं है।
(ve) paṛhẽge.
(they) read-3p-fut
They'll read.

Notice that -ना *-na:* is added to the verb stem in the formation of the infinitive form.

15. मेरा पढ़ना उसे पसंद नहीं आया।
mera: paṛhna: use pasand nahĩ: a:ya:.
my read-inf he-dat like neg came
He did not like me to read.

16. मुझे पढ़ना पसंद है।
mujhe paṛhna: pasand hɛ.
I-obl read-Inf like is
I like to read.

Noun clauses can function as subjects, direct objects, postpositional objects, and adverbials.

Verbs are made non-finite by the processes of infinitivization and participialization. Infinitivizaton is the result of adding the suffix –ना *-na:* to the verbal stem. There are three groups of participial constructions: (i) present participle, (ii) past participle, and (iii) agentive participle. The present participle indicates ongoing action or process, the past participle indicates completed action or process, and the agentive participle indicates a habitual or potential action or process.

17. वह पढ़ा - लिखा लड़का है।
vah paṛha: - likha: laṛka: hɛ.
he read-past-ms write-past-ms boy is
He is a literate boy.

17a. वह पढी - लिखी लड़की है।
vah paṛhi: - likhi: laṛki: thi:.
she read-past-fs write- past-fs girl was
She was a literate girl.

17b. पढ़ने लिखने वाला लड़का समय बर्बाद नहीं करता।
paṛhne likhne va:la: laṛka: samay barba:d nahĩ: karta:.
read-inf-obl write-inf-obl gen boy time waste neg do-ptc
The boy who studies does not waste time.

Notice that participial forms remain unaltered in the present and past participles. It is the auxiliary which takes person, gender, number, and tense markers. The participial forms agree with the following nouns in number and gender.

Masculine		Feminine	
Sg	Pl	Sg	Pl
का ka:	के ke	की ki:	की ki:

18. उसका उमा को कल यह कहना अच्छा नहीं था।
uska: uma: ko kal yeh kahna: accha: nahĩ: tha:.
he-gen Uma-dat yesterday this say-inf good neg was
His telling this to Uma yesterday was not proper.

The word order of non-finite noun clauses remains unchanged. The focus-related movements to the left of the non-finite verb yield well-formed sentences. Examples of various movements of non-finite noun clauses are given as follows:

Leftward movements of indirect objects

18a. उमा को उसका कल यह कहना अच्छा नहीं था।
uma: ko uska: kal yah kahna: accha: nahĩ: tha:.
Uma-dat his yesterday this say-inf good neg was
His telling this to Uma yesterday was not proper.

Leftward movement of the time adverb

18b. कल उसका उमा को यह कहना अच्छा नहीं था।
kal uska: uma: ko yah kahna: accha: nahĩ: tha:.

Notice that no constituent of the non-finite noun clauses can be moved to a position following the non-finite verb कहना *kahna:* 'to say' as below.

Rightward movement of indirect object

18c. *उसका कल यह कहना अच्छा नहीं था उमा को।
uska: kal yah kahna: accha: nahĩ: tha: uma: ko.

Rightward movement of time adverb

18d. *उसका उमा को यह कहना अच्छा नहीं था कल।
uska: uma: ko yah kahna: accha: nahĩ: tha: kal.

4.2.3. Relative Clauses

There are two types of relative clause constructions: finite and non-finite participial relative clauses. The finite relative clauses maintain full sentence structures with subject verb agreement and are very common. Participial relative clauses exhibit the non-finite form of the verb. The former is more explicit than the latter. The former type is also labeled as the real relative clause.

In the formation of finite relative clauses, the relative marker जो *jo* 'who', which is placed in front of the relativized element, the correlative marker वह *vah* 'that' is placed at the beginning of the head noun, and the second identical or co-referential noun phrase may be deleted. The forms of relative and correlative markers are given below.

Relative markers			
Direct		Oblique	
Sg	Pl	Sg	Pl
जो jo	जो jo	जिस jis	जिन jin

Correlative markers			
वह vah	वे ve	उस us	उन un

The relative marker begins with a ज /j/ sound, whereas correlative markers begin with व / v/ and उ /u/ sounds. In the direct case, the noun is not followed by a postposition and when it is, it is in the oblique case. The relative and correlative markers change for the number and case of the noun. The forms are as follows.

Direct			
Relative Pronouns		Correlative Pronouns	
Sg	Pl	Sg	Pl
जो jo	जो jo	वह vah	वे ve

Oblique			
जिस jis	जिन jin	उस us	उन un
जिसे jise	जिन्हें jinhẽ	उसे use	उन्हें unhẽ
जिसको jisko	जिनको jinko	उसको usko	उनको unko
जिससे jisse	जिनसे jinse	उससे usse	उनसे unse
जिसने jisne	जिन्होंने jinhõne	उसने usne	उन्होंने unhõne

In the examples given below, the symbol ø indicates the presumed site of relativized and head NP prior to deletion.

1. जो लड़का दिल्ली में रहता है वह ø मेरा भाई है।
jo laṛka: dilli mẽ rahta: hɛ vah ø mera: bha:i: hɛ.
rel boy Delhi-loc live-ptc is cor -ø my brother is
The boy, who lives in Delhi, is my brother.

Sentence (1) consists of two clauses which share an identical and co-referential noun phrase.

Main clause:
लड़का मेरा भाई है।
laṛka: mera: bha:i: hɛ.
The boy is my brother.

Relative clause:

लड़का दिल्ली में रहता है।
laṛka: dilli: mẽ rahta: hɛ.
The boy lives in Delhi.

Here the relative clause takes the relative pronoun जो *jo*, whereas the correlative clause takes the correlative pronoun वह *vah*. When the relative clause precedes the main clause it results in the sentence (1a):

1a. [जो लड़का दिल्ली में रहता है] वह लड़का मेरा भाई है।
[jo laṛka: dilli mẽ rahta: hɛ] vah laṛka: mera: bha:i: hɛ.

The second occurrence of लड़का *laṛka:* is deleted to yield sentence (1b). There are two other possibilities for relative clauses: (i) the relative clause may follow the head noun phrase (1b), and (ii) the relative clause may follow the correlative clause (1c).

1b. वह लड़का [जो दिल्ली में रहता है] मेरा भाई है।
vah laṛka: [jo dilli: mẽ rahta: hɛ] mera: bha:i: hɛ.

1c. वह लड़का मेरा भाई है [जो दिल्ली में रहता है]।
vah laṛka: mera: bha:i: hɛ [jo dilli: mẽ rahta: hɛ].

Notice that the participial relative clause is formed by (i) deleting the relativized noun phrase, and (ii) changing the verb into a participial form by adding the suffix -ता *-ta:* for the present participle and -ने वाला *-ne va:la:* for the agentive participle.

4.2.3.1. Restrictive and Non-restrictive Clauses

The restrictive relative clauses allow three possible word orders as given above (1a-1c). The non-restrictive relative clauses are those where some extra but relevant information is provided about the antecedent head noun. They allow only one word order in which the additional information follows the head noun.

2. नेहरू [जो भारत के पहले प्रधानमंत्री थे]
nehru: [jo bha:rat ke pradha:n mantri: the]
Nehru who India-gen first prime minister was

इल्हाबाद में जन्मे।
ilha:ba:d mẽ janme.
Allahabad in born
Nehru, who was the first prime minister of India, was born at Allahabad.

2a. *नेहरू जन्मे इल्हाबाद में [जो भारत के पहले प्रधानमंत्री थे]
**nehru: janme ilha:ba:d mẽ [jo bha:rat ke pahle pradha:n mantri: the].*

2b. *[जो भारत के पहले प्रधानमंत्री थे] वे नेहरू इलहाबद में जन्मे।
**[jo bha:rat ke pahle pradha:n mantri: the] ve nehru: illha:ba:d mẽ janme.*
There are no word order differences between a restrictive and a non-restrictive participial relative clause.

3. [ø दिल्ली में रहने वाला लड़का] मेरा भाई है।
[ø dilli: mẽ rahne va:la: laṛka:] mera: bha:i: hɛ.
Delhi in live-inf-obl gen boy my brother is
The boy who lives in Delhi is my brother.

4. इल्हाबाद में जन्म लेने वाले नेहरू भारत के पहले प्रधानमंत्री थे।
ilha:ba:d mẽ janm lene va:le nehru: bha:rat ke pahle pradha:n mantri: the.
Born at Allahabad, Nehru was the first prime minister of India.

The relative clause may precede or follow the head noun. The non-restrictive relative clause always follows the head noun. In general, the participial relative clauses precede the head noun.

The form of the relativized element in the relative clause corresponding to the head noun (i.e., the relativized element) is usually preserved in full when the relative clause precedes the main clause. Alternately, it is deleted. It is pronominalized when the head is a pronoun.

5. वह [जो मेहनत करता है] उन्नति करता है।
vah [jo mehnat karta: hɛ] unnati: karta: hɛ.
He who hard work do-pr is progress do-pr is
He who works hard progresses.

Here the second occurrence of the identical noun phrase is nominalized. The antecedent noun phrase may undergo deletion too, as in sentence (6).

6. [जो दिल्ली में रहता है] वह लड़का मेरा भाई है।
[jo dilli: mẽ rahta: hɛ] vah laṛka: mera: bha:i: hɛ.
Who Delhi in stay is he boy my brother is
The boy who lives in Delhi is my brother.

The original position of the relativized element usually remains unchanged. In case the relative constituent is placed in the beginning of the clause, the effect is that of contrastive focus.

7. मैंने वह लेख पढ़ा [जो सरिता ने लिखा है।]
mɛ̃ne vah lekh paṛha: [jo sarita: ne likha: hɛ].
I-erg that essay read which Sarita-erg write is
I read the essay which was written by Salim.

The place of the relativized direct object is usually in the preverbal position. The placement of the relativized object NP to the relative clause initial position indicates focus on the relativized NP. The relativized adverbials and indirect objects can undergo similar movement.

7a. [मैंने वह लेख पढ़ा] जो सरिता ने लिखा है।
[mɛ̃ne vah lekh paṛha:] jo sarita: ne likha: hɛ.
I-erg that essay read which Salim-erg wrote is
I read the essay which Sarita wrote.

If the relative clause occurs to the left of the main clause, the relativized element can be placed in the sentence initial position.

7b. [जो लेख सरिता ने लिखा है] मैंने पढ़ा वह।
[jo lekh sarita: ne likha: hɛ] mɛ̃ne paṛha: vah.
which essay sarita-erg wrote I read that
I read the essay which was written by Sarita.

In the third order, the relative clause follows immediately after the head NP.

7c. मैंने पढ़ा वह लेख जो सरिता ने लिखा है।
mɛ̃ne par̩ha: vah lekh jo sarita: ne likha: hɛ.
I read that write which Sarita-erg wrote is
I read the essay written by Sarita.

In a headless relative clause, the relative clause cannot be placed immediately after the head NP.

8. [राज ने जो सुना] मैंने सुना नहीं।
[ra:j ne jo suna:] mɛ̃ne suna: nahĩ:.
Raj-erg rel heard I-erg hear not
I didnt hear what Raj heard.

However, it is possible to place the relative clause to the right of the main clause.

8a. मैंने सुना नहीं [जो राज ने सुना।]
mɛ̃ne suna: nahĩ: [jo ra:j ne suna:.].
I didnt hear what Raj heard.

All the constituents of a main clause except the verb can be relativized in a finite relative clause.

Relativization of subject

9. वह आदमी [जो ø आया:]
vah a:dmi: [jo ø a:ya:]
cor person rel came
the person who came

Relativization of direct object

10. वह आदमी [जिसे ø मैं यहां लाया:]
vah a:dmi: [jise ø mɛ̃ yahã: la:ya:]
cor person rel I here brought
the person whom I brought here

Relativization of indirect object

11. वह आदमी [जिसे ø मैंने किताब दी]
vah a:dmi: [jise ø mɛ̃ne kita:b di:]
cor person rel I-erg watch gave
the person who I gave the book

Relativization of adjunct (object of associative postposition)

12. वह आदमी [जिसके ø साथ मैं दिल्ली गया]

vah a:dmi: [jiske ø sa:th mɛ̃ dilli: gaya:]

cor person rel with I Delhi went

the person with whom I went to Delhi

Relativization of adjunct (object of a locative postposition)

13. वह दफ़्तर [जिसमें ø मैं काम करता हूँ]

vah daftar [jis ø mẽ mɛ̃ ka:m karta: hũ:]

cor office rel in I work do-ptc am

the office in which I work

Relativization of possessor noun

14. वह आदमी [जिसका ø यह मकान है]

vah a:dmi: [jiska: ø yeh maka:n hɛ]

cor person rel-poss this house is

the man whose house this is

Relativization of object of comparison

15. वह मकान [जिससे ø यह मकान बड़ा है]

vah maka:n [jisse ø yeh maka:n baṛa: hɛ]

cor house rel than this house big is

the house which is smaller than this house

Relativization of a subordinate subject

16. वह लड़का [जो ø उमा ने कहा हाकी खेलता है] गया।

vah laṛka: [jo ø uma: ne kaha: ha:ki: khelta: hɛ] gaya:.

rel boy cor Uma-erg said play-ptc hockey is went

The boy that Uma said plays hockey has gone.

Relativization of a subordinate direct object

17. वह टोपी [जो ø [राजा ने कहा [उमा ने बुनी है]]

vah ṭopi: [jo ø [ra:ja: ne kaha: [uma: ne buni: hɛ]]

rel cap that Raja-erg said Uma-erg has knitted

मेरे पास है।

mere pass hɛ.

me-poss is

The cap that Raja said Uma knitted is with me.

Relativization of subordinate indirect object

18. वह लड़का [जिसे ø [मोहन ने कहा कि राजा ने किताब दी]] आया।

vah laṛka:[jiseø[mohan ne kaha: ki ra:ja: ne kita:b di:]a:ya:.

rel boy cor Mohan-erg said that Raja-erg book gave

The boy that Mohan said Raja gave a book to came.

Relativization of object of a postpositional adverbial phrase

19. वह कालेज [जिस ø में [अजीत ने कहा [कि उमा

vah ka:lej [jis ø mẽ [aji:t ne kaha: [ki uma:

rel college cor in Ajit-erg said that

काम कर रही है]]] छोटा है।

ka:m kar rahi: hɛ]]] choṭa: hɛ.

Uma work do-ing is small is

The college that Ajit said Uma works at is small.

Relativization of object of comparison in subordinate clause

20. वह मकान [जिस ø से [अजीत ने कहा [कि मेरा मकान

vah maka:n [jis ø se [aji:t ne kaha: [ki mera: maka:n

rel house cor than Ajit-erg said that

बड़ा है]]] दूर नहीं है।

baṛa: hɛ]]] du:r nahĩ: hɛ.

my office is big is far not is

The house that Ajit said that my house is bigger than it is not far way.

4.2.3.2. Non-finite Relative Clauses

Participial/non-finite relative clauses allow the subject and the direct object constituent to undergo the process of relativization. However, the indirect object etc. cannot undergo relativization.

Relativization of subject

21. [ø बढ़ता (हुआ)] बच्चा

[ø baṛhta: (hua:)] bacca:

grow-pst-ms (part.) child

the growing child

22. [ø पढ़ने लिखने वाला] लड़का
[ø paṛhne likhne va:la:] laṛka:
read-inf-obl write-inf-obl gen boy
the boy who is studying (Lit. the studying boy)

Relativization of direct object
23. [उसकी ख़रीदी हुई] किताब
[uski: xari:di: hui:] kita:b
his buy-pst-fs book
the book bought by him

Indirect object
24. *[ø किताब दी हुई] लड़की
**[ø kita:b di: hui:] laṛki:*
the girl to whom the book is given

Any constituent of a subordinate relative clause, except the verbs, can be relativized.

4.2.3.3. Finite Relative Clauses

In finite relative clause modifiers, the possessor elements of the noun phrase can be subjected to further relativization. Also any constituent of a relative clause can be subjected to further relativization.

Relativization of possessor
25. वह डाक्टर [जिसका मोहन दवाई खाता है] अच्छा नहीं है।
vah ḍa:kṭar [jiska: mohan dava:i: kha:ta: hɛ] accha: nahĩ: hɛ.
rel doctor cor-poss Mohan medicine eating is good neg is
The doctor whose (prescribed) medicine Mohan is taking is not good.

Relativization of modifier
26. यह दूध उतना गर्म नहीं है जितना (गर्म) मैं चाहता था।
yeh du:dh utna: garm nahĩ: hɛ jitna: (garm) mɛ̃ ca:hta: tha:.
this milk rel hot neg is cor hot I wanted
This milk is not as hot as I wanted.

Relativization of a constituent of a relative clause

27. वह मेज़ [जो ø [मुझे पता था [कि आपने ख़रीदा]

vah mez [jo ø [mujhe pata: tha: [ki a:pne xari:da:]

that table cor I know was that you-erg bought

उतना बड़ा नहीं है जितना मेरा है।

utna: baṛa: nahĩ: hɛ jitna: mera: hɛ.

rel big neg is cor mine is

The table that I know you bought is not as big as mine.

The participialization, however, does not allow relativization of any constituent of a relative clause.

The noun phrases in postpositional phrases can be relativized by the finite relativization strategy. The constituents within coordinate noun phrases can be relativized.

28. वह लड़का [जो ø मेरे भाई का दोस्त है] चालाक है।

vah laṛka: [jo ø mere bha:i: ka: dost hɛ] ca:la:k hɛ.

cor boy rel my brother of friend is clever is

The boy who is a friend of my brother is clever.

Elements within coordinate verb phrases and coordinate sentences can also be relativized. In (29) an element of the first conjunct of a coordinate verb phrase is conjoined.

29. वह लेख [जो ø मैंने पढ़ा और पत्र लिखा] अच्छा है।

vah lekh [jo ø ɛ̃ne paṛha: ɔr patr likha:] accha: hɛ.

cor article rel I-erg read and letter wrote good is

The article which I read and wrote a letter about is good.

This sentence can be interpreted as the joining of two actions in which the first stimulates the second one. The two actions, thus joined, are not independent of each other. In (30) an element of the second conjunct of a coordinate verb phrase is relativized.

30. मैंने लेख पढ़ा और जो पत्र लिखा वह अच्छा है।

mɛ̃ne lekh paṛha: ɔr jo patr likha: vah accha: hɛ.

I-erg article read and cor letter wrote rel good is

I read an article and the wrote a good letter about it.

This sentence can be interpreted as the joining of two actions in which the meaning after doing one thing the second one is done is implied. Therefore it appears like a participial construction. The preferred version will be (30a).

30a. लेख पढ़कर जो पत्र मैंने लिखा वह अच्छा है ।
     lekh paṛhkar jo patr mɛ̃ne likha: vah accha: hɛ.
     article read-cp cor letter I-erg wrote rel good is
     After reading the article, I wrote a good letter about it.

The relativization of the first or second conjunct elements of a coordinate sentence result in ill-formed sentences.

31. *वह लेख [जो मैंने पढ़ा और मोहन ने पत्र लिखा] अच्छा है ।
     vah lekh jo mɛ̃ne paṛha: ɔr mohan ne patr likha: accha: hɛ.
     *The essay which I read and Mohan wrote a letter is good.

31a. *मैंने लेख पढ़ा और मोहन ने जो पत्र लिखा वह अच्छा है ।
     mɛ̃ne lekh paṛha: ɔr mohan ne jo patr likha: vah accha: hɛ.
     *I read the essay and the letter which Mohan wrote is good.

The order of pre-sentential and post-sentential positions of relative with reference to a correlative clause, also yield well-formed sentences.

32. [जो ø मैंने पढ़ा और पत्र लिखा] वह लेख अच्छा है ।
     [jo ø mɛ̃ne paṛha: ɔr patr likha:] vah lekh accha: hɛ.
     which I-erg read and letter wrote rel essay good is
     The essay which I read, and wrote a letter about is good.

32a. वह लेख अच्छा है [जो ø मैंने पढ़ा और पत्र लिखा ।]
     vah lekh accha: hɛ [jo ø mɛ̃ne paṛha: ɔr patr likha:].
     he write good is which I read and letter write
     That essay is good which I read and wrote a letter about.

Notice that a conjunct intervening between a relative and a correlative clause is less preferred. Therefore, sentence (32a) more preferred than (32). The relativized element can be moved within the constituents and sometimes to the initial position for the consideration of focus.

Mostly the relative clauses favor the finite relativization strategy. The participilization strategy, which is non-finite in nature, is subject to various syntactic and semantic constraints as pointed out above.

4.2.4. Adverbial Clauses

Adverbial clauses are marked by (a) the finite form of the verb, or (b) the non-finite form of the verb. Finite adverbial clauses can be placed in pre-sentential as well as post-sentential position. The unmarked order of a nonfinite adverbial clause is at the pre-verbal or post-verbal position. There are time, manner, purpose, cause, condition, concession, and degree adverbial clauses.

4.2.4.1. Adverbial Clauses of Time

There are three kinds of the adverbial clauses: (a) finite clauses with relative clauses like time markers such as यदि *yedi* 'if', (b) participial (non-finite) adverbial constructions, and (c) the infinitival constructions.

(a) Finite clauses with relative clause time markers

Some of the adverbial markers in this category are जब *jab* 'when', जब से *jab se* 'since', and ज्योंही *jyõhi:* 'as soon as'.

1. जब वह आएगा मैं भी आऊँगा।
   jab vah a:yega: mɛ̃ bhi: a:ũ:ga:.
   when he come-fut I too come-fut
   When he comes, I'll come too.

2. जब मैं जाता हूँ (तब) वह भी जाता है।
   jab mɛ̃ ja:ta: hũ: (tab) vah bhi: ja:ta: hɛ.
   when I go-ptc am (then) he too go-ptc is
   When I go, (then) he goes too.

3. जबसे वह यहां आया (तबसे) हम साथ साथ काम करते हैं।
   jabse vah yahã: a:ya: (tabse) ham sa:th-sa:th ka:m karte hɛ̃.
   cor-from he came here rel-from we together work do-ptc are
   Weve worked together since he came here.

In sentences (2) and (3), time adverbial clauses are introduced by the markers जब *jab* and जब से *jab se* respectively. Like relative clauses, they distinguish themselves from question words which begin with क *k*. The time clause contains a finite verb with tense aspect information. The time marker जब *jab* denotes a sequence of events (2) and simultaneous events (3) respectively. It is important to note that the relative clause time markers जब *jab* or जब से *jab se* do not undergo deletion as do the correlative markers तब *tab* and तब से *tab se*.

(b) Participial (non-finite) constructions

Four participial constructions, present participle, past participle, absolutive and the as soon as participle, also act as time adverbials. The present and past participles agree in gender and number with the subject of the main clause, whereas the last two do not undergo any agreement changes.

4. मोहन दौड़ता आया।
mohan dɔṛta: a:ya:.
Mohan run-ptc came
Mohan came running.

5. अफ़सर ने कुर्सी पर बैठकर पूछा
afsar ne kursi: par bɛṭhkar pu:cha:
officer chair on sit-cp asked
the officer asked, sitting on the chair

6. घर पहुँचकर उसने टेलीफोन किया।
ghar pahũckar usne ṭeliphon kiya:.
home reach-pp she-erg telephone did
She telephoned after reaching home.

7. आते ही उसने यह सवाल पूछा।
a:te hi: usne yah sava:l pu:cha:.
come-emp he-erg this question asked
As soon as he came, he asked this question.

A present participle expresses an ongoing action or process. It takes the progressive aspect in the subordinate clause.

8a. मोहन उस समय आया जिस समय वह दौड़ रहा था।
mohan us samay a:ya: jis samay vah dɔṛ raha: tha:.
Mohan at that time came when he run-prog was
Mohan came at the time when he was running.

The participle forms can be reduplicated as in (8b).

8b. मोहन दौड़ता - दौड़ता आया।
mohan dɔṛta: - dɔṛta: a:ya:.
Mohan run-ptc run-ptc came
Mohan came running.

(c) Infinitival construction

A verbal noun followed by पहले *pahle* 'before', बाद में *ba:d mẽ* 'after', or पर *par* 'on' results in a time adverbial.

9. उसके आने से पहले कोई नहीं आएगा।
uske a:ne se pahle koi: nahĩ: a:yega:.
he-gen-obl come-inf-obl before none neg come-fut
No one will come before he comes.

10. उसके जाने के बाद मैं जाऊँगा।
uske ja:ne ke ba:d mɛ̃ ja:ũ:ga:.
he-gen-obl go-inf-obl after I go-fut
I'll go after his departure.

11. उसके आने पर सारे खुश हुए।
uske a:ne par sa:re khuš hue.
he-gen-obl come-inf-obl on all happy became
All were happy on his coming.

4.2.4.2. Manner Clauses

Manner clauses also employ relative-like and participial constructions. They are not expressed by infinitival or gerundive constructions. The relative clause-like manner markers जैसे वैसे *jɛse - vɛse* 'as/which way' indicates the manner reading.

12. जैसे मैं कहूँगा वैसे ही करो।
jɛse mɛ̃ kahũ:ga: vɛse hi: karo.
as-rel I tell-you the same way-cor emp do
Do as I tell you.

The word order of the relative manner clause and correlative manner clause can be altered.

12a. वैसे करो जैसे मैं कहूँगा।
vɛse karo jɛse mɛ̃ kahũ:ga:

The following participial constructions express manner rather than tme.

13. वह रोते - रोते आया।
vah rote - rote a:ya:.
he weep-ptc weep-ptc came
He came (while) crying.

14. वह फर्श पर बैठकर रोया।
vah faraš par bɛṭhkar roya:.
he floor on sit-cp wept
He cried sitting on the floor.

15. वह शरारत के साथ बोला।
vah šara:rat ke sa:th bola:.
he anger-gen with said
He said with anger.

The negativized participial form is formed by adding -ए बिना *-e bina:.*

16. वह हँसे बिना बोला।
vah hãse bina: bola:.
he laugh-obl without said
He said without laughing.

Infinitival constructions also express manner.

17. उसका नाचना मुझे पसंद है।
uska: na:cna: mujhe pasand hɛ.
(s)he-gen dance-inf me-dat like is
I like his/her manner of dancing.

17a. उसके नाचने का तरीका मुझे पसंद है।
uske na:cne ka: tari:ka: mujhe pasand hɛ.
(s)he-gen-obl dance-inf-gen manner I-dat like is
I like his/her manner of dancing.

4.2.4.3. Purpose Clauses

Purpose clauses are formed in two ways: (a) infinitival form followed by ए *e* or the oblique form plus the postposition के लिए *ke liye* 'for', and (b) the क्योंकि *kyõki* 'because/ as' clause modifying इस लिए *is liye* 'therefore'.

18. वह नाटक देखने गया।
vah na:ṭak dekhne gaya:.
he play see-inf-obl for
He went to see a play.

18a. वह नाटक देखने के लिए गया।
vah na:ṭak dekhne ke liye gaya:.
he play see-inf-obl for went
He went to see a play.

Notice that in (18) the oblique case marker *e* is added to the infinitive form of the verb, which expresses the meaning for. In (18a), the oblique case marker -ए *-e* is added before the postposition के लिए *ke liye* 'for'. In the above construction, there is an option between the two alternatives. If the verb is not a motion verb the oblique form and postposition must be used.

19. मैंने उसे किताब पढ़ने के लिए कहा।
mɛ̃ne use kita:b paṛhne ke liye kaha:.
I-erg he-dat book read-inf-obl for said
I told him to read the book.

19a. *मैंने उसे किताब पढ़ने कहा।
**mɛ̃ne use kita:b paṛhne kaha:.*

The co-referential phrases *kyõki* because and *is liye* 'therefore' can also be used.

20. क्योंकि आज गर्मी थी इसलिए मैं बाज़ार नहीं गया।
kyõki a:j garmi: thi: isliye mɛ̃ ba:za:r nahĩ: gaya:.
because today hot was therefore I market neg went
Because it was hot, I didnt go to market.

The elements of co-referential phrases क्योंकि *kyõki* and इसलिए *is liye* can be deleted. The word order undergoes a change as in (20a) and (20b) below.

20a. आज गर्मी थी इसलिए मैं बाज़ार नहीं गया।
a:j garmi: thi: isliye mɛ̃ ba:za:r nahĩ: gaya:.
Today hot was therefore ार नहीं I market neg go-past
It was hot, therefore, I couldnt go to market.

20b. क्योंकि आज गर्मी थी मैं बाज़ार नहीं गया।
kyõki a:j garmi: thi: mɛ̃ ba:za:r nahĩ: gaya:.
because today hot was I market neg go-past
Because it was hot, I didnt go to market.

4.2.4.4. Cause Clauses

Cause is expressed by using these constructions: (a) finite clauses marked by क्योंकि *kyõki* 'because', (b) participles, and (c) infinitival plus से *se* from.

(a) Finite clauses

21. वह पढ़ नहीं सकता क्योंकि वह अनपढ़ है।
vah paṛh nahĩ: sakta: kyõki vah anpaṛh hɛ.
he read not able because he illiterate is
He cannot read because he is illiterate.

21a. क्योंकि वह अनपढ़ है वह पढ़ नहीं सकता।
kyõki vah anpaṛh hɛ, vah paṛh nahĩ: sakta:.
Because he is illiterate, he cannot read.

(b) Participles

22. चलते चलते वह थका और बैठ गया।
calte calte vah thaka: ɔr bɛṭh gaya:.
walk-ptc he tired and sat aux
Because of walking (constantly), he was tired and sat down.

23. मैं प्रतीक्षा करते करते थक गया।
mɛ̃ prati:kša: karte karte thak gaya:.
I wait do-ptc tired aux
I got tired of waiting.

The cause is expressed in (22) and (23) by reduplicated present and past participles respectively. Cause can be expressed by other participles, too.

24. अधिक शराब पीकर वह बीमार हुआ।
adhik šara:b pi:kar vah bi:ma:r hua:.
more liquor drink-cp he sick was
Because he drank a lot (of liquor), he was sick.

25. दवाई खाते ही वह ठीक हुआ।
dava:i: kha:te hi: vah ṭhi:kh hua:.
medicine eat-ptc emp he alright became
Immediately upon taking the medicine, he recovered (from illness).

(c) Infinitive plus *se* with

26. बच्चे के आने से सभी खुश हुए।
bacce ke a:ne se sabhi: khuš hue.
child-obl-gen come-inf-obl with all happy were
Because of the arrival of the child, all were happy.

4.2.4.5. Condition Clauses

Condition clauses are marked by the conjunction *agar/yadi* 'if'.

27. अगर/यदि वह बाज़ार जाएगा फिर मैं नहीं जाऊँगा।
agar/yadi vah ba:za:r ja:yega:, phir mɛ̃ nahĩ: ja:ũ:ga:.
if he market go-fut-ms then I neg go-fut.1s
If he goes to market, (then) I won't go.

28. अगर/यदि बारिश होगी फिर अच्छी फसल होगी।
agar/yadi ba:riš hogi:, phir acchi: fasal hogi:.
if rain fall-fut then good crop be-fut
If it rains, then the crops will be good.

The sequence of if - then clause can be reversed.

27a. फिर मैं बाज़ार नहीं जाऊँगा अगर वह जाएगा।
phir mɛ̃ ba:za:r nahĩ: ja:ũ:ga: agar vah ja:yega:.
again I market neg go-fut if he go-fut
I will not go to the market if he goes.

28a. फिर अच्छी फसल होगी अगर बारिश होगी।
phir acchi: fasl hogi: agar ba:riš hogi:.
again good harvest will if rain comes
The crop will be good if it rains.

It is to be noted that the condition marker अगर *agar* is not deleted, whereas its co-referential marker फिर *phir* can be deleted. The conjunction marker वर्ना *varna:* 'otherwise' also is used in condition clauses.

29. कल जल्दी आ जाना वर्ना मैं अकेले जाऊँगा।
kal jaldi: a: ja:na: varna: mɛ̃ akele: ja:ũ:ga:.
tomorrow soon come otherwise I alone-obl go-fut
Come early tomorrow, otherwise I will go alone.

The same tense reference is marked in both constituents conjoined by the markers अगर *agar* and वर्ना *varna:*.

4.2.4.6. Concession Clauses

A concession clause is marked by subordinate conjunction markers such as यध्यपि *yadhypi*/ हालांकि *ha:lã:ki*/ चाहे *ca:he* 'although', अगर - फिर भी *agar - phir bhi:* 'even if', and क्यों नहीं *kyõ nahĩ:* 'why not'.

30. यध्यपि/ हालंकि वह बहुत अमीर है फिर भी वह कंजूस है।
yadhypi/ha:lã:ki vah bahut ami:r hɛ phir bhi: vah kanju:s hɛ.
although he very rich is still he miser is
Although he is very rich, he is a miser.

31. चाहे आप उसको पीटोगे भी वह यह काम नहीं करेगा।
ca:he a:p usko pi:ṭoge bhi:, vah yah ka:m nahĩ: karega:.
even if you he-dat beat-fut too he this work not do-fut
Even if you beat him/her up, he/she won't do this work.

31a. चाहे आप उसको पीटोगे भी वह फिर भी यह काम
ca:he a:p usko pi:ṭoge bhi:, vah phir bhi: yah ka:m
even if you he-dat beat-fut too even then this work
नहीं करेगा।
nahĩ: karega:.
not do-fut
Even if you'll beat him/her up, even then he/she won't do this work.

32. वह क्यों न काफी अनुरोध करे फिर भी मैं उसके साथ
vah kyõ na ka:phi: anurodh kare phir bhi: mɛ̃ uske sa:th
he why do much insist do even then I he-gen with
दिल्ली नहीं जाऊँगा।
dilli: nahĩ: ja:ũ:ga:.
Delhi not go-fut
Even if he insists, I'll not go to Delhi with him.

4.2.4.7. Result Clauses

In result clauses, the main clause contains a cause marked by an oblique infinitive followed by the postposition के कारण *ke ka:raṇ* / की वजह *ki: vajah* 'because of the reason'. This expresses the result of a sentence. In a sentence sequence, the cause is usually given in the first sentence, followed by another sentence giving the result of it. The second sentence usually contains the phrase इस लिए *is liye* 'therefore'.

33. बारिश होने के कारण / की वजह से मैं बाज़ार न जा सका।
ba:riš hone ke ka:raṇ/ki: vajah mɛ̃ ba:za:r na ja: saka:.
rain fall-inf-obl reason I market neg go able
I could not go to market because of the rain.

34. कल अच्छा मौसम था इसलिए मैं घूमने गया।
kal accha: mɔsam tha: isliye mɛ̃ ghu:mne gaya:.
yesterday good weather was therefore I walk-inf-obl went-1s
The weather was good yesterday, therefore, I went for a walk.

4.3. Sentence Construction

Here we will discuss the different types of sentence constructions: copular, verbal, negation, interrogatives, imperatives, anaphora, reflexives, reciprocals, equatives, comparison, superlatives, and coordination.

4.3.1. Copular Sentences

The verb होना *hona:* 'to be' is employed in copular sentences. The copula may take a predicate noun, predicate adjective, participle, or a predicate adverb as a complement.

Predicate noun

1. वह वकील है।
   vah vaki:l hɛ.
   he lawyer is
   He is a lawyer.

Predicate adjective

2. सुषमा लंबी है।
   sušma: lambi: hɛ.
   Sushma tall is
   Sushma is tall.

Predicate adverbial (participle)

3. मोहन खड़ा है।
   mohan khaṛa: hɛ.
   Mohan stand is
   Mohan is standing.

Predicate adverbial

4. उसकी आवाज़ मीठी है।
   uski: a:va:z mi:ṭhi: hɛ.
   his/her voice sweet is
   His/her voice is sweet.

The unmarked order of constituents in the examples given above is subject - complement - copula.

There are two types of predicate adjectival copular sentences: (a) those which change for gender and number of the nouns they modify and (b) those which do not. The adjective लंबा *lamba:* 'tall' falls into the first category, and the adjective सफेद *safed* 'white' falls into the second.

5. यह लंबा लड़का है।
yah lamba: laṛka: hɛ.
this tall boy is
This is a tall boy.

5a. ये लंबे लड़के हैं।
ye lambe laṛke hɛ̃.
these tall boys are
These are tall boys.

5b. यह लंबी लड़की है।
yeh lambi: laṛki: hɛ.
this tall girl is
This is a tall girl.

5c. ये लंबी लड़कियाँ हैं।
ye lambi: laṛkiyã: hɛ̃.
these tall girls are
These are tall girls.

6. यह सफेद फूल है।
yeh safed phu:l hɛ.
this white flower is
This is a white flower.

6a. ये सफेद फूल हैं।
ye safed phu:l hɛ̃.
these white flowers are
These are white flowers.

6b. यह सफेद कमीज़ है।
yeh safed kami:z hɛ.
this white shirt is
This is a white shirt.

6c. ये सफेद कमीज़ें हैं।
ye safed kami:zẽ hɛ̃.
these white shirts are
These are white shirts.

The copular verb must be retained in both affirmative (positive) as well as negative sentences. In the case of co-ordinate structures, it is optionally deleted.

7. मोहन डॉक्टर है।
mohan ḍa:kṭar hɛ.
Mohan doctor is
Mohan is a doctor.

8. सोहन वकील नहीं है।
sohan vaki:l nahĩ: hɛ.
Sohan lawyer not is
Sohan is not a lawyer.

9. मोहन और अजीत डॉक्टर हैं।
mohan aur aji:t ḍa:kṭar hɛ̃.
Mohan and Ajit doctors are
Mohan and Ajit are doctors.

9a. मोहन डॉक्टर है और अजीत भी।
mohan ḍa:kṭar hɛ ɔr aji:t bhi:.
Mohan doctor is and Ajit too
Mohan is a doctor and so is Ajit.

9b. न मोहन वकील है और न अजीत।
na mohan vaki:l hɛ ɔr na aji:t.
neg Mohan lawyer is and neg Ajit
Neither Mohan nor Ajit is a lawyer.

The copular verb is used for definition, identity, existence, and role functions. It is also used as a second member (explicator) in the compound verb sequences.

10. आजकल सूर्य जल्दी चढ़ता है।
a:jkal su:rya jaldi: caṛhta: hɛ.
nowadays sun quick rise-ptc is
The sun rises early these days.

11. दिन प्रति दिन हालात सुधर रहे हैं।
din prati din ha:la:t sudhar rahe hɛ̃.
day after day situation improve-prog are
The situation is improving day by day.

12. आजकल जल्दी अंधेरा होता है।
a:jkal jaldi: andhera: hota: hɛ.
nowadays early dark be-ptc is
It becomes dark early (in the evening) these days.

13. ईश्वर है।
i:švar hɛ.
God is

14. भगवान अपना अपना है।
bha:gya apna: apna: hɛ.
luck self self is
One is born with his/her own luck.

15. सत्य छिपता नहीं।
satya chipta: nahĩ:.
truth hidden neg
The truth (eventually) comes out. *Or*
The truth cannot be hidden.

16. समय बलवान है।
samay balva:n hɛ.
time strong is
Time is strong.

The copular verb always takes a complement. In sentence (13) the complement does not appear at the surface and is understood as विध्यमान *vidhyma:n*/ मौजूद *mɔju:d* 'exists/omnipresent' and/or हर स्थान *har stha:n*/ कण कण में *kaṇ kaṇ mẽ* 'everywhere'.

16a. ईश्वर विध्यमान/मौजूद /हर स्थान पर/ कण कण में है।
i:švar vidhyma:n/mauju:d /har stha:n par/kaṇ kaṇ mẽ hɛ.
God present/every where particles in is
God exists. *Or* God is present everywhere.

In Hindi the copula verb होना *hona:* 'to be' is used as a non-stative verb and is translated as to become/happen/take/occur. This meaning is expressed by using the verb होना *hona:* or हो जाना *ho ja:na:* 'to become'.

17. देर हुई /हो गई।
der hui:/ho gai:.
late be-pst-fs/be aux-fs
It became late.

18. बातचीत हुई।
ba:tci:t hui:.
conversation be-pst-fs
The conversation took place.

19. काम हुआ।
ka:m hua:.
work be-pst-ms
The work was done.

4.3.2. Verbal Sentences

Verbal phrases can be grouped into three categories based on the classification of their verbs as simple, conjunct, or compound. The first category has only one verbal root as in (1).

1. मैंने किताब पढ़ी।
mɛ̃ne kita:b paṛhi:.
I-erg book read
I read a book.

The second category is formed by combining a noun/adjective plus the verb करना *karna:* 'to do', or होना *hona:* 'to be'. (i.e. काम करना *ka:m karna:* 'to work', मेहनत करना *mehnat karna:* 'to work hard', साफ होना *sa:ph hona:* 'to be clear' ताकत होना *ta:kat hona:* 'to be strong/healthy'.)

2. मुझे काम करना है।
mujhe ka:m karna: hɛ.
I-dat work do-inf be
I have to work.

3. यह मामला साफ है।
yeh ma:mla: sa:f hɛ.
this matter clear is
This matter is clear. *or* It is clear.

4. उसने मेहनत की।
usne mehnat ki:.
he-erg hard work did
He worked hard.

5. उसमें ताकत है।
usmẽ ta:kat hɛ.
he-obl-loc strength be
(S)he is strong/healthy. *or* (S)he has strength.

The third category employs a sequence of verbs like पढ़ लेना *paṛh lena:* 'to read', and लिख देना *likh dena:* 'to write'.

6. उसने अखबार पढ़ लिया।
usne axba:r paṛh liya:.
he-erg newspaper read took-explicator-ms
He read the newspaper.

7. मैंने चिट्ठी लिख दी।
mɛ̃ne ciṭṭhi: likh di:.
I-erg letter write gave-explicator-fs
I wrote the letter.

The subject of a transitive verb in the past tense is in the oblique case, followed by the case sign or the postposition ने *ne.*

8. लड़के ने लेख लिखा।
laṛke ne lekh likha:.
boy-erg essay-ms wrote-ms
The boy wrote an essay.

9. लड़की ने पत्र लिखा।
laṛki: ne patr likha:.
girl-erg letter-ms wrote-ms
The girl wrote a letter.

10. लड़कों/लड़कियों ने अखबार पढ़ा।
laṛkõ/laṛkiyõ ne axba:r paṛha:.
boys-/girls-erg newspaper read
The boys/girls read the newspaper.

11. मैंने/हमने फिल्म देखी।
mɛ̃ne/hamne film dekhi:.
I-erg/we-erg film-fs saw-fs
I/we saw a film.

12. तूने/तुमने/आपने किताब पढ़ी।
tu:ne/tumne/a:pne kita:b paṛhi:.
you-erg book-fs read-fs
You read a book.

13. तुमने/आपने कुर्सी देखी।
tumne/a:pne kursi: dekhi:.
you-erg chair saw-fs
You saw a chair.

The plural forms of personal pronouns are used as honorific singular/plural subjects as well.

Psychological predicates such as गुस्सा आना *gussa: a:na:* 'to be angry or irritated', and लगना *lagna:* 'seem' always take a dative subject using a dative case marker and the postposition को *ko.*

14. लड़के को गुस्सा आया।
laṛke ko gussa: a:ya:.
boy-obl to anger came
The boy was angry.

15. उसे चोट लगी।
use coṭ lagi:.
he-dat injury struck
He got injured.

4.3.2.1. Direct Object

Verbs are conventionally divided into intransitive and transitive on the basis of whether they take a noun phrase as an object. Transitive verbs take noun phrases as their object and intransitive verbs do not. In certain cases, the objects are understood and they do not appear at the surface level. For example, see the use of the transitive verbs कहना *kahna:* 'to say' and पूछना *pu:chna:* 'to ask' in sentences (16) and (17) below.

16. मैंने कही।
mẽne kahi:.
I-erg said-fs
I said (it) to him/her.

17. उसने पूछा।
usne pu:cha:.
he-erg asked-fs
He asked (it to) him/her.

In (16), the verb कहना *kahna:* is inflected for an implied generic feminine object. Similarly, in (17), the verb पूछना *pu:chna:* is inflected for an implied generic masculine object. These sentences can be completed as follows.

16a. मैंने उससे अपनी बात कही।
mẽne usse apni: ba:t kahi:.
I-erg him/her selfs matter-fs told-fs
I told him/her my story.

17a. उसने हालचाल पूछा।
usne ha:lca:l pu:cha:.
he/she-erg welfare-ms asked-ms
He/she asked (him/her) welfare.

4.3.2.2. Indirect Object

Whenever direct and indirect objects occur in a sentence, the indirect object receives the dative case markings. The order of the direct and indirect object in a sentence mainly depends on the emphasis given to these constituents in a given sentence. When animate indirect objects precede direct objects, they get extra emphasis. Notice the following examples of sentences using indirect objects in the dative case.

18. मैंने अजीत को किताब दी।
mɛ̃ne aji:t ko kita:b di:.
I-erg Ajit-dat book-fs gave-fs
I gave Ajit a book.

18a. मैंने किताब अजीत को दी।
mɛ̃ne kita:b aji:t ko di:.

19. अजीत ने अपनी पत्नी के लिए शाल ख़रीदा।
aji:t ne apni: patni: ke liye ša:l xari:da:.
Ajit-erg selfs wife for shawl bought
Ajit bought his wife a shawl.

19a. अजीत ने शाल अपनी पत्नी के लिए ख़रीदा।
aji:t ne ša:l apni: patni: ke liye xari:da:.
Ajit-erg shawl selfs wife for bought
Ajit bought a shawl for his wife.

20. उमा ने मुझे खाना खिलाया।
uma: ne mujhe kha:na: khila:ya:.
Uma-erg I-obl food feed-fs
Uma offered the food to me.

20a. मुझे उमा ने खाना खिलाया।
mujhe uma ne kha:na: khila:ya:.
I-obl Uma-erg food feed-fs
Uma offered the food to me.

In (18), (19) and (20) the indirect objects receive more emphasis than in (18a), (19a) and (20a).

4.3.2.3. Other Types of Verb Argument

Other types of verb arguments appear in the form of various postpositional phrases. They include locatives, instruments, benefactives, and comitatives.

There are no restrictions regarding the number of arguments (subject, direct/indirect object, and optional arguments) put together in a sentence. There are, of course, certain semantic restrictions, including the selection of their cases (nominative, dative, and ergative subjects), imposed by the choice of verbs and tense.

In Hindi, the verb occurs in the final position. The unmarked word order is subject, indirect object, direct object, adverbial (time, locative), and verb. The direct object may occur before the indirect object depending on the emphasis given to it. Consider sentences (21)- (21c) below.

21. मोहन ने पीटर को अजीत के लिए कल घर पर किताब दी।
mohan ne pi:ṭar ko aji:t ke liye kal ghar par kita:b di:.
Mohan-erg Peter to Ajit for yesterday home at book gave
Mohan gave Peter a book for Ajit yesterday at home.

21a. मोहन ने अजीत के लिए पीटर को कल घर पर किताब दी।
mohan ne aji:t ke liye pi:ṭar ko kal ghar par kita:b di:.

21b. मोहन ने पीटर को अजीत के लिए घर पर कल किताब दी।
mohan ne pi:ṭar ko aji:t ke liye ghar par kal kita:b di:.

21c. मोहन ने कल पीटर को अजीत के लिए घर पर किताब दी।
mohan ne kal pi:ṭar ko aji:t ke liye ghar par kita:b di:.

In sentence (21), the direct object gets more emphasis than the indirect object. The order of emphasis is reversed in sentence (21a). Similarly, the adverbial phrase can also precede the direct or indirect object for emphasis.

4.3.3. Negation

4.3.3.1. Sentential Negation

Sentential negation is expressed by the negative particles नहीं *nahĩ:* not, मत *mat* don't, and न *na* no. The negative particle नहीं *nahĩ:* is added before the main verb, which may or may not be followed by an auxiliary verb.

1. वह आजकल दफ़्तर नहीं जाता है।
vah a:jkal daftar nahĩ: ja:ta: hɛ.
he nowadays office neg go-ptc is
He doesn't go to the office nowadays.

2. मैंने यह किताब नहीं पढ़ी (है)।
mẽne yeh kita:b nahĩ: paṛhi: (hɛ).
I-erg this book neg read (have)
I have not read this book.

The particle मत *mat* 'don't' is used with imperative constructions. It is added in the preverbal position.

3. अखबार मत पढ़ो।
axba:r mat paṛho.
newspaper neg read
Don't read the newspaper.

4. आज घर मत जाइए।
a:j ghar mat ja:iye.
today home neg go-pl
Please don't go home today.

The negative particle मत *mat* can be replaced by न *na* 'no', but it is not used frequently.

3a. अखबार न पढ़ो।
axba:r na paṛho.
Don't read the newspaper.

4a. आज घर न जाइए।
a:j ghar na ja:iye.
Please don't go home today.

4.3.3.2. Constituent Negation

A number of devices are employed to mark constituent negation. The main constituents are the stress and the use of a negative particle after the negated constituent. Sometimes stress is used to negate the constituent.

5. उसे कल पत्नी से लड़ना नहीं चाहिए था।
use kal patni: se laṛna: nahĩ: ca:hiye tha:.
he-dat yesterday wife with quarrel neg should was
He should not have quarreled with his wife yesterday.

6. उसे हर रोज़ शराब नहीं पीनी चाहिए।
use har roz šara:b nahĩ: pi:ni: ca:hiye.
he every day liquor neg drink should
He should not drink (liquor) daily.

In sentences (5) and (6), the negated constituents are stressed by stressing the adverbs.

The negative marker follows the negated constituent.

7. वह घर नहीं गया वह अस्पताल गया।
vah ghar nahĩ: gaya:, vah aspata:l gaya:.
he home neg went he hospital went
He did not go home; he went to the hospital.

7a. वह घर नहीं गया अस्पताल गया।
vah ghar nahĩ: gaya:, aspata:l gaya:.

The negative constituent is also expressed by the use of the negative markers सिवा *siva:* except and बिना *bina:* without added after the main verbs as given below.

8. वह खाना खाए बिना कालेज गया।
vah kha:na: kha:ye bina: ka:lej gaya:.
he food eat without college went
He went to college without eating.

9. उमा के सिवा सारे समय पर आए।
uma: ke siva: sa:re samay par a:ye.
Uma gen without all time on came
All came on time except Uma.

In sentences (7) and (8), the negative markers cannot be replaced by नहीं *nahĩ:.*

The indefinite markers कोई *koi:* 'someone' and कुछ *kuch* 'something' and the question words कहीं भी *kahĩ: bhi:* 'anywhere' and कभी भी *kabhi: bhi:* 'ever' are also used with negative constituents.

10. कोई लड़का स्कूल नहीं गया।
koi: laṛka: sku:l nahĩ: gaya:.
someone student school neg went
No child went to school.

11. इतने पैसे से कुछ नहीं होगा।
itne pɛse se kuch nahĩ: hoga:.
this-obl money with something neg be-fut
This money is not sufficient.

12. उसने कल से कोई काम नहीं किया।
usne kal se koi: ka:m nahĩ: kiya:.
he-erg yesterday from any work neg did
He has done no work since yesterday.

13. अमित कहीं नहीं गया।
amit kahĩ: nahĩ: gaya:.
Amit anywhere neg went
Amit went nowhere.

14. यह काम कभी भी व्यर्थ नहीं होगा।
yeh ka:m kabhi: bhi: vyarth nahĩ: hoga:.
this work ever waste neg be-fut
This work will never go waste.

Participles are also used along with negated constituents.

15. अमित दौड़ते - दौड़ते नहीं आया।
amit dɔṛte - dɔṛte nahĩ: a:ya:.
Amit run-ptc neg came
Amit did not come running.

The negative prefixes *be-* and *an-,* borrowed from Persian (morphological negation) negate the constituent to which they are prefixed.

16. वह बेरहम है।
vah beraham hɛ.
he without-mercy is
He is merciless.

17. वह बेदिल काम करता है।
vah bedil ka:m karta: hɛ.
he without-heart work do-ptc is
He works uninterestingly.

4.3.3.3. Double/Multiple Negation

Hindi allows only one negative particle per clause. Double or multiple negation markers are not used.

18. मैं हैदराबाद नहीं गया हूँ।
mɛ̃ hɛdara:ba:d nahĩ: gaya: hũ:.
I Hyderabad neg went be
I have not gone to Hyderabad.

It is, however, possible to use double negation markers for emphasis.

19. मैं मास्को नहीं न गया हूँ।
mɛ̃ ma:sko nahĩ: na gaya: hũ:.
I Moscow neg neg went be
Have I ever gone to Moscow? *Or*
I have never gone to Moscow.

4.3.3.4. Negation and Coordination

Negation occurs in coordinate structures as it does in simple sentences. The negative element is not moved to the co-ordinate position unless the identical element is deleted from the second negative conjunct. It is only in the न *na* ... न *na* 'neither … nor' situation that negative elements are used sentence initially.

20. न अमित नौकरी करता है और न कारोबार।
na amit nɔkri: karta: hɛ ɔr na karoba:r.
neg Amit service do-prt is and neg business
Amit has neither a job nor a business.

20a. अमित नौकरी नहीं करता है।
amit nɔkri: nahĩ: karta: hɛ.
Amit job neg do-pr is
Amit is not doing a job.

20b. अमित कारोबार नहीं करता है।
amit ka:roba:r nahĩ: karta: hɛ.
Amit business neg do-ptc is
Amit is not doing a business.

4.3.3.5. Negation and Subordination

With predicates expressing opinion (पता होना *pata: hona:* 'to know', expectation/ intention (चाहना *ca:hna:* 'to want'), or perception (लगना *lagna:* 'to seem' and विचार होना *vica:r hona:* 'to have an opinion/to think'), the matrix verb can be negated to express subordinate negation.

21. मुझे पता है कि वह नहीं आएगा।
mujhe pata: hɛ ki vah nahĩ: a:yega:.
I-obl know is that he neg come-fut
I know that he will not come.

22. मुझे लगता है कि आज बारिश नहीं होगी।
mujhe lagta: hɛ ki a:j ba:riš nahĩ: hogi:.
I-dat seem-ptc is that today rain neg be-fut
It seems to me that it won't rain today.

23. मैं चाहता हूँ कि वह कारोबार नहीं करे।
mɛ̃ ca:hta: hũ: ki vah karoba:r nahĩ: kare.
I want-ptc am that he business neg do-subjunctive
I don't want him to do business.

24. मेरा विचार है कि उसे वह नौकरी नहीं करनी चाहिए।
mera: vica:r hɛ ki use vah nɔkri: nahĩ: karni: ca:hiye.
my opinion is that he-obl this job neg do-inf should
In my opinion, he should not take this job.

The negative particle नहीं *nahĩ:* can occur before the modal verbs पता होना *pata: hona:*, लगना *lagna:* and चाहना *ca:hna:* but not before विचार होना *vica:r hona:*. Thus, sentences (21-23) can be rephrased as (21a-23a) but not as (24a).

21a. मुझे नहीं पता कि वह आएगा (कि नहीं)।
mujhe nahĩ: pata: ki vah a:yega: (ki nahĩ:).

22a. मुझे नहीं लगता है कि आज बारिश होगी।
mujhe nahĩ: lagta: hɛ ki a:j ba:riš hogi:.

23a. मैं नहीं चाहता कि वह कारोबार करे।
mɛ̃ nahĩ: cahta: ki vah ka:roba:r kare.

24a. *मुझे नहीं विचार है कि
**mujhe nahĩ: vica:r hɛ ki.*

4.3.4. Interrogative

There are two types of interrogative sentences: yes-no questions and information questions using question-words. These questions are marked by certain intonation characteristics.

4.3.4.1. Yes-No Questions

On the basis of the expected answer, yes-no questions can be put into two categories: (a) neutral yes-no questions (where a definite answer is not expected) and (b) leading yes-no questions (where either an affirmative or a negative answer is expected).

4.3.4.1.1. Neutral Yes-No Questions

Neutral yes-no questions are formed by the optional placement of the question word क्या *kya:* what in the sentence initial position of a declarative sentence. Note that the use of the question marker क्या *kya:* in neutral questions is different from its use in the question-word questions. In question-word questions, क्या *kya:* usually occurs in the second position, and in yes-no questions it occurs only in the initial position.

1. तुम कल दिल्ली जाओगे।
tum kal dilli: ja:oge.
you tomorrow Delhi go-fut tomorrow
You will go to Delhi tomorrow.

1a. (क्या) तुम कल दिल्ली जाओगे?
(kya:) tum kal dilli: ja:oge?
(Q-word) you tomorrow Delhi go
Will you go to Delhi tomorrow?

1b. तुम क्या कल दिल्ली जाओगे?
tum kya: kal dilli: ja:oge?

A declarative sentence can be converted to a neutral yes-no question without adding any question marker by raising the intonation at the end of the verb.

A negative declarative sentence is changed to a yes-no question by adding the negative morpheme before the verb.

2. तुम कल दिल्ली जाओगे।
tum kal dilli: nahĩ: ja:oge.
you tomorrow Delhi neg go-fut
You won't go to Delhi tomorrow.

2a. (क्या) तुम कल दिल्ली नहीं जाओगे?
(kya:) tum kal dilli: nahĩ: ja:oge?
(Q) you tomorrow Delhi neg go-fut
Won't you go to Delhi tomorrow?

2b. तुम क्या कल दिल्ली नहीं जाओगे?
tum kya: kal dilli nahĩ: ja:oge?
Aren't you going to Delhi tomorrow?

A negativized yes-no question invokes multiple answers. Consider the answers to questions (3) and (4):

3. तुम यह फ़िल्म नहीं देखोगे?
tum yah film nahĩ: dekhoge?
you this picture neg watch-fut
Won't you watch this film?

3a. हाँ, मैं देखूँगा (यह फ़िल्म).
hã:, mɛ̃ dekhũ:ga: (yeh film).
yes I watch-1s-fut (this film).
Yes, I'll see (this film).

3b. नहीं, मैं देखूँगा नहीं (यह फ़िल्म).
nahĩ:, mɛ̃ dekhũ:ga: nahĩ: (yeh film).
neg I see-fut neg (this film)
No, I won't watch (this film).

3c. हाँ, मैं देखूँगा नहीं।
hã:, mɛ̃ dekhũ:ga: nahĩ:.
yes, I watch-1s-fut neg
Yes, I won't watch.

3d. नहीं, मैं देखूँगा।
nahĩ:, mɛ̃ dekhũ:ga:.
neg I watch-fut
No, I'll watch.

4. आज सर्दी है ना?
a:j sardi: hɛ na:?
today cold is neg-Q
Isn't it cold today?

4a. हाँ, आज सर्दी है।
hã:, a:j sardi: hɛ.
yes today cold is
Yes, it is cold today.

4b. नहीं, आज सर्दी नहीं है।
nahĩ:, a:j sardi: nahĩ: hɛ.
Neg today cold neg is
No, it isn't cold today.

4c. हाँ, आज सर्दी नहीं है।
hã:, a:j sardi: nahĩ: hɛ.
yes today cold neg is
Yes, it isn't cold today.

4d. नहीं, आज सर्दी नहीं है।
nahĩ:, a:j sardi: nahĩ: hɛ.
neg today cold neg is
No, it isn't cold today.

In these examples, the (a-b) answers indicate positive-negative and the (c-d) indicate agreement-disagreement answering systems. The agreement-disagreement answering systems are less frequently used than the positive-negative ones.

4.3.4.1.2. Leading Questions

Leading questions are formed by adding the repetitive form of the verb negative or positive question markers नहीं *nahĩ:* and हाँ *hã:* respectively at the end of a declarative sentence to serve as tag questions. The tag question comprising of the verb + ना *na:* is preceded by a positive proposition and the tag question of the verb + हाँ *hã:* is preceded by the negative proposition.

The expectation of a positive answer is expressed by an affirmative proposition preceding the verb + ना *na:* as a tag question.

5. आज गर्मी है, है ना?
   a:j garmi: hɛ, hɛ na:?
   today hot is is neg-q
   It is hot today, isn't it?

6. वह किताब पढ़ेगा, पढ़ेगा ना?
   vah kita:b paṛhega:, paṛhega: na:?
   he book read-3s-fut read-3s-fut neg-q
   He will read a letter, won't he?

The expectation of a negative answer is expressed by a negative proposition preceding the verb + ना *na:* or the repetition of the verb form as a tag question.

7. आज गर्मी नहीं है, ना?
   a:j garmi: nahĩ: hɛ, na:?
   today hot neg is neg-q
   It isn't hot today, is it?

8. वह पत्र नहीं पढ़ेगा, पढ़ेगा?
   vah patr nahĩ: paṛhega:, paṛhega:?
   he letter neg read-3s-fut read-3s-fut-q
   He won't read a letter, will he?

Note that the occurrence of certain negative polarity markers such as पहले *pahle,* थोड़े *thoṛe* 'ever' in the interrogative sentence also invoke a negative answer.

9. वह पहले/थोड़े काम करता है?
vah pahle/thoṛe ka:m karta: hɛ?
he ever work do-ptc.ms is
Does he ever work?

Alternative questions are formed by adding the expression कि नहीं *ki nahĩ:* 'or not' at the end of an interrogative yes-no question.

10. तुम पत्र लिखोगे कि नहीं?
tum patr likhoge ki nahĩ:?
you letter write-3s or not
Will you write a letter or not?

An alternative form of this question will be:

10a. तुम पत्र लिखोगे कि नहीं लिखोगे?
tum patr likhoge ki nahĩ: likhoge?
you letter write-fut or neg write-fut
Will you write the letter or not?

4.3.4.2. Question-Word Questions

Interrogative sentences with *wh-* question words are referred to as क- *k*-questions in Hindi because question words begin with the क- *k*-sound. Question words always occur in the second position of interrogative sentences. The main question words are क्या *kya:* what, कौन *kɔn* 'who', कहाँ *kahã:* 'where', कैसा *kɛsa:* how, क्यों *kyõ* 'why', कितना *kitna:* 'how much', कब *kab* 'when' and किधर *kidhar* 'in what direction'. The question word is always stressed.

11. यह क्या है?
yeh kya: hɛ?
this what is
What is this?

12. मोहन कहाँ है?
mohan kahã: hɛ?
Mohan where is
Where is Mohan?

13. तुम क्यों आए?
tum kyõ a:ye?
you why come-2pl
Why did you come?

14. तुम कब आओगे?
tum kab a:oge?
you when come-2s-fut
When will you come?

15. वह किधर जाएगा?
vah kidhar ja:yega:?
he where go-3s-fut
Where will he go?

The question words कैसा *kaisa:* and कितना *kitna:* agree with the following or preceding noun in number and gender. They have the following three forms.

Masculine		Feminine	
Sg	Pl	Sg / Pl	
कैसा kɛsa:	कैसे kɛse	कैसी kɛsi:	how
कितना kitna:	कितने kitne	कितनी kitni:	how much

16. यह लड़का कैसा है?
yeh laṛka: kɛsa: hɛ?
this boy how is
How is this boy?

17. ये लड़के कैसे हैं?
ye laṛke kɛse hɛ̃?
these boys how are
How are these boys?

18. यह घड़ी कैसी है?
yeh ghaṛi: kɛsi: hɛ?
this watch-f how is
How is this watch?

19. ये घड़ियाँ कैसी हैं?
ye ghaṛiyā̃: kɛsi: hɛ̃?
these watches how are
How are these watches?

20. यह पुल कितना लंबा है?
yeh pul kitna: lamba: hɛ?
this bridge how much long is
How long is this bridge?

21. ये कितने बच्चे हैं?
ye kitne bacce hɛ̃?
these how many children are
How many children are there?

22. वह कितनी बड़ी किताब है?
vah kitni: baṛi: kita:b hɛ?
that how big-fs book-f is
How big is that book?

23. वे कुर्सियाँ कितनी छोटी हैं?
ve kursiyā̃: kitni: choṭi: hɛ̃?
those chairs how small are
How small are those chairs?

The question words क्या *kya:* what and कौन *kɔn* who have the oblique forms किस *kis* (Sg) and किन *kin* (Pl) which are followed by case suffixes and postpositions. The oblique forms of postpositions are inflected for number as follows.

Masculine/Feminine		
Sg	Pl	
किसे kise	किन्हें kinhẽ	to what/whom
किस को kis ko	किन को kin ko	to whom
किस से kis se	किन से kin se	by what/whom
किस ने kis ne	किनहोंने kinhõne	who
किस के साथ kis ke sa:th	किन के साथ kin ke sa:th	with whom
किस पर kis par	किन पर kin par	on
किस का kis ka:	किन का kin ka:	whose

24. यह किताब किसे/किस को देनी है?
yeh kita:b kise/kis ko deni: hɛ?
this book who give-inf-f aux
To whom is this book to be given? *Or*
Who is this book to be given to?

25. किस लड़के/लड़की को जाना है?
kis laṛke/laṛki: ko jana: hɛ?
who-obl boy-dat/girl-dat go-Inf aux
Which boy/girl has to go?

26. किन लड़कों/लड़कियों को आना है?
kin laṛkõ/laṛkiyõ ko a:na: hɛ?
who.pl-dat boys-dat/girls-dat come-inf is
Which boys/girls have to come?

27. वह किस शहर/किन शहरों से आएगा?
vah kis šahar/kin šahrõ se a:yega:?
he which-abl city-abl/cities-abl from come-3s-fut
Which city/cities will he come from?

28. यह किसने /किन्होंने सेब खाया?
yeh kisne/kinhõne seb kha:ya:?
this who-erg-ms/-fs/-p apple ate-ms
Who ate this apple?

29. यह किसका बना है?
yeh kiska: bana: hɛ?
this what-of made is
What is it made of?

30. ये किसके बने हैं?
ye kiske bane hɛ̃?
these which-gen-ms made-mp are
What are these made of?

31. यह किसकी बनी हैं?
ye kiski: bani: hɛ̃?
these which-gen-fp are
Which are these made of?

32. यह किसका/किनका मकान है?
yeh kiska:/kinka: maka:n hɛ?
this who-s-gen-ms/-p-gen-ms house is
Whose house is this?

33. यह किस की/किन की किताब है?
yeh kiski:/kinki: kita:b hɛ?
this who-s-gen-fs/-p-gen-fs book is
Whose book is this?

34. ये किसके/किनके पर्दे हैं?
ye kiske/kinke parde hɛ̃?
these who-s-gen-mp/-p-gen-mp curtains are
Whose curtains are these?

35. ये किसकी/किनकी कमीज़ें हैं?
ye kiski:/kinki: kami:zẽ hɛ̃?
these who-gen-fp shirts are
Whose shirts are these?

When question words are combined with postpositions they create adverbials like कहाँ से *kahã: se* 'in which direction', कैसे *kɛse/* किस तरह *kis tarah* 'in what manner', and कहाँ *kahã:/* कहाँ पर *kahã: par* 'wherein'.

36. वह कहाँ जाएगा?
vah kahã: ja:yega:.
vah where go-fut
Where will he go?

37. वह किस तरह आएगा?
vah kis tarah a:yega:.
he what manner come-fut
How will he come?

38. आप कहाँ से जाएँगे?
a:p kahã: se ja:ẽge?
you-p which direction go-2p-fut
Where will you go from? *Or*
In which direction will you go?

39. आप कैसे आएँगे?
a:p kεse a:ẽge?
you how (manner) come-2p-fut
How will you come?

40. वह कहाँ (पर) बैठा होगा?
vah kahã: (par) bεṭha: hoga:?
He where (at) sit-PP be-fut
Where will he be sitting?

The question words are reduplicated when the expected answer provide a list (of more that one thing, person, event, etc.). Reduplication is obligatory with plural nouns.

41. आपने क्या क्या देखा?
a:pne kya: kya: dekha:?
you-p-erg what what saw-2p-Pa
What items did you see?

42. वह कहाँ कहाँ गया?
vah kahã: kahã: gaya:?
he where where went
Which places did he visit?

The masculine plural forms of pronouns are used for honorific singular subjects as well.

Different constituents of the main clause can be questioned as may be seen in sentence (43) below.

43. अमर ने कल शीला को अपने घर एक कमीज़ दिखाई।
amar ne kal ši:la: ko apne ghar ek kami:z dikha:i:.
Amar-erg yesterday Shiela to selfs house a shirt showed-fs
Amar showed a shirt to Shiela at his home yesterday.

Subject

43a. किसने कल शीला को अपने घर एक कमीज़ दिखाई?
kisne kal ši:la: ko apne ghar ek kami:z dikha:i:?
Who showed a shirt to Shiela at his home yesterday?

Direct object

43b. अमर ने कल शीला को अपने घर क्या दिखाया?
amar ne kal ši:la: ko apne ghar kya: dikha:ya:?
What did Amar show Shiela at his home yesterday?

Indirect object

43c. अमर ने किसको कल अपने घर एक कमीज़ दिखाई?
amar ne kisko kal apne ghar ek kami:z dikha:i?
To whom did Amar show a shirt at his home yesterday?

Time adverbial

43d. अमर ने कब शीला को अपने घर एक कमीज़ दिखाई?
amar ne kab ši:la: ko apne ghar ek kami:z dikha:i:?
When did Amar show Shiela a shirt at his home?

Location adverbial

43e. अमर ने कहाँ कल शीला को एक कमीज़ दिखाई?
amar ne kahã: kal ši:la: ko ek kami:z dikha:i:?
Where did Amar show a new shirt to Shiela?

It is not possible to use simple questions word for questioning a constituent of a verb. Usually the verb phrase क्या किया *kya: kiya:* 'do what' is used for transitive verbs and क्या हुआ *kya: hua:* 'what happened' is used for intransitive verbs.

43f. अमर ने कल अपने घर क्या किया?
amar ne kal apne ghar kya: kiya:?
Amar-erg yesterday self-obl-home what did
What did Amar do at his home yesterday?

43g. अमर के घर कल क्या हुआ'?
amar ke ghar kal kya: hua:?
Amar-gen home yesterday what happened
What happened at Amars house yesterday?

In non-equational copular interrogative sentences, all the elements except the verb may be questioned. In examples (44-47) the subject, the accompanier, locative, and time adverbial have been questioned. The copular verb cannot be deleted as shown in in (44a-47a).

44. कौन है?
kɔn hɛ?
who is-3s
Who is (there)?

44a. *कौन?
*kɔn?

45. तुम किसके साथ हो?
tum kiske sa:th ho?
you who-gen with are-2s
Who are you with?

45a. तुम किसके साथ?
**tum kiske sa:th?*

46. किताब कहाँ है?
kita:b kahã: hɛ?
book-fs where-abl is
Where is the book?

46a. *किताब कहाँ?
**kita:b kahã:?*

47. छुट्टी कब है?
chuṭṭi: kab hɛ?
holiday when is
When is the holiday?

47a. *छुट्टी कब?
*chuṭṭi: kab?

In equational copular interrogative sentences, either the subject noun phrase or the predicate nominal can be questioned. The demonstrative pronoun used as a subject cannot be questioned. Consider the following examples.

48. यह पर्दा है।
yeh parda: hɛ.
it curtain is
It is a curtain.

48a. यह क्या है?
yeh kya: hɛ?
it what is-3s
What is it?

48b. *क्या पर्दा है?
**kya: parda: hɛ?*

49. यह किताब है।
yeh kita:b hɛ.
this book is
This is a book.

49a. यह क्या है?
yeh kya: hɛ?
this what is-f
What is this?

49b. *क्या किताब है?
*kya: kita:b hɛ?

Different constituents of subordinate clauses can be questioned. There are two types of subordinate clauses: finite and non-finite. As is the case with matrix sentences, all elements of these clauses can be questioned. Constituents, which undergo deletion in the process of non-finitization, however, cannot be questioned. This supports the argument that the question formation rule applies after the rules for non-finitization of the subordinate clauses take place.

50. (क्या) आपको पता है मोहन ने अमर को कल
kya: a:pko pata: hɛ mohan ne amar ko kal
Q you-dat knowledge is Mohan-erg Amar-dat yesterday
किताब दी?
kita:b di:?
book gave-f
Do you know that Mohan gave a book to Amar yesterday?

Subject

50a. (क्या) आपको पता है अमर को किसने कल किताब दी?
(kya:) a:pko pata: hɛ amar ko kisne kal kita:b di:?
You know who gave a book to Amar yesterday?

Direct object

50b. (क्या) आपको पता है कि मोहन ने कल अमर को क्या दिया?
(kya:) a:pko pata: hɛ ki mohan ne kal amar ko kya: diya:?
Do you know what Mohan gave to Amar yesterday?

Indirect object

50c. (क्या) आपको पता है कि मोहन ने किसको कल किताब दी?
(kya:)a:pko pata: hɛ mohan ne kisko kal kita:b di:?
You know to whom Mohan gave a book yesterday?

Time adverbial

50d. (क्या) आपको पता है कि मोहन ने कब अमर को किताब दी?
(kya:) a:pko pata: hɛ ki mohan ne kab amar ko kita:b di?
You know when Mohan gave the book to Amar?

The questioning of the constituent clauses may also involve questioning of the matrix clause.

Note that no constituent of a finite relative clause can be questioned.

51. रमेश से जो दोस्त आज मिला वह चालाक है।
rameš se jo dost a:j mila: vah ca:la:k hɛ.
Ramesh-abl rel friend today met he clever is
The friend who met Ramesh is clever.

51a. *रमेश से कौन दोस्त आज मिला चालाक है?
**rameš ka: kɔn dost a:j mila: ca:la:k hɛ?*

Constituents of non-finite subordinate clauses which comprise infinitival and participial phrases can be questioned.

52. वह खाना खाते हुए अख़बार पढ़ रहा था।
vah kha:na: kha:te hue akhba:r paṛh raha: tha:.
he food eating-part newspaper read-prog was
He was reading a newspaper while eating his meal.

Direct object

52a. वह क्या खाते हुए अख़बार पढ़ रहा था?
vah kya: kha:te hue akhba:r paṛh raha: tha:?
What was he eating while reading a newspaper?

53. वह चाय पीते हुए बच्चे को पढ़ा रहा था।
vah ca:y pi:te hue bacce ko paṛha: raha: tha:.
he tea drinking-part child-dat teach-prog was
He was teaching the child while drinking his tea?

Indirect object

53a. वह किस को चाय पीते हुए पढ़ा रहा था?
vah kis ko ca:y pi:te hue paṛha: raha: tha:?
Who was he teaching while drinking his tea?

54. वह राज के साथ बातें करते हुए जा रहा था।
vah ra:j ke sa:th ba:tẽ karte hue ja: raha: tha:.
he Raj with talk do-ptc go-prog was
He was talking to Raj while going.

Object of a postposition

54a. वह किसके साथ बातें करते हुए जा रहा था?
vah kiske sa:th ba:tẽ karte hue ja: raha: tha:?
Who was he talking to while going?

The subject of the subordinate clauses undergoes deletion in sentences (52a-54a) because it is co-referential to the subject of the matrix sentence. All the constituents of gerundive and infinitival clause can be questioned.

55. वह क्या करने दिल्ली गया?
vah kya: karne dilli: gaya:?
he what do-inf-obl Delhi went
Why did he go to Delhi?

56. मास्टर ने लड़के को पत्र लिखने के लिए कहा।
ma:sṭar ne laṛke ko patr likhne ke liye kaha:.
teacher-erg student-dat letter write-inf-obl for told
The teacher asked the student to write a letter?

56a. मास्टर ने लड़के को क्या करने के लिए कहा?
ma:sṭar ne laṛke ko kya: karne ke liye kaha:?
What did the teacher ask his student to do?

56b. मास्टर ने लड़के को क्या लिखने के लिए कहा?
ma:sṭar ne laṛke ko kya: likhne ke liye kaha:?
What did the father ask his son to write?

Different constituents of a noun phrase can be questioned. A noun phrase may be made up of any of the following: (a) demonstrative pronoun, (b) quantifier, (c) intensifier, (d) descriptive adjective, (e) classifier/specifier, (f) possessive adjective, (g) possessor, (h) particle and a noun. Nouns may also modify relative clauses and objects of comparison.

Demonstrative pronoun

57a. यह छोटी लड़की घर जाएगी।
yeh choṭi: laṛki: ghar ja:yegi:.
this little girl home go-3s-fut
This little girl will go home.

57b. कौन सी छोटी लड़की घर जाएगी?
kɔn si: choṭi: laṛki: ghar ja:yegi:?
Which little girl will go home?

Quantifier (cardinal number)

58a. मोहन के तीन दोस्त कल आएँगे।
mohan ke ti:n dost kal a:yẽge.
Mohan-gen three friends tomorrow come-3p-fut
Mohans three friends will come tomorrow.

58b. मोहन के तीन दोस्त कल आएँगे?
mohan ke kitne dost kal a:yẽge?
How many friends of Mohan will come tomorrow?

Quantifier (ordinal number)

59a. उसका तीसरा बेटा दिल्ली में है।
uska: ti:sra: beṭa: dilli: mẽ hɛ.
he-gen third son Delhi in is
His third son is in Delhi.

59b. उसका कौन सा बेटा दिल्ली में है?
uska: kɔn sa: beṭa: dilli: mẽ hɛ?
Which son of his is in Delhi?

Quantifier (proportional number)

60a. वह हमेशा चौगुना खर्च करता है।
vah hameša: cɔguna: kharc karta: hɛ.
he always four times expenditure do-pr is
He always incurs four times the expenses of everyone else.

60b. वह कितने गुना खर्च करता है?
vah kitne guna: kharc karta: hɛ?
How many times the expenditure of everyone else does he incur?

Descriptive adjective

61a. पतला लड़का घोड़े पर नहीं चढ़ सकता।
patla: laṛka: ghoṛe par nahĩ: caṛh sakta:.
slim boy horse on neg ride can-ptc
The slim boy cannot ride the horse.

61b. कौन सी लड़की कार नहीं चला सकती?
kɔn si: laṛki: ka:r nahĩ: cala: sakti:?
Which girl cannot drive the car?

Intensifier

62a. रमा बहुत ही लंबी लड़की है।
rama: bahut hi: lambi: laṛki: hɛ.
Rama very (intensifier) tall-fs girl is
Rama is a very tall girl.

62b. रमा कितनी लंबी लड़की है?
rama: kitni: lambi: laṛki: hɛ?
How tall a girl is Rama?

Possessive adjective

63a. मोहन का कालेज दिल्ली में है।
mohan ka: ka:lej dilli: mẽ hɛ.
Mohan-gen college is Delhi-loc is in
Mohan’s college is in Delhi.

63b. किसका कालेज दिल्ली में है?
kiska: ka:lej dilli: mẽ hɛ?
Whose college is in Delhi?

Specifier/classifier
64a. मोहन का बड़ा वाला बेटा बीमार है।
mohan ka: baṛa: va:la: beṭa: bi:ma:r hɛ.
Mohan-gen elder (specifier) son sick is
Mohan's elder son is sick.

64b. मोहन का कौन सा बेटा बीमार है?
mohan ka: kɔn sa: beṭa: bi:ma:r hɛ?
Which of Mohans sons is sick?

Particles ही *hi:* and भी *bhi:* cannot be questioned.

65a. तुम ही जाओ।
tum hi: ja:o.
you-par go-3s-fut
Only you go.

65b. *कौन ही जाओ।
**kɔn hi: ja:o.*

66. वह भी आपके साथ आएगा।
vah bhi: a:pke sa:th a:ega:.
he-part you-gen with come-3s-fut
Hell also come with you.

66a. *कौन भी आपके साथ आएगा।
**kɔn bhi: a:pke sa:th a:ega:.*

A comparative phrase can also modify a noun phrase.

Object of comparison
67a. मैंने रजनी से लंबी लड़की देखी।
mɛ̃ne rajini se lambi: laṛki: dekhi:.
I-erg Rajni-abl than tall-fs girl saw-fs
I saw a girl taller than Rajni.

67b. मैंने किससे लंबी लड़की देखी।
mε̃ne kis-se lambi: laṛki: dekhi:?
I-erg who-abl tall girl saw-fut
I saw a girl taller than whom?

There are two types of relative clauses: non-finite and finite. No constituent of a finite relative clause can be questioned. Any element of a non-finite relative clause, except the subject, can be questioned.

68. यह बच्चों को पैसे देने वाला है।
yeh baccõ ko pεse dene va:la: hε.
he children-dat money give-inf aux
He is going to give money to the children.

Direct object of a non-finite relative clause
68a. यह बच्चों को क्या देने वाला है?
yeh baccõ ko kya: dene va:la: hε?
What is he going to give to the children?

Indirect object of a non-finite relative clause
68b. यह किनको पैसे देने वाला है?
yeh kinko pεse dene va:la: hε?
Who he is going to give money to?

Elements of a postpositional phrase can also be questioned. A postpositional phrase consists of a head noun followed by a postposition. The postposition assigns the case to the head noun. The noun phrase elements of a postpositional phrase can be questioned. The noun phrase, which is followed by a postposition, is in the oblique case.

69. इस मेज़ पर काकज़ है।
is mez par ka:kaz hε.
this-obl table on paper is
There is paper on this table.

69a. किस मेज़ पर काकज़ है?
kis mez par ka:kaz hε?
Which table is the paper on?

69b. काकज़ किस पर है?
ka:kaz kis par hɛ?
What is the paper (placed) on?

70. मोहन के घर के पास दुकान है।
mohan ke ghar ke pa:s duka:n hɛ.
Mohan-poss house near shop is
There is a shop near Mohans house.

70a. किसके घर के पास दुकान है?
kiske ghar ke pa:s duka:n hɛ?
Near whose house is there a shop?

70b. किसके पास दुकान है?
kiske pa:s duka:n hɛ?
Near which place is a shop?

It is only the noun phrase elements of a postpositional phrase which can be questioned, not the postpositions.

Elements of a coordinate structure can be questioned. The coordinate structures are formed either by juxtaposition or by the use of a conjunction.

Juxtaposition

71. शीला चिट्ठी लिखने के लिए काकज़ कलम लाई।
ši:la: ciṭṭhi: likhne ke liye ka:kaz kalam la:i:.
Shiela letter write-inf for paper pen brought
Shiela brought paper and pen for writing a letter.

71a. शीला काकज़ कलम क्या लिखने के लिए लाई?
ši:la: ka:kaz kalam kya: likhne ke liye la:i:?

71b. शीला चिट्ठी लिखने के लिए क्या लाई?
ši:la: ciṭṭhi: likhne ke liye kya: la:i:?

Conjunction

72. मोहन और अजीत दिल्ली गए।
mohan ɔr aji:t dilli: gae.
Mohan and Ajit Delhi went
Mohan and Ajit went to Delhi.

72a. मोहन और कौन गए?
mohan ɔr kɔn gae?
Mohan and who went? (Mohan went with whom?)

72b. *कौन और अजीत दिल्ली गए?
**kɔn ɔr aji:t dilli: gae?*
Who and Ajit went to Delhi?

72c. कौन कौन दिल्ली गए?
kɔn kɔn dilli: gae?
Who (are the ones who) went to Delhi?

73. शीला और मोहन ने अपना अपना काम समाप्त किया।
ši:la: ɔr mohan ne apna: ka:m sama:pt kiya:.
Shiela and Mohan-erg self's work finish did
Shiela and Mohan finished their work.

73a. शीला और किसने अपना काम समाप्त किया?
ši:la: ɔr kisne apna: apna: ka:m sama:pt kiya:?
Shiela and who finished their work?

73b. *किसने और शीला ने अपना काम समाप्त किया?
**kisne ɔr ši:la: ne apna: ka:m sama:pt kiya:?*
Who and Shiela finished their work?

73c. किस किस ने काम समाप्त किया?
kis kis ne ka:m sama:pt kiya:?
Who (are the ones who) finished their work?

74. उसने चिट्ठी लिखी और किताब पढ़ी।
usne ciṭṭhi: likhi: ɔr kita:b paṛhi:.
he-erg letter wrote-fs and book read-fs
He wrote a letter and read a book.

74a. *उसने चिट्ठी लिखी और क्या पढ़ी?
**usne ciṭṭhi: likhi: ɔr kya: paṛhi:?*

74b. *उसने क्या लिखी और किताब पढ़ी?
**usne kya: likhi: ɔr kita:b paṛhi:?*

74c. उसने चिट्ठी लिखी और क्या किया?
usne ciṭṭhi: likhi: ɔr kya: kiya:?
He wrote a letter and what else did he do?

74d. उसने क्या क्या किया?
usne kya: kya: kiya:?
What are the things he did?

75. उसने रोटी खाई और दूध पिया।
usne roṭi: kha:i: ɔr du:dh piya:.
He-erg bread ate-fs and milk drank-ms
He ate bread and drank milk.

75a. उसने रोटी खाई और क्या पिया?
usne roṭi: kha:i: ɔr kya: piya:?
He ate bread and what did he drink?

75b. *उसने क्या खाया और दूध पिया?
usne kya: kha:ya: ɔr du:dh piya:?

No part of the juxtaposition phrase can be questioned. The questioning of the first element of a coordinate noun phrase results in the formation of ill-formed sentences as in (73b) and (75b). Similarly, in the coordinate verb phrases, the object of the first verb phrase cannot be questioned.

There is no constraint on the number of constituents of a sentence that can be questioned at one time. The multiple question-word questions are normally used at the end of the narration of a story, especially a folk tale, for checking the comprehension of the listeners.

76. मोहन कल अमर के साथ बाग देखने गया।
mohan kal amar ke sa:th ba:g dekhne gaya:.
Mohan yesterday Amar with garden see-inf-obl went
Mohan went to see the garden with Amar yesterday.

76a. मोहन कल क्या देखने गया अमर के साथ?
mohan kal kya: dekhne gaya: amar ke sa:th?
What did Mohan go to see with Amar yesterday?

76b. मोहन कब क्या देखने गया अमर के साथ?
mohan kab kya: dekhne gaya: amar ke sa:th?
What did Mohan go to see with Amar and when?

76c. मोहन किसके साथ क्या देखने कल गया?
mohan kiske sa:th kya: dekhne kal gaya:?
Who did Mohan go with to see what yesterday?

76d. मोहन कब किसके साथ क्या देखने गया?
mohan kab kiske sa:th kya: dekhne gaya:?
When did Mohan go with whom (and) for seeing what?

Question-words are reduplicated when the expected answer is a listing of persons, items, or events. Multi-question-word questions are used when information about different things is wanted all at the same time in one answer.

77. कौन कौन कब कब किन किन के पास जाता है?
kɔn kɔn kab kab kin kin ke pa:s ja:ta: hɛ?
who when whom near go-ptc is
Who (which individual) goes with whom (which individual) where/what places (and) when?

This sentence can be used by an employer seeking information regarding his/her employees. Question-words which are not used in plural cannot be reduplicated. For example, the question word *kyõ* why cannot be used in its reduplicated form.

78. *कौन कौन कब कब क्यों क्यों जाता है?
**kɔn kɔn kab kab kyõ kyõ ja:ta: hɛ?*

The constituents of both the main and subordinate clauses can be questioned at the same time and the question words can be reduplicated.

79. किसकी राय में कौन कौन कहाँ कहाँ किस किस के पास जाता है?
kiski: ra:y mẽ kɔn kɔn kahã: kahã: kis kis ke pa:s ja:ta: hɛ.
who-obl opinion in who where who-obl near go-ptc is
Who thinks that who (which individual) goes (near) to whom (which individual) and where (what place)?

There is a flexibility as far as the placement of the questioned constituent is concerned. The movement of the questioned elements is related to their focus. Consider the following examples:

80. रमेश कब आएगा?
rameš kab a:yega:?
Ramesh when come-3s-fut
When will Ramesh come?

80a. कब आएगा रमेश?
kab a:yega: rameš?

80b. रमेश आएगा कब?
rameš a:yega: kab?

80c. आएगा कब रमेश?
a:yega: kab rameš?

81. सरला कहाँ जाएगी?
sarla: kahã: ja:yegi?
Sarla where go-fs
Where will Sarla go?

81a. सरला जाएगी कहाँ?
sarla: ja:yegi: kahã:?

81b. कहाँ जाएगी सरला?
kahã: ja:yegi: sarla:?

81c. जाएगी कहाँ सरला?
ja:yegi: kahã: sarla:?

The question-word in the sentence initial position carries a stronger focus than when it is in the second position. In other words, it is marked by more stress in the sentence initial position than in other positions. Interrogative sentences (80) and (81) are in natural word order. In (80a) and (81a), the subject is stressed, in (80b) and (81b) the question words are stressed, and in (80c) and (81c) the verb is stressed. The interrogative sentences (80c) and (81c) do not necessarily invoke an answer.

Usually the question-word क्यों *kyõ* why occurs in the pre-verbal position. It follows the verb within the sentence. The movement of this question- word influences the meaning of the sentence. The placement of this question word in the post-verbal position is possible, but it does not necessarily invoke an answer.

82. आपने उसे किताब क्यों दी?
a:pne use kita:b kyõ di:?
you-erg book he-dat why gave?
Why did you give him a book?

82a. किताब क्यों दी?
kita:b kyõ di:?

82b. क्यों किताब दी?
kyõ di: kita:b?

82c. दी किताब क्यों?
di: kyõ kita:b?

In (82a) there is stress on the direct object; in (82b) the stress is on the question-word; and in (82c) the stress is on the verb and the indirect object.

4.3.4.3. Echo-Questions

There are two types of echo-questions: (a) yes-no echo-questions, and (b) question-word echo-questions.

4.3.4.3.1. Yes-No Echo-Questions

A yes-no echo-question usually repeats one or more elements of the statement uttered by the previous speaker. The element/elements chosen for clarification is/are retained with a rising intonation and other elements are deleted. For example, the response to a statement made in (83) can be in different forms (83a-83e) in yes-no echo-questions.

83. मोहन कल बाज़ार जाएगा।
mohan kal ba:za:r ja:yega:
Mohan tomorrow market go-3s-fut
Mohan will go to market tomorrow.

83a. मोहन कल बाज़ार जाएगा?
mohan kal ba:za:r ja:yega:?
Will Mohan go to market tomorrow?

83b. बाज़ार जाएगा?
ba:za:r ja:yega:?
Will (Mohan) go to market?

83c. मोहन कल जाएगा?
mohan kal ja:yega:?
Will Mohan go tomorrow?

83d. मोहन जाएगा?
mohan ja:yega:?
Will Mohan go (to the market tomorrow)?

83e. मोहन?
mohan?
(Will) Mohan (go to market tomorrow)?

The yes-no echo-questions may be preceded by the term *accha:* 'it is so'.

84. वह कल दिल्ली से आएगा?
vah kal dilli: se a:yega:.
he tomorrow Delhi-abl from come-fut
He will come from Delhi tomorrow.

84a. अच्छा, वह कल दिल्ली से आएगा?
accha:, vah kal dilli: se a:yega:?
Is it so that he'll come from Delhi tomorrow?

Using the same intonational patterns as in yes-no questions echoing a statement, yes-no question echo-questions are formed either by asking the previous speaker whether he/she asked the question or by replacing the constituent under focus. Yes-no questions are prompted by the previous speakers question and they do not merely seek clarification of the previous speakers statement.

85. आपने किताब पढ़ी?
a:pne kita:b paṛhi:?
you-erg book read-fs-pst book
Did you read the book?

85a. मैंने किताब पढ़ी?
mɛ̃ne kita:b paṛhi:?
Did I read the book?

85b. आप पूछ रहे हैं कि मैंने किताब पढ़ी?
a:p pu:ch rahe hɛ̃ (ki) mɛ̃ne kita:b paṛhi:?
You are asking if I read the book?

The focused constituent receives stress if the speaker chooses to retain unfocused elements.

4.3.4.3.2. Question-Word Echo-Questions

A question-word may also be used in echo questions and elements of the statement may be repeated depending on the clarification sought.

86. वह पत्र लिख रहा है।
vah patr likh raha: hɛ.
he letter write-pr is
He is writing a letter.

86a. क्या लिख रहा है?
kya: likh raha: hɛ?
What is he writing?

86b. क्या?
kya:?
What (is he writing)?

86c. पत्र।
patr
(He is writing a) letter.

Question-word echo-questions are uttered with a slightly rising intonation at the end of the phrase or sentence in yes-no questions. It is not so in question-word questions. The questioner may also use the expected answer in his/her question with a rising intonation.

86d. क्या लिख रहा है, पत्र?
kya: likh raha: hɛ, patr?
What is he writing, a letter?

86e. हाँ हाँ, पत्र।
hã: hã:, patr.
Yes, a letter.

In (86d), a pause (indicated by a comma) separates the two rising intonation patterns. A statement containing more than one constituent permits the use of more than one echo-question.

87. हाँ, उसने कल किताब पढ़ी।
hã:, usne kal kita:b paṛhi:.
yes he-erg yesterday book read-fs
Yes, he read a book yesterday.

87a. किसने (कल) किताब पढ़ी।
kisne (kal kita:b) paṛhi:?
Who read (a book yesterday)?

87b. किसने क्या पढ़ी?
kisne kya: paṛhi:?
Who read what?

87c. किसने क्या किया?
kisne kya: kiya:?
Who did what?

Question-word echo-questions follow the same pattern.

88. आप क्या कर रहे हैं?
a:p kya: kar rahe hɛ̃?
you what are-2s doing
What are you doing?

88a. मैं क्या कर रहा हूँ?
mɛ̃ kya: kar raha: hũ:?
I what am-ms doing
What am I doing?

All elements in a sentence, including the verb and any possible combination thereof, can be questioned.

89. मैं पूछ रहा हूँ किसने किसे और कब कमीज़ दी?
mɛ̃ pu:ch raha: hũ: kisne kisko ɔr kab kami:z di:?
I ask-pr am who-erg who-dat and when shirt gave
Im asking you who gave a shirt to whom and when?

89a. किसने किसे और कब कमीज़ दी?
kisne kise kab kami:z di:?
Who gave a shirt to whom and when?

89b. किसने किसे कब क्या दिया?
kisne kise kab kya: diya:?
Who gave what to whom and when?

In (89b), the verb is echo-questioned.

4.3.4.4. Answers

Not all types of answers can be formally distinguished from other declarative statements. Answers to yes-no questions require the use of the agreement and disagreement markers हाँ *hã* 'yes' and नहीं *nahĩ:* 'no' respectively in the sentence initial position, which may be followed with certain honorific markers. Answers to question-word questions involve the stating of the constituent required by the question. The rest of the elements of the sentence are usually deleted.

90. वह कब आगरा जाएगा?
vah kab a:gra: ja:yega:?
When will he go to Agra?

90a. परसों जाएगा।
parsõ ja:yega:.
(He) will go day after tomorrow.

90b. परसों।
parsõ.
Day after tomorrow.

The minimum answers to a yes-no question include हाँ *hã:* 'yes', नहीं *nahĩ:* 'no' शायद *ša:yad* 'perhaps', मालूम *ma:lu:m/* पता नहीं *pata: nahĩ:* 'it is not known'. The short answers may optionally be followed by polite or honorific particles or terms. The polite particle जी *ji:* can be added to both positive and negative short answers. It usually precedes the answers. In speech under the influence of Punjabi, it follows the affirmative or negative short answers. It is added to indicate politeness for any questioner older or younger than the respondent. Other formal honorific markers used are जिनाब *jina:b* or साहब *sa:hab* 'sir/madam' for addressing people of all communities. The English honorific terms, sir and madam are also frequently used by the educated community.

91. वह आज आएगा आगरा से?
vah a:j a:yega a:gra: se?
he come-fut today Agra-abl from
Will he come from Agra today?

91a. हाँ /जी हाँ /हाँ जिनाब/ हाँ साहब/ हाँ सर/ हाँ मैड्म
hã:/ji: hã:/hã: jina:b/hã: sa:hab/hã: sar/ hã: mɛḍam
Yes/ yes sir/madam.

91b. नहीं / जी नहीं /नहीं जिनाब/ नहीं साहब/ नहीं सर/ नहीं मैड्म
nahĩ:/ji: nahĩ:/nahĩ: jina:b/nahĩ: sa:hab/nahĩ: sar/ nahĩ: mɛḍam
No/no sir/madam.

91c. शायद।
ša:yad.
Perhaps.

91d. क्या मालूम /क्या पताा/ जी क्या पता?
kya: ma:lu:m/kya: pata:/ ji: kya: pata:?
Who knows?

91e. पता नहीं /मालूम नहीं / जी मालूम नहीं ।
pata: nahĩ: /ma:lu:m nahĩ:/ ji: ma:lu:m nahĩ:.
It is not known.

91f. पता नहीं /मालूम नहीं ।
pata:/ma:lu:m nahĩ:.
I don't know.

The honorific terms जिनाब *jina:b* and साहब *sa:hab* can also be added in the sentence initial position.

91dd. जिनाब / साहब क्या पता?
jina:b/sa:hab kya: pata:?
Sir, who knows?

91ee. जिनाब / साहब क्या पता?
jina:b/sa:hab kya: pata:?
Sir, it is not known.

91ff. जिनाब / साहब पता/मालूम नहीं ।
jina:b/sa:hab pata:/ma:lu:m nahĩ:.
Sir, I don't know.

The agreement or affirmative response is sometimes indicated merely by using the honorific terms जिनाब *jina:b* and साहब *sa:hab* as in the following examples:

92. वह चालाक नहीं है?
vah ca:la:k nahĩ: hɛ?
he clever neg-Q is
Isn't he clever?

92a. जी /जी है/ हाँ, वह चालाक नहीं है?
ji:/ ji: hɛ/ hã:, jina:b/hã: sa:hab hɛ.
Yes, he is.

As shown above, answers to yes-no questions may be yes, or no, or other response terms or expressions. The positive and negative response particles हाँ *hã:* yes and नहीं ɪ*nahĩ:* no can be reduplicated for emphasis. They may be followed by certain expressions for greater emphasis.

93. आप मेरा यह काम करेंगे?
a:p mera: yeh ka:m karẽge?
you my this work-ms do fut-q
Will you do this work for me?

93a. हाँ हाँ, ज़रूर/ अवश्य।
hã: hã:, zaru:r/avašya.
yes yes definitely.
Yes, I'll do it, definitely.

93b. हाँ हाँ, क्यों नहीं?
hã: hã:, kyõ nahĩ:?
yes yes why not
Yes, why not?

94. आप आगरा नहीं आएँगे?
a:p a:gra: nahĩ: a:yẽge?
you Agra neg come-2p-fut
Won't you come to Agra?

94a. नहीं नहीं, बिल्कुल नहीं।
nahĩ: nahĩ:, bilkul nahĩ:
no no absolutely not
No, not at all.

The expression बिल्कुल *bilkul* is followed by the negative marker. It is to be noted that affirmative and negative particles only are reduplicated, not other response terms and expressions.

94b. *नहीं (नहीं), शायद शायद नहीं।
**nahĩ: (nahĩ:) ša:yad ša:yad nahĩ:.*

94c. *नहीं (नहीं), क्या पता क्या पता।
**nahĩ: (nahĩ:) kya: pata:, kya: pata:*

Answers to positive and negative leading questions are determined by the proposition underlying the question and not by the tag question.

95. आप यह काम करेंगे, करेंगे ना?
a:p yah ka:m karẽgẽ, karẽge na:?
you this work do-fut, do-fut neg-q
You will do this work, won't you?

95a. हाँ, करूँगा।
hã:, karũ:ga:.
yes do-1s-fut
Yes, I'll do it.

96. आप यह काम नहीं करेंगे, करेंगे?
a:p yah ka:m nahĩ: karẽge, karẽge?
You won't do this work, will you?

96a. नहीं (मैं नहीं करूँगा)।
nahĩ: (mɛ̃ nahĩ: karũ:ga).
No (I will not do it).

4.3.5. Imperatives

Imperative sentences are marked for number, gender, person, and degree of politeness. There are three types of imperative constructions: (a) unmarked or true imperatives, (b) prohibitive imperatives and (c) obligative imperatives.

4.3.5.1. Unmarked or True Imperatives

The unmarked imperative takes the second person subjects तू *tu:* 'you' (non honorific intimate singular), तुम *tum* 'you' (non-honorific/plural), and आप *a:p* 'you' (honorific plural/singular). Notice that the honorific plural and the honorific singular forms are the same. The singular imperative consists of the verbal stem. Whereas the singular non-honorific form remains unchanged, the suffix -ओ *-o* is added to derive the plural non-honorific forms and the suffix – इए *-iye* is added to derive the singular/plural honorific forms. If the verb stems end in the vowels ई /*i:*/ or ए /*e*/, the suffix – ईजिए *-i:jiye* is added to the honorific singular and plural forms. The stem final vowels ई /*i:*/ and ए /*e*/ are dropped before the imperative suffixes or the plural non-honorific -ओ *-o* and singular/plural honorific suffix – ईजिए *-i:jiye* are added.

1.

Sg non hon		Pl non-hon	Pl/hon	
(तू tu:)		(तुम tum)	(आप a:p)	
पढ़		पढ़ो	पढ़िए	
paṛh	read	paṛho	paṛhiye	Please read.
लिख		लिखो	लिखिए	
likh	write	likho	likhiye	Please write.
ला		लाओ	लाइए	
la:	bring	la:o	la:iye	Please bring.
खा		खाओ	खाइए	
kha:	eat	kha:o	kha:iye	Please eat.
पी		पिओ	पीजिए	
pi:	drink	piyo	pi:jiye	Please drink.
ले		लो	लीजिए	
le	take	lo	li:jiye	Please take.

The polite markers जी *ji:,* साहब *sa:hab,* and जिनाब *jina:b* can be added to the honorific imperative forms.

1a. Polite pl./hon. sg.
पढ़िए जी paṛhiye ji:/ साहब sa:hab/ जिनाब jina:b Please read.
लिखिए जी likhiye ji:/ साहब sa:hab/ जिनाब jina:b Please write.
लाइए जी la:iye ji:/ साहब sa:hab/ जिनाब jina:b Please bring.
खाइए जी kha:iye ji:/ साहब sa:hab/ जिनाब jina:b Please eat.
पीजिए जी pi:jiye ji:/ साहब sa:hab/ जिनाब jina:b Please drink.
लीजिए जी li:jiye ji:/ साहब sa:hab/ जिनाब jina:b Please take.

With an object, the order will be as follows:

1b. आप किताब पढ़िए।
a:p kita:b paṛhiye.
you book read-pl
Please read the book.

4.3.5.2. Prohibitive Imperatives

Prohibitive imperatives are formed by adding the negative particle *mat* don't in the pre verbal position.

2. किताब पढ/पढ़ो/ पढ़िए।
kita:b paṛh / paṛho / paṛhiye.
Read a book.

2a. किताब मत पढ/पढ़ो/ पढ़िए।
kita:b mat paṛh / paṛho/ paṛhiye.
Don't read a book.

3. पत्र लिख/लिखो/ लिखिए।
patr likh/likho/likhiye.
Write a letter.

3a. पत्र मत लिख/लिखो/ लिखिए।
patr mat likh/likho/likhiye.
Don't write a letter.

Prohibitive imperatives can also be formed by using the verb form मना *mana:/* वर्जित होना *varjit hona:* to be prohibitive as in (4-4a).

4. शराब पीना मना /वर्जित है।
šara:b pi:na: mana:/varjit hɛ.
liquor drink-Inf prohibited is
Drinking (of liquor) is prohibited.

4a. सिगरेट पीना मना है।
sigreṭ pi:na: mana: hɛ.
cigarette smoke-inf prohibited is
Smoking is prohibited.

Prohibitive imperatives are also constructed from expressions like ख़बरदार *xabarda:r*/सावधान *sa:vadha:n* 'beware'.

5. ख़बरदार / सावधान देर से न आना।
xabarda:r/sa:vadha:n der se na a:na:.
beware late-abl neg come-inf
Beware, don't come late.
(You better not come late.)

The expressions ख़बरदार *xabarda:r/* सावधान *sa:vadha:n* are followed by conditional clauses.

4.3.5.3. Degrees of Imperatives

The unmarked ordinary imperative is stronger than the polite imperative. The obligatives of compulsion are stronger than the obligatives of prescription and the polite imperatives. Certain devices are used to strengthen or weaken the force of the imperative. Intonation and tone play an important role in the degree of the imperative. A soft tone of persuasion weakens and a hard authoritative tone strengthens the degree of the imperative.

Certain lexical items or phrases, such as कृपया *krapaya:* kindly कृपा *kripa:/* मेहरबानी करके *meharba:ni: karke* 'after being kind', and भगवान सावधान खुदा के लिए *bhagva:n/xuda: ke liye* 'for God's sake' are added to imperative sentences to add politeness. They weaken the imperative.

6. कृपया घर जाइए।
   krapaya: ghar ja:yiye.
   kindly home go-pol-fut
   Kindly go home.

7. कृपा / मेहरबानी करके पैसे दीजिए।
   krapa:/meharba:ni: karke pɛse di:jiye.
   kindness do-cp money give-pol-fut
   Kindly give money.
8. भगवान के लिए समय बरबाद मत कीजिए।
   bhagva:n ke liye samay barba:d mat ki:jiye.
   God-abl sake/for time waste neg do-pol-fut
   For Gods sake, don't waste time.

The vocative forms may also be used in the sentence initial position to strengthen and weaken the degree of imperative. The vocative forms are as follows.

Masculine				Feminine			
Sg		Pl		Sg		Pl	
ओ	o	ओ	o	ओ	o	ओ	o
अरे	are	अरे	are	अरी	ari:	अरे	are

9. अरे, दरवाज़ा बंद करो।
are darva:za: band karo.
hey door do-2s-fut close-2s-imp
Hey, close the door.

9a. अरे, मेरी बात तो सुनिए।
are, meri: ba:t to suniye.
O, my talk emp listen-2p-imp
Hey, listen to me.

The vocative address forms may be followed by kinship terms like भाई*bha:i:* 'brother', यार *ya:r*/दोस्त *dost*/मित्र *mitr* 'friend', प्यारे *pya:re* 'dear one' बहिन *bahin* 'sister', and माई *ma:i:* 'mother'.

10. अरे भाई/यार/दोस्त/मित्र/प्यारे दूध लाओ।
are bha:i:/ya:r/dost/mitr/pya:re du:dh la:o.
hey brother/friend/dear one milk bring-2s-imp
Hey brother/friend/dear one, bring the milk.

10a. अरी बहिन, अपना काम कर।
ari: bahan, apna: ka:m kar.
hey-f sister selfs work do-2s-imp
Hey sister, do your work.

10b. हे भाई साहब यह अख़बार पढ़िए।
he bha:i: sa:hab yah akhba:r paṛhiye.
oh-hon brother hon this newspaper read-pol
Oh brother, please read this newspaper.

The vocatives may also be followed by derogative terms like पागल *pa:gal* 'mad', abusive terms like साले *sa:le* 'brother-in-law', and सुसरे *susre* 'father-in-law' or other derogative expressions of address. The use of such derogative terms and abusive kinship terms strengthen the imperative.

11. अरे साले, क्या बोलता है?
are sa:le, kya: bolta: hɛ?
hey-mas brother-in-law what say-ptc be
Hey (my) brother-in-law, what are you saying?

11a. ओ पागल, यहाँ आओ।
o pa:gal, yahã: a:o
hey mad person here come-2s-imp
O mad one, come here.

The use of reduplicated forms of imperatives reinforces the impolite force.

12. जा जा, सुन लिया।
ja: ja:, sun liya:.
go go listened
Go, I have listened.

Yes-no positive and negative questions in the future tense may also convey the force of imperative form.

13. (आप)तस्वीर देंगे?
(a:p) tasvi:r dẽge?
you picture give-fut-q
Would you give the picture?

13a. आप देंगे क्या तस्वीर?
a:p dẽge kya: tasvi:r?
you give-fut-q picture

13b. तस्वीर देंगे क्या?
tasvi:r dẽge kya:?
Would you give (me) the picture?

Performative verbs such as निवेदन करना *nivedan karna:* 'to make a request', and (हाथ जोड़कर *ha:th joṛ kar*) प्रार्थना करना *pra:rthana: karna:* 'to make a request (with folded hands') also render imperative force in their complement clause.

14. मैं हाथ जोड़कर प्रार्थना करता हूँ मुझपर कृपा करो।
mɛ ʃha:th joṛkar pra:rthana: karta: hũ: mujhpar kripa: karo.
I hands fold-cp request do-ptc am me-dat on kindness do
I humbly request you to be kind to me.

4.3.6. Anaphora

Here we will discuss (i) the means of expressing anaphora and (ii) the domains of anaphora. Anaphora in Hindi may be personal pronouns, reflexives, zero pronouns (i.e., null elements PRO or pro) or quasi-pronouns.

In a narrative text or natural discourse, deletion is a prominent device in expressing the anaphora, e.g.,

1. एक दिन मैंने एक बच्चे को रास्ते पर रोते देखा,
   ek din mɛ̃ne ek bacce ko ra:ste par rote hue dekha:,
   one day I-erg one child-dat road-obl on weep-ptc saw
   पूछा तुम कौन हो?
   pu:cha: tum kɔn ho?
   asked you who are
   One day I saw a child crying on the road; I asked (him),
   Who are you?

In the above example, the anaphoric subject and object (the child) become accessible by means of deletion or zero anaphora in the second sentence. They are recoverable from the first sentence.

Since the verb agrees with the subject and/or object in gender, number, and person, depending on various kinds of constructions, the subject and object can be deleted.

2. मोहन छे बजे घर पहुँचा, कपड़े बदले और आया।
   Mohan che baje ghar pahũca:, kapṛe badle ɔr a:ya:.
   Mohan reached home six-abl hour clothes changed and came
   Mohan reached home at six oclock; (he) changed his clothes and he came here.

Anaphoric elements are frequently in the third person, and they are often expressed by personal pronouns.

3. मोहन और उसकी पत्नी सैर करने गए, उसको ठोकर लगी
   mohan ɔr uski: patni: sɛr karne gaye, usko ṭhokar lagi:
   Mohan and his wife walk do-inf-obl went he-dat stumbled
   और गिर गया।
   ɔr gir gaya:

and fell
Mohan and his wife went for a walk. He stumbled and fell down.

Anaphora is expressed by possessive and reflexive pronouns as given in (4) and (5).

4. उसने अपने मित्र से पैसे उधार लिए।
usne apne mitr se pɛse udha:r liye.
he-erg refl friend-from money credit took
He took money from his friend on loan.

5. अमित घर आया और स्वयं पत्नी को दवाई दी।
amit ghar a:ya: ɔr svayam patni: ko dava:i: di:
Amit home came and self wife-dat medicine gave
Amit came home and gave medicine to his wife himself.

Certain other devices like the use of सारा *sa:ra:* all, and the use of ordinals like पहला *pahla:* 'first' and दूसरा *du:sra:* 'second', are also employed to denote anaphora.

6. मेहन बाज़ार से सेब लाया। सारे सड़े हुए थे।
mohan ba:za:r se seb la:ya:. sa:re saṛe hue the.
Mohan market from apples brought all rotten-ptc were
Mohan brought apples from the market. All were rotten.

7. उमा और शोभा बहनें हैं। पहली चालाक है,
uma: ɔr šobha: bahnẽ hɛ̃. pahli: ca:la:kh hɛ,
Uma and Shobha: sisters are first clever is
और दूसरी सीधी सादी।
ɔr du:sri: si:dhi: sadi:.
and second simple
Uma and Shobha are sisters. The former is clever and the latter is simple.

The anaphora occurs within the clause with reflexive pronouns. Personal pronouns are not employed for this purpose.

8. वकील को अपने पर पूरा भरोसा है।
vaki:l ko apne par pu:ra: bharosa: hɛ.
advocate-dat refl-obl on full confidence is
The advocate has full confidence in himself.

9. वह अपनी पत्नी के साथ दिल्ली गया।
vah apni: patni: ke sa:th dilli: gaya:.
he refl-dat wife with Delhi went
He went to Delhi with his wife.

Anaphora between coordinate structures is usually forward. It is marked by deletion or pronominalization.

10. मोहन समय पर पहुँचा और ø अपना काम किया।
mohan samay par pahũca: ɔr ø apna: ka:m kiya:
Mohan time on reached and ø refl work did
Mohan reached in time and did his work.

10a. मोहन (i) समय पर पहुँचा और ø उसने (i) अपना काम किया।
mohan (i) samay par pahũca: ɔr ø usne (i) apna: ka:m kiya:
Mohan time on reached and ø he-erg self work did
Mohan reached (office) in time and did his work.

It is possible to have an anaphora between superordinate and subordinate clauses. Usually, subordinate clauses (except for subject complementation, relative clauses and if … then clauses) follow superordinate clauses. Deletion indicates anaphora between a superordinate and a following subordinate clause.

11. माँ ने बेटे (i) को ø (i) पत्र लिखने के लिए कहा।
mã: ne beṭe (i) ko ø (i) patr likhne ke liye kaha:
mother-erg son-dat ø letter write-inf-abl for said
The mother asked her son to write a letter.

11a. माँ ने बेटे (i) को कहा वह (i) पत्र लिखे।
mã: ne beṭe(i) ko kaha: vah (i) patr likhe.
mother-erg son-dat said he letter write-subj
The mother asked her son to write a letter.

Backward deletion is not possible.

11b. *माँ ने कहा कि ø/वह (i) बेटा (i) पत्र लिखे।
mã: ne kaha: ki ø /vah (i) beṭa: (i) patr likhe.

Backward as well as forward deletion and pronominalization are used to express anaphora.

12. [जो ø किताब पढ़ रही है] वह लड़की मेरी बहिन है।
[jo ø kita:b paṛh rahi: hɛ] vah laṛki: meri: bahan hɛ.
rel ø book read-prog is cor girl my sister is
The girl who is reading a book is my sister.

12a. [जो लड़की किताब पढ़ रही है] वह ø मेरी बहिन है।
[jo laṛki: kita:b paṛh rahi: hɛ] vah ø meri: bahan hɛ.
rel girl book read-prog is cor ø my sister is
The girl who is reading a book is my sister.

Anaphora between different sentences also uses the strategy of deletion and pronominalization. No other strategy is employed.

4.3.7. Reflexives

A reflexive pronoun occupies the same position within a clause as any other type of a pronoun. The only restriction is that the antecedent of a reflexive pronoun must be the subject of its clause. There is no other change except the selection of a dative case marker or a postposition in its use as an indirect object. Emphatic possessive pronouns do not require a co-referential antecedent.

1. वह लड़की उसकी अपनी बेटी है।
vah laṛki: uski: apni: beṭi: hɛ.
that girl his emp/*refl
That girl is his/her own.

Emphatic pronouns are sometimes completely homophonous with possessive pronouns as in (2).

2. दुल्हन अपने दूल्हे को पसंद है।
dulhan apne du:lhe ko pasand hɛ.
bride refl-obl bridegroom-dat like is
The bride is liked by her bridegroom.

Sentence (2) is not passive. The conjunct verb पसंद होना *pasand hona:* to like takes a dative subject. Sentence (2), using the emphatic pronoun, can be interpreted as follows:

2a. दुल्हन उसके अपने दूल्हे को पसंद है।
dulhan uske apne du:lhe ko pasand hɛ.
bride her refl-obl bridegroom-dat like is
The bride is liked by her own bridegroom.

Reflexivity is expressed by the use of agentive reflexive pronouns. This term is used to distinguish between the possessive reflexive अपना *apna:* and non-possessive reflexive अपने आप *apne a:p* 'self'. The reflexive अपने आप *apne a:p* represents the main reflexive pronoun, which when followed by a postposition, has the oblique form अपने *apne*. It also functions as an emphatic pronoun as in (1). The emphatic form is also derived by adding the emphatic suffix -ही *-hi:* to it. The result is आप ही *a:p hi:*. The reduplicated form अपने आप *apne a:p* also occurs as a reflexive.

3. अमित आप/ अपने आप/ आप ही यहाँ आया।
amit a:p/apne a:p/a:p hi: yahã: a:ya:.
Amit self -emp here came
Amit came here by himself.

4. मैं अपने आप खाना बनाता हूँ।
mɛ̃ apne a:p kha:na: bana:ta: hũ:.
I am refl food cook-pr am
I cook my meals myself.

5. हम अपने आप कपड़े धोते हैं।
ham apne a:p kapṛe dhote hɛ̃.
we refl clothes wash-ptc are
We wash our clothes ourselves.

6. सुमन अपने आप कपड़े इस्त्री करती है।
suman apne a:p kapṛe istri: karti: hɛ.

Suman refl clothes iron do-ptc is
Suman irons the clothes herself.

There are no separate pronominal reflexive pronouns for each pronoun. The person information is obtained from the antecedent subject.

7. अमित ने अपने लिए / भाई के लिए जूते खरीदे।
amit ne apne liye/bha:i: ke liye ju:te: khari:de:.
Amit-erg refl-obl for/brother for shoes bought
Amit bought a pair of shoes for himself/his brother.

Sentence (7) shows that a non co-referential object does not take a reflexive form, but selects a non-reflexive form. The reflexivization is also controlled by dative and ergative subjects.

8. उमा को अपने आप काम करना पसंद है।
uma: ko apne a:p ka:m karna: pasand hɛ.
Uma-dat refl work do-inf like is
Uma likes to do (her) work herself.

9. अमित ने अपने आप दिन भर आराम किया।
amit ne apne a:p din bhar a:ra:m kiya:.
Amit-erg refl day-whole rest did
Amit rested the whole day.

Examples (8-9) can be interpreted as emphatic reflexives as well. Reflexivization can allow backward movement as well.

10. अपने आप अमित ने आराम किया।
apne a:p amit ne a:ra:m kiya:.
refl Amit-erg rest did
Amit rested himself.

In possessive structures, the possible reflexive form अपना *apna:* 'self' is used in place of possessive pronouns such as the English my and your. When the possessive reflexive is used, the possessor is the same as the agent of the action or the subject. अपना *apna:* agrees with the following head NP in number and gender. Following are its forms:

Masculine				Feminine			
Sg		Pl		Sg		Pl	
अपना	apna:	अपने	apne	अपनी	apni:	अपनी	apni:

11. मैं अपना /*मेरा कमरा साफ कर रहा हूँ।
*mɛ̃ apna:/*mera: kamra: sa:f kar raha: hũ:.*
I-m sefl/*my room clean do-prog am
I am cleaning my room.

12. मैं अपने /*मेरे पैसे गिन रहा हूँ।
*mɛ̃ apne/*mere pɛse gin raha: hũ:.*
I refl /*my money count-prog am
I am counting my money.

13. आप अपनी /*आपकी किताव पढ़ रहे हैं।
*a:p apni:/*a:p ki: kita:b paṛh rahe hɛ̃.*
you refl/*yours book read-prog are
You are reading your book.

14. वे अपनी /*उनकी कमीज़ें धो रहे हैं।
*ve apni:/*unki: kami:zẽ dho rahe hɛ̃.*
he refl/*his shirts wash-prog are
He is washing his shirts.

15. वह अपना /*उसका लाभ जानता हैं।
*vah apna:/*uska: la:bh ja:nta: hɛ.*
he refl/*his profit know-ptc is
He is aware of his benefit.

16. वे अपनी /* उनकी किस्मत पर रो रहे हैं।
*ve apni:/*unki: kismat par ro rahe hɛ̃.*
they refl/*selfs luck on cry-prog are
They repent on their own work.

The use of non-reflexive pronouns yield well-formed sentences provided the subject and possessive pronoun are not co-referential.

17. वह (i) उसकी (j) कमीज़ सी रहा है।
vah (i) uski: (j) kami:z si: raha: hɛ.

he his shirt stitch-prog is
He (i) is stitching his (j) shirt.

18. वह (i) उनके (j) बच्चे पढ़ा रहा है।
vah (i) unke (j) bacce paṛha: raha: hɛ.
he their children teach-prog is
He(i) is teaching their (j) children.

Similar to nominative and ergative subjects, the dative subject also controls the possessive reflexive अपना *apna:*. The possessive structure also permits reduplicated reflexives.

19. वे अपना अपना काम कर रहे हैं।
ve apna: apna: ka:m kar rahe hɛ̃.
they refl work do-prog are
They are doing their respective jobs.

The scope of reflexivity is usually restricted to the clause in which it is used.

20. मोहन ने कहा कि वह /*अपने आप समय पर आएगा।
*mohan ne kaha: ki vah/*apne a:p samay par a:yega:.*
Mohan-erg said that he/*refl time at come-fut
Mohan (i) said that he (i) would come on time.

21. मोहन ने पूछा कि उसकी/*अपनी पत्नी कब आएगी।
*mohan ne pu:cha: ki uski:/*apni: patni: kab a:yegi:.*
Mohan-erg asked that his/*refl wife when come-fut
Mohan (i) asked when his (i) wife would come.

Sentences (20) and (21) show that reflexivization does not go down into subordinate clauses. Notice that reflexivization does not always meet clausemate constraint, as shown in (22).

22. अमित मोहन को अपना शत्रु मानता है।
amit mohan ko apna: šatru: ma:nta: hɛ.
Amit Mohan-dat refl enemy consider-ptc is
Amit (i) considers Mohan (j) his (i,j) enemy.

Sentence (22) is ambiguous because the reflexive pronoun is co-referential with the subject of the subordinate as well as with the subject of the subordinate clause. It has two readings.

22a. अमित (i) मानता है [कि मोहन अमित (j) का शत्रु है]।
amit (i) ma:nta: hɛ [ki mohan amit (i) ka: šatru: hɛ].
Amit consider-ptc is that Mohan Amit of enemy is
Amit considers Mohan Amits enemy.

22b. अमित मानता है [कि मोहन (i) मोहन (j) का शत्रु है]।
amit ma:nta: hɛ [ki mohan (i) mohan (i) ka: šatru: hɛ.
Amit consier-prog that Mohan Mohans enemy is
Amit considers Mohan Mohans enemy.

Here, the reflexive pronoun cannot occur in (22a), but it can occur in sentence (22b) due to its clause boundaries. It shows that the finite subordinate clause becomes finite and is raised to the object position of the matrix sentence.

Reflexive relations occur within nominalized clauses.

23. उसका स्वयं को मारना ठीक नहीं था।
uska: svayam ko ma:rna: ṭhi:kh nahĩ: tha:.
his self kill-inf proper neg was
His killing himself was not proper.

Reflexive relations cannot exist within an ordinary noun phrase. It is possible to have reflexive antecedents under two conditions: (i) when the logical antecedent is deleted at the surface level and (ii) when the antecedent is either generic or contextually implied.

(i) Deletion of an underlying antecedent

24. तुम अपना कमरा साफ करो।
tum apna: kamra: sa:f karo.
you refl room clean do
Clean your room.

24a. अपना कमरा साफ करो।
apna: kamra: sa:f karo.
refl room clean do
Clean your room.

(ii) Generic/implied antecedent

25. अपना समय नष्ट करना ठीक नहीं है।
apna: samay našṭ karna: ṭhi:k nahĩ: hɛ.
refl time waste do-inf good neg is
It is not proper (for someone) to waste ones time.

Notice that in (25) the generic antecedent someone is implied.

4.3.8. Reciprocals

The primary way of expressing a reciprocal relationship is the expression एक दूसरे को *ek du:sre ko* 'to one another'. It is the combination of the cardinal एक *ek* 'one' and the oblique case form of the ordinal दूसरा *du:sra:* followed by को *ko*. Reciprocals can also be formed with आपस में *a:pas mẽ* 'mutual'. The scope of reciprocity is restricted to the clause.

1. हमने एक दूसरे के साथ बात की।
hamne ek du:sre ke sa:th ba:t ki:.
we-erg one another-obl with talk did
We talked to each other.

2. उन्होंने एक दूसरे की बहुत सहायता की।
unhõne ek du:sre ki: bahut saha:yta: ki:.
they-erg one another-obl very help did
They helped each other very much.

In these sentences, the scope of the reciprocal expression does not extend to the matrix subject.

Reciprocals usually require an antecedent subject. They may be used as a direct object, an indirect object, an adverb, or a possessive adjective in different types of constructions.

Direct object

3. वे एक दूसरे से कई बार मिले।
ve ek du:sre se kai: ba:r mile.
they one another-obl many times lot-abl met
They met each other many times.

Indirect object

4. उन्होंने एक दूसरे को उपहार दिए।
unhõne ek du:sre ko upha:r diye.
they-erg one another-obl presents gave
They gave presents to each other.

Adverb

5. वे एक दूसरे पर ज़ोर से चिल्ला रहे हैं।
ve ek du:sre par zor se cilla: rahe hɛ̃.
they one another-obl with shout-prog are
They are shouting at each other.

Possessive adjective

6. हम एक दूसरे के घर नहीं जाते।
ham ek du:sre ke ghar nahĩ: ja:te.
we one another-poss home neg go-ptc
We don't visit each others houses.

7. वे आपस में बात नहीं करते (हैं)।
ve a:pas mẽ ba:t nahĩ: karte (hɛ̃).
they among themselves talk neg do-pre (are)
They do not talk to each other.

The same range of reciprocals occur in nominalized clauses.

8. उनका एक दूसरे के घर न जाना ठीक नहीं है।
unka: ek du:sre ke ghar na ja:na: ṭhi:k nahĩ: hɛ.
their one another-gen house not go-inf good neg is
Their not visiting each others homes is not right.

9. उनकी एक दूसरे की टोपियाँ बराबर नहीं हैं।
unki: ek du:sre ki: ṭopiyã: bara:bar nahĩ: hɛ̃.
their one another-poss caps equal/fit neg are
Each others caps do not fit them.

It is possible to have reciprocal structures without antecedent, if the antecedent is understood either syntactically, as in the case of imperative constructions, or contextually.

10. एक दूसरे के साथ बातें मत करो।
ek du:sre ke sa:th ba:tẽ mat karo.
one another-obl with talk don't do
Don't talk to each other.

11. अमित के दो बेटे हैं। वे एक दूसरे के साथ हमेशा लड़ते हैं।
amit ke do beṭe hɛ̃. ve ek du:sre ke sa:th hameša: laṛte hɛ̃.
Amit-gen two sons are they one-another-gen with always fight-pr
Amit has two sons. (They) always quarrel with each other.

4.3.9. Equatives

Like comparatives, there are two types of equatives: (i) syntactic and (ii) phrasal. The former type is composed of two clauses called as इतना *itna:* 'this much' and उतना *utna:* 'that much' clauses. The main difference between these clauses and the comparative clause is that in equative clauses, an equative adjective or adverb is used with the subject and the standard of comparison. A comparative sentence can be transformed into an equative sentence by the deletion of the negative particle.

1. अजय उतना चालाक है जितना उसका भाई (है)।
ajay utna: ca:la:k hɛ jitna: uska: bha:i: (hɛ).
Ajay that much-cor clever as much-rel his brother
Ajay is as clever as his brother.

Equative structures can also be formed by using the clause जैसा *jɛsa:* as/which way and वैसा *vɛsa:* like/that way.

2. जैसा अजय चालाक है, उतना उसका भाई (भी)है।
jɛsa: ajay ca:la:k hɛ, utna: uska: bha:i: (bhi:) hɛ.
as-rel Ajay clever is that much his brother (also) is
Ajay is as clever as his brother.

Phrasal type equatives are formed using adjectives such as बराबर *bara:bar*/समान *sama:n* 'equal', and जैसा *jɛsa:* 'like'. The forms agree with the standard of comparison in number and gender.

3. विजय अपने पिताजी के बराबर/ समान लंबा है।
vijay apne pita:ji: ke bara:bar/sama:n lamba: hɛ.
Vijay selfs father-gen like tall is
Vijay is as tall as his father.

4. ये दो भाई अपनी माँ जैसे सीधे हैं।
ye do bha:i: apni: mã: jɛse si:dhe hɛ̃.
these two brothers selfs mother like simple are
These two brothers are as simple as their mother.

5. यह लड़की अपनी बहिन जैसी सुंदर है।
yeh laṛki: apni: bahan jɛsi: sundar hɛ.
this girl selfs sister like beautiful is
This girl is as beautiful as her sister.

6. ये दो बहिनें अपनी माँ की तरह सुंदर हैं।
ye do bahnẽ apni: mã: ki: tarah sundar hɛ̃.
these two sisters selfs mother like beautiful is
These two sisters are as beautiful as their mother.

7. विजय बच्चे के समान है।
vijay bacce ke sama:n hɛ.
Vijay child-gen equal is
Vijay is like a child.

8. उमा अनु के बराबर लंबी है।
uma: anu ke bara:bar lambi: hɛ.
Uma Anu-gen equal tall is
Uma is as tall as Anu.

Notice that a copular/equational sentence employs only the plural adjectival forms of एक जैसे *ek jɛse*/एक जैसी *ek jaisi:* that agree with the number and gender of the subject of comparison.

9. अजय और विजय एक जैसे ही हैं।
ajay ɔr vijay ek jɛse hi: hɛ̃.
Ajay and Vijay alike emp are
Ajay and Vijay are alike.

10. उमा और अनु एक जैसी हैं।
uma: ɔr anu ek jɛsi: hɛ̃.
Uma and Anu alike are
Uma and Anu are alike.

Equative adjectives may be modified by adding the particle –ही *-hi:* to these forms: जैसे ही *jɛse hi:*, जैसी ही *jɛsi: hi:* 'alike'. The particle –ही *-hi:* is also added to singular forms for emphasis as well.

11. विजय अजय जैसा ही है।
vijay ajay jɛsa: hi: hɛ.
Vijay Ajay like emp is
Vijay is like Ajay.

12. उमा अनु जैसी ही है।
uma: anu jɛsi: hi: hɛ.
Uma Anu alike emp is
Uma is like Anu.

A number of fixed adjectival phrases are used in Hindi.

13. फूल सा/ जैसा कोमल
phu:l sa:/jɛsa: komal
flower like delicate
as delicate as a flower

14. पत्थर सा दिल
patthar sa: dil
stone like heart
a stone-hearted (person)

It is possible to delete the identical elements in equative structures. Deletion is always forward and not backward.

15. उमा उतनी लंबी है जितनी (लंबी) अनु (है)।
uma: utni: lambi: hɛ jitni: (lambi:) anu (hɛ).
Uma cor tall is rel (tall) Uma (is)
Uma is as tall as Anu.

The bracketed elements can be deleted to yield (15a).

15a. उमा उतनी लंबी है जितनी अनु।
uma utni: lambi: hɛ jitni: anu.
Uma is as tall as Anu.

The backward deletion generates ungrammatical sentences, as (15b).

15b. *उमा उतनी ø ø जितनी लंबी है।
**uma: utni: ø ø jitni: lambi: anu hɛ.*

Correlative equatives are formed by syntactic strategy only. They are formed by using the correlative marker उतना *utna:*.

4.3.10. Comparison

Comparison is usually expressed by sentential, phrasal, and morphological strategies. Two types of comparative structures are very common, phrasal comparative structures and non-phrasal ones. Both use postpositions followed by the standards of comparison. Sentential comparison is carried out by the use of two finite clauses introduced by the relative marker उतना *utna:* 'as much as' and the correlative marker जितना *jitna:* 'that much'.

1. वह उतना सीधा नहीं है [जितना सीधा उसका भाई है]।
vah utna: si:dha: nahĩ: hɛ[jitna: si:dha: uska: bha:i: hɛ]
he is not that-cor simple as much as-rel simple his brother is
He is not as simple as his brother.

The relative clause can be placed at the sentence initial position as well.

1a. [जितना सीधा उसका भाई है] वह उतना सीधा नहीं है।
[jitna: si:dha: uska: bha:i: hɛ] vah utna: si:dha: nahĩ: hɛ

2. वह जितना परिश्रम करता है उतना पैसा नहीं कमाता।
vah jitna: parišram karta: hɛ utna: pɛsa: nahĩ: kama:ta:
he as much hard work do-ptc is that much money earn-ptc neg is
He doesn't earn as much as he works.

The relative clause can follow the correlative clause.

2a. वह उतना पैसा नहीं कमाता, जितना परिश्रम करता है।
vah utna: pɛsa: nahĩ: kama:ta:, jitna: parišram karta: hɛ

Most of the morphological markers of comparison are borrowed from Perso-Arabic sources. They are not very productive in Hindi.

3. उसका वहाँ जाना बेहतर रहेगा।
uska: vahã: ja:na: behtar rahega:
his there go-inf better remain-fut
It is better for him to go there.

4. यह उसके लिए बदतरीन बात है।
yah uske liye badtari:n ba:t hɛ.
this is he-for worst matter is
This is the worst thing for him.

Phrasal comparison is expressed by a postposition associated with the standard of comparison. The postposition से *se* is added to the standard of comparison.

5. अमित अनु से लंबा है।
amit anu: se lamba: hɛ.
Amit Anu than tall is
Amit is taller than Anu.

6. अनु उमा से गोरी है।
anu uma: se gori: hɛ.
Anu Uma than fair-complexioned is
Anu is more fair-complexioned than Anu.

The phrasal comparison is also expressed by the use of the phrase के मुकाबले में *ke muka:ble mẽ* 'in comparison with' following the standard of comparison.

7. विजय के मुकाबले में राज पढ़ने में कमज़ोर है।
vjay ke muka:ble mẽ ra:j paṛhne mẽ kamzor hɛ.
Vijay-gen comarison in Raj studies-obl in weak is
Raj is weak in his studies in comparison to Vijay.

8. वह पेड़ इस पेड़ के मुकाबले में लंबा नहीं है।
vah peṛ is peṛ ke muka:ble mẽ lamba: nahĩ: hɛ.
that tree this tree-gen comparison in tall neg is
That tree is not taller than this tree.

9. उस लड़की के मुकाबले में यह लड़की बुद्धिमान है।
us laṛki: ke muka:ble mẽ yah laṛki: buddhima:n hɛ.
that girl-gen comparison-obl in this girl wise is
This girl is wiser than that girl.

Adjectives used in a comparison can be modified by the adverb of degree अधिक *adhik* more.

10. यह घर उस घर से अधिक बड़ा है।
yeh ghar us ghar se adhik baṛa: hɛ.
this house that-obl house comparison more big is
This house is bigger than that one.

11. वह पुस्तक इस पुस्तक से अधिक अच्छी है।
vah pustak is pustak se adhik acchi: hɛ.
that book this book comparison more good is
That book is better than this one.

When two sentences are joined, the identical elements in the second conjunct are usually deleted. Whereas forward deletion is possible, backward deletion is not.

12. अमित उतना चालाक नहीं है जितना (चालाक) उसका भाई है।
amit utna: ca:la:k nahĩ: hɛ jitna: (ca:la:k) uska: bha:i: hɛ.
Amit that much clever neg is as much (clever) his brother is
Amit is not as clever as his brother.

12a. *अमित उतना नहीं है जितना उसका भाई चालाक है।
*amit utna: nahĩ: hɛ jitna: uska: bha:i: ca:la:k hɛ

The deletion of the first occurrence of चालाक *ca:la:k* in sentence (12a) results in the sentence being grammatically incorrect. The relative correlative markers जितना *jitna:* उतना *utna:* cannot be deleted under any circumstance.

4.3.11. Superlatives

Superlatives are usually expressed by substituting सब से अधिक *sab se adhik* 'most', सर्वोतम *sarvotam* 'best', or हर एक में से *har ek mẽ se* 'out of all' for the standard of comparison. Superlative constructions are also formed by the use of कोई दूसरा *koi: du:sra:* 'anyone else' plus the negative particle.

1. अमित कक्षा में सब से अधिक बुद्धिमान है।
   amit kakša: mẽ sab se adhik buddhima:n hɛ.
   Amit class in out of all more wise is
   Amit is wisest of all in his class.

2. उमा सब से अधिक तेज़ दौड़ती है।
   uma: sab se adhik tez dɔṛti: hɛ.
   Uma out of all more fast run-pr is
   Uma runs faster than everyone else.

3. विजय से चतुर और कोई दूसरा नहीं है।
   vijay se catur ɔr koi: du:sra: nahĩ: hɛ.
   Vijay than clever anyone else neg is
   No one else is more clever than Vijay.

Superlative constructions are also formed by substituting an adjective of comparison for सब से अधिक *sab se adhik*.. It also serves as the standard of comparison.

4. वह बड़ी से बड़ी समस्या आसनी से हल करता है।
   vah baṛi: se baṛi: samasya: a:sa:ni: se hal karta: hɛ.
   he big-f more big-f problem easy with solve do-ptc is
   He solves the biggest problems easily.

5. हमारे पास अच्छे से अच्छा कपड़ा यही है।
   hama:re pa:s acche se accha: kapṛa: yahi: hɛ.
   we-obl with good-obl than good cloth this is
   This is the best cloth we have.

Notice that in these constructions, the first part of the phrase is put in the oblique case as it is followed by से *se*.

4.3.12. Coordination

Sentence coordination is marked mainly by the use of the conjunction morphemes और *ɔr* 'and' या *ya:* 'or', and मगर *magar/*पर *par/*किंतु *kintu* 'but'.

1. मैं दिल्ली गया और मेरा भाई आगरा (गया)।
   mɛ̃ dilli: gaya: aur mera: bha:i: agra: (gaya:).
   I Delhi went and my brother Agra went
   I went to Delhi and my brother went to Agra.

2. सोहन मोहन के घर गया मगर/ पर/ किंतु मोहन
   sohan mohan ke ghar gaya: magar/par/kintu mohan
   Sohan Mohan gen home went but Mohan
   घर पर नहीं था।
   ghar par nahĩ: tha:.
   home at neg was
   Sohan went to Mohans home, but Mohan was not there.

The conjunction morpheme और *ɔr* 'and' can be followed by another particle, भी *bhi:* 'also'.

3. मोहन कल बनारस जाएगा और सोहन भी (जाएगा)।
   mohan kal bana:ras ja:yega: ɔr sohan bhi: (ja:yega:).
   Mohan tomorrow Banaras go-fut and Sohan also go-fut
   Mohan will go to Banaras tomorrow and Mohan will also go.

The conjunction compound morphemes या *ya:* -या *-ya:* 'either – or' are also used in sentence conjunctions.

4. या आज वर्षा होगी या हिमपात होगा।
   ya: a:j varša: hogi: ya: himpa:t hoga:.
   either today rain fall-fut or snowfall be-fut
   Either it rains today or it will snow.

Notice that the word order of the constituent sentences undergo a change when conjoined by the use of the conjunction morphemes या - या *ya: - ya:*. Sentence (4) is obtained by conjoining (4a) and (4b).

4a. आज वर्षा होगी।
a:j varša: hogi:.
It will rain today.

4b. आज हिमपात होगा।
a:j himpa:t hoga:.
It will snow today.

And coordination is commonly expressed by the conjunction marker और *ɔr*. It can join two or more sentences or phrases. This conjunction morpheme occurs before the last conjunct.

5. शीला किताब पढ़ रही है और उमा चिट्ठी लिख रही है।
ši:la: kita:b paṛh rahi: hɛ ɔr uma: ciṭṭhi: likh rahi: hɛ.
Shiela book read-prog is and Uma letter write write-prog is
Shiela is reading a book and Uma is writing a letter.

6. अमर खेल रहा है, मोहन गाने सुन रहा है और
amar khel raha: hɛ, mohan ga:ne sun raha: hɛ, ɔr
Amar play-prog is Mohan songs listen-prog is and
शाम टी वी देख रहा है।
ša:m ṭi:vi: dekh raha: hɛ.
Sham TV see-prog is
Amar is playing, Mohan is listening to songs, and Sham is watching television.

5a. *और शीला किताब पढ़ रही है उमा पत्र लिख रही है।
**ɔr ši:la: kita:b paṛh rahi: hɛ, uma: patr likh rahi: hɛ.*

6a. *अमर खेल रहा है और मोहन गाने सुन रहा है, शाम टी वी देख रहा है।
**amar khel raha: hɛ ɔr mohan ga:ne sun raha: hɛ, ša:m ṭi:vi: dekh raha: hɛ.*

The misplacement of the coordination conjunction morpheme और *ɔr* renders the sentences (5a) and (6a) ungrammatical.

Coordination does not merely involve juxtaposition of two or more independent sentences. There are various syntactic and semantic constraints on the construction of coordinate structures. In general, coordinate sentences express contrast, cumulative effect, cause and effect, sequential action, and contingency. Again, the order of the conjuncts is interchangeable if a coordinate sentence expresses contrast or cumulative effect. Consider the following examples of various types of coordinate structures as listed above.

Contrast

7. यह लड़का मोटा है और वह लड़का दुबला।
yeh laṛka: moṭa: hɛ ɔr vah laṛka: dubla:.
this boy fat is and that boy slim
This boy is fat and that boy is slim.

7a. वह लड़का दुबला है और याह लड़का मोटा।
vah laṛka: dubla: hɛ ɔr yah laṛka: moṭa:.
That boy is slim and this boy is fat.

Cumulative effect

8. वह रोज़ व्यायाम करता है और सैर करता है।
vah roz vya:ya:m karta: hɛ aur sɛr karta: hɛ.
he daily exercise do-ptc is and walk do-ptc is
He exercises daily and goes for a walk (daily).

8a. वह रोज़ व्यायाम करता है और सैर भी।
vah roz vya:ya:m karta: hɛ ɔr sɛr bhi:.
he daily exercise do-ptc is and walk also
He exercises daily and goes for a walk, too.

9. वह दवाई खाता है और आराम करता है।
vah dava:i: kha:ta: hɛ ɔr a:ra:m karta: hɛ.
he medicine eat-ptc is and rest do-ptc is
He is taking medicine and relaxing.

9a. वह आराम करता है और दवाई खाता है।
vah a:ra:m karta: hɛ ɔr dava:i: kha:ta: hɛ.
He is relaxing and taking medicine.

Cause and effect

10. उसने दवाई खाई और वह स्वस्थ हुआ।
usne dava:i: kha:i: ɔr vah svasth hua:.
he-erg medicine ate and he healthy became
He took medicine and recovered from the illness.

10a. *वह स्वस्थ हुआ और उसने दवाई खाई।
*vah svasth hua: ɔr usne dava:i: kha:i:.

11. चोर को गोली लगी और वह आहत हुआ।
cor ko goli: lagi: ɔr vah a:hat hua:.
thief-dat bullet struck and he injured was
The thief was hit by a bullet and he was injured.

11a. *चोर आहत हुआ और उसको गोली लगी।
*cor a:hat hua: aur usko goli: lagi:.

Sequential action

12. वह आया और हमें घर आने के लिए न्योता दिया।
vah a:ya: ɔr hamẽ ghar a:ne ke liye nyota: diya:.
he came and we-obl home come-inf-obl invitation gave
He came and invited us to visit his home.

12a. *उसने हमें घर आने के लिए न्योता दिया और आया।
*usne hamẽ ghar a:ne ke liye nyota: diya: ɔr a:ya:.

13. मोहन घर आया और उसने दरवाज़े का ताला खोला।
mohan ghar a:ya: ɔr usne darva:ze ka: tala: khola:.
Mohan home came and he-erg door-gen lock opened
Mohan came home and unlocked the door.

13a. *मोहन ने दरवाज़े का ताला खोला और घर आया।
*mohan ne darva:ze ka: ta:la: khola: ɔr ghar a:ya:.

14. तुम एक अच्छी लड़की ढूँढ़ो और विवाह करो।
tum ek acchi: laṛki: ḍhũ:ḍho ɔr viva:h karo.
you-fem one good girl search and marriage perform
You find a good girl and get married.

14a. तुम विवाह करो और एक अच्छी लड़की ढूँढ़ो।
*tum viva:h karo ɔr ek acchi: laṛki: ḍhũ:ḍho.

Notice that sentences (7), (8), and (9) permit the reverse order of (7a), (8a), and (9a) respectively. In sentences (10), (11), (12), (13) and (14), the reverse order of the conjuncts results in ungrammatical sentences as shown above because of the constraints on cause and effect, sequential action, and contingency the conjoined structures are marked for. The coordinate sentences (10-14) can be paraphrased to indicate that they are related with the subordination process as well. Consider the following sentences.

10b. वह दवा खाकर स्वस्थ हुआ।
vah dava: kha:kar swasth hua:.
he medicine take-cp healthy became
He recovered (from illness) after taking the medicine.

11b. चोर गोली लगने से आहत हुआ।
cor goli: lagne se a:hat hua:.
thief bullet hit-inf-obl with injured became
The thief was injured by a bullet.

12b. उसने आकर हमें घर आने का न्योता दिया।
usne a:kar hamẽ ghar a:ne ka: nyota: diya:.
he-erg come-cp us-dat home go-inf-gen invitation gave
On arrival, he invited us to his home.

13b. मोहन ने घर आकर दरवाज़े का ताला खोला।
mohan ne a:kar darva:ze ka: ta:la: khola:.
Mohan-erg came-cp door-gen lock opened
On arrival, Mohan unlocked the door.

14b. एक अच्छी लड़की ढूँढ़कर तुम विवाह करो।
ek acchi: laṛki: ḍhũ:ḍhkar tum viva:h karo.
a good girl find-cp you marriage do-imp
Find a good girl and get married.

In the above sentences, cause and effect, sequential action, and contingency are expressed without using conjunction morphemes. The paraphrases indicate that the first conjuncts of the sentences represent the adverbial complements of the second conjuncts.

Besides conjoining sentences, the coordinating conjunction marker *ɔr* can be used to coordinate nouns (subjects, direct and indirect objects), verbs, adjectives, and adverbs.

Coordinate nominal subjects

15. लड़का और लड़की खेल रहे हैं।
laṛka: ɔr laṛki: khel rahe hɛ̃.
boy and girl play-prog are
A boy and a girl are playing.

Coordinate verbs

16. शीला ने कपड़े धोए और खाना पकाया।
ši:la: ne kapṛe dhoye ɔr kha:na: paka:ya:.
Shiela-erg clothes washed and food cooked
Shiela washed clothes and cooked meals.

Coordinate adjectives

17. शीला लंबी और गोरी है।
ši:la: lambi: aur gori: hɛ.
Shiela tall and fair complexioned is
Shiela is tall and fair-complexioned.

Coordinate adverbials

18. मैं कल और परसों घर नहीं जाऊँगा।
mɛ̃ kal ɔr parsõ ghar nahī: ja:ũ:ga:.
I tomorrow and day after tomorrow home neg go-fut
I will not go home tomorrow nor the day after tomorrow.

The coordination of two noun phrases yields a plural noun phrase and therefore, verb agreement is affected. In the case of coordinate subjects, the verb takes a masculine plural concord, whereas, in the case of coordinate objects, the verb agrees with the nearest object.

19. मोहन और शीला बाज़ार गए।
mohan ɔr ši:la: ba:za:r gaye.
Mohan and Shiela market went-mp
Mohan and Shiela went to the market.

20. मैंने सेब और ख़ोबानियाँ ख़रीदीं।
mɛ̃ne seb ɔr xoba:niyã: xari:di:
I-erg apples-mp and apricots-fp bought-fs
I bought apples and apricots.

But coordination is expressed by the conjunction marker पर *par*/मगर *magar*/किंतु *kintu* 'but'. This marker is placed in the beginning of the second conjunct.

21. मोहन अध्यापक है, मगर वह पढ़ाता नहीं।
mohan adhya:pak hɛ, magar vah paṛha:ta: nahĩ:.
Mohan is a teacher, but he teaches neg
Mohan is a teacher, but he does not teach.

22. उमा अनपढ़ है, पर वह बड़ी बुद्धिमान है।
uma: anpaṛh hɛ, par vah baṛi: budhima:n hɛ.
Uma is illiterate, but she very wise is
Uma is illiterate, but she is very wise.

In sentence coordination, as mentioned earlier, the conjunct marker और *ɔr* occurs before the second or the last conjunct. The conjunct marker पर *par* precedes the second or subsequent coordinated sentences. Among the disjunctive markers, या *ya:* can precede the first as well as subsequent disjuncts.

23. या वह दिल्ली जाएगा, या आगरा।
ya: vah dilli: ja:yega:, ya: a:gra:.
either he Delhi go-fut or Agra
Either he will go to Delhi or Agra.

But coordination is usually used with adjectives and adverbials.

24. मीरा बुद्धिमान है पर सुस्त है।
mi:ra: budhima:n hɛ par sust hɛ.
Mira is intelligent but lazy is
Mira is intelligent but lazy.

25. वह सैर करता है पर केवल शाम को।
vah sɛr karta: hɛ par keval ša:m ko.
she walk do-ptc is but only evening-loc at
He goes for a walk, but only in the evenings.

But coordination of nouns and verbs may involve a negative particle preceding or following the adversative conjuncts.

26. अमर चालाक लड़का है पर सोहन नहीं है।
amar ca:la:k lar̥ka: hɛ par sohan nahĩ: hɛ.
Amar clever boy is but Sohan neg is
Amar is a clever boy but Sohan is not.

27. हमने उसकी सुंदरता के बारे में सुना है पर
hamne uski: sundarta: ke ba:re mẽ suna: hɛ par
we-erg his beauty about heard but
कभी देखा नहीं है।
kabhi: dekha: nahĩ: hɛ.
but never use him saw neg is
We have heard about her beauty, but have never seen her.

28. वह पत्र नहीं लिखेगा पर टेलीफ़ोन ज़रूर करेगा।
vah patr nahĩ: likhega: par ṭeliphon zaru:r karega:.
He letter neg write-fut but telephone certainly do-fut
He will not write a letter but hell certainly call.

Or coordination uses the disjunctive markers *ya:* or and वरना *varna:/* अपितु *apitu* 'or' to conjoin nouns, adjectives, adverbs, and verbs.

29. मोहन या सोहन कपड़े सिएगा।
mohan ya: sohan kapr̥e siyega:.
Mohan or Sohan clothes stitch-fut
Mohan or Sohan will stitch the clothes.

30. उमा आज बाज़ार जाएगी या कल।
uma: a:j ba:za:r ja:yegi: ya: kal.
Uma today market go-fut or tomorrow
Uma will go to the market today or tomorrow.

31. कमीज़ के लिए नीला या लाल कपड़ा ख़रीदिए।
kami:z ke liye ni:la: ya: la:l kapr̥a: xari:diye.
shirt for blue or red cloth buy
Buy blue or red cloth for the shirt.

32. (आप) सेब खाएँगे या केला?
(a:p) seb kha:yẽge ya: kela:?
(you-p) apple eat-fut or banana
Would you like to take an apple or a banana?

4.3.12.1. Coordination and Accompaniment

Accompaniment is expressed by the postposition साथ *sa:th* with or in the company of. It can also be expressed by the conjunction morpheme और *ɔr* and.

33. सोहन और मोहन आए।
    sohan ɔr mohan a:ye.
    Sohan and Mohan came
    Sohan and Mohan came.

33a. सोहन मोहन के साथ आया।
    sohan mohan ke sa:th a:ya:
    Sohan Mohan with came
    Sohan came with Mohan.

Sentence (33) is an example of coordination, whereas sentence (33a) denotes accompaniment. Notice that the accompaniment uses a singular verb as in (33a). A single unit cannot be formed using accompaniment, but can be formed by using coordination. The term दोनों *donõ* 'both' can, therefore, be used with coordination, but not with accompaniment.

33b. सोहन और मोहन दोनों आए।
    sohan ɔr mohan donõ a:ye.
    Sohan and Mohan both came
    Sohan and Mohan both came.

33c. *सोहन मोहन के साथ आया दोनों।
    **sohan mohan ke sa:th a:ya: donõ.*

The unity of the conjoined phrase cannot be distorted, and this unity is expressed only by coordination and not by accompaniment.

33d. बेटा पिता के साथ आया।
    beṭa: pita: ke sa:th a:ya:.
    son father-obl with came
    The son came with the father.

33e. बेटा और पिता घर आए।
beṭa: ɔr pita: ghar a:ye.
The son and father came home.

33f. *बेटा घर और पिता आए।
**beṭa: ghar ɔr pita: a:ye.*

33g. *बेटा और घर पिता आए।
**beta: ɔr ghar pita: a:ye.*

This explains the ungrammaticalness of sentences (33f) and (33g). The commutative postposition के साथ *ke sa:th* follows the noun of accompaniment. It is possible to form coordinate sentences using the co-ordinate conjunction और *ɔr* the comitative postposition साथ *sa:th* in one of the conjuncts.

34. अजीत और मोहन अमर के साथ जाएँगे।
aji:t ɔr mohan amar ke sa:th ja:yẽge.
Ajit and Mohan Amar-obl with go-fut
Ajit and Mohan will accompany Amar.

34a. अमर के साथ अजीत और मोहन जाएँगे।
amar ke sa:th aji:t ɔr mohan ja:yẽge.
Ajit and Mohan will accompany Amar.

4.3.12.2. Structural Constraints

There are various structural constraints in coordination. In general, members in the same class can be conjoined but not those that belong to different classes.

Adjective and noun

35. *वह सुंदर और लड़की है।
**vah sundar ɔr laṛki: hɛ.*
she is beautiful and girl.

35a. वह सुंदर और बुद्धिमान लड़की है।
vah sundar ɔr budhima:n laṛki: hɛ.
she beautiful and intelligent girl is
She is a beautiful and an intelligent girl.

Adjective and adverb

36. *यह कपड़ा अच्छा और कल है।
yeh kapṛa: accha: ɔr kal hɛ.
this cloth good and yesterday is

36a. यह कपड़ा अच्छा और सस्ता है।
yeh kapṛa: accha: ɔr sasta: hɛ.
this cloth good and inexpensive is
This cloth is good and inexpensive.

As exemplified above in sentences (35) and (36), it is not possible to conjoin adjectives and nouns, nor adjectives and adverbs. Other types of constraints are indicated below.

Present and past participles and adjectives can be conjoined using coordinate conjunction morphemes.

37. अमित पढ़ा-लिखा और शरीफ लड़का है।
Amit paṛha: - likha: ɔr šari:ph laṛka: hɛ.
Amit educated and gentle boy is
Amit is an educated and a gentle boy.

Similarly, it is possible to conjoin the conjuncts with adverbial construction and an adjective phrase.

38. मेरा मित्र शहर में रहता है और बहुत चालाक है।
mera: mitr šahar mẽ rahta: hɛ ɔr bahut ca:la:k hɛ.
my friend city in live-ptc is and very clever is
My friend lives in the city and is clever.

A relative clause and an adjective phrase cannot be conjoined.

38a. *जो शहर में रहता है और बहुत चालाक मित्र है।
jo šahar mẽ rahta: hɛ aur bahut ca:la:k mitr hɛ.
who city-abl is live-pr is and clever friend tomorrow

Nouns and nominalized constructions can be conjoined, provided the semantic and pragmatic conditions are met.

39. उसे उपन्यास पढ़ना और नाटक देखना पसंद है।
use upanya:s paṛhna: ɔr na:ṭak dekhna: pasand hɛ.

he-dat novel read-inf and play watch-inf like is
He likes to read novels and watch plays.

40. मैंने उसे और उसके घर को सपने में देखा।
mε̃ne use ɔr uske ghar ko sapne mẽ dekha:.
I-erg he-obl and his house-dat dream-obl in saw
I saw him and his house in the dream.

It is possible to coordinate related adverbials in a coordinated structure.

41. वह हँसते - हँसते और जल्दी हर एक काम करता है।
vah hãste - hãste ɔr jaldi: har ek ka:m karta: hε.
he laugh-ptc and quickly every work do-ptc is
He gives his opinion smilingly and quickly.

Time adverbials and manner adverbials cannot be conjoined.

42. *वह कल रोया और ज़ोर-ज़ोर से।
**vah kal roya: ɔr zor - zor se*
he yesterday wept and loudly

Active and passive verbs can be coordinated provided they are appropriate in a pragmatic situation. In Hindi, passive constructions can mean capability as well.

43. अनु ने सेब खरीदे और उससे खाए नहीं गए।
anu ne seb xari:de aur usse kha:ye nahĩ: gaye.
Anu-erg apples bought and she-pass eat-pass neg aux-pass
Anu bought apples and she was not able to eat.

44. मैंने यह काम किया और उससे नहीं किया गया।
mε̃ne yeh ka:m kiya: ɔr usse nahĩ: kiya: gaya:.
I-erg this work did and he-pass neg do-pa went-pass
I did this work and it could not be done by him.

Simple verbs can be conjoined with infinitives in a coordinate structure.

45. मैंने यह नावल पढ़ा और इसे पढ़ना आसान है नहीं।
mε̃ne yeh na:val paṛha: ɔr ise paṛhna: a:sa:n hε nahĩ:.

I-erg this novel read and this-obl read-inf easy neg is
I read this novel and it is not easy to read.

It is also possible to conjoin different types of verbs.

46. मेरा हँसना और हँसाना किसी को पसंद नहीं आया।
mera: hãsna: ɔr hãsa:na: kisi: ko pasand nahĩ: a:ya:.
my laugh-inf and laugh-caus anyone-dat like neg came
My laughing and making others laugh was not liked by anyone.

47. गुस्सा आना और गुस्सा प्रकट करना अच्छा नहीं।
gussa: a:na: ɔr gussa: prakaṭ karna: accha: nahĩ:.
anger come-inf and anger express do-inf good neg
It is not good to be angry nor to express ones anger.

When two sentences are conjoined, any number of elements, including verbs, can be deleted under identity. The deletion can be both forward as well as backward. However, backward deletion is less frequent than forward deletion.

48. अमित ने किताब खरीदी और रजत ने कमीज़।
amit ne kita:b xari:di: ɔr rajat ne kami:z.
Amit-erg book bought and Rajat-erg shirt
Amit bought a book and Rajat a shirt.

48a. अमित ने किताब ø और रजत ने कमीज़ खरीदी।
amit-ne kita:b ø ɔr rajat ne kami:z xari:di:.
Amit-erg book ø and Rajat-erg shirt bought
Amit bought a book and Rajat bought a shirt.

The coordinating morpheme और *ɔr* conjoins sentences and parts of sentences of similar syntactic and semantic structure. Due to such constraints, the following pairs of sentences cannot be conjoined by merely deleting the identical elements.

49a. मुझे चाय पसंद है।
mujhe ca:y pasand hɛ.
I-obl tea like is
I like tea.

49b. मुझे काम करना पसंद है।
mujhe ka:m karna: pasand hɛ.
I-obl work do-inf like is
I like to do work.

49c. *मुझे चाय और काम करना पसंद है।
**mujhe ca:y ɔr ka:m karna: pasand hɛ.*

50a. अमित अवश्य आएगा।
amit avašy a:yega:
Amit definitely come-fut
Amit will definitely come.

50b. अमित मोहन के साथ आएगा।
amit mohan ke sa:th a:yega:.
Amit Mohan with come-fut
Amit will come with Mohan.

50c. *अमित अवश्य आएगा और मोहन के साथ।
**amit avašy a:yega: aur mohan ke sa:th*

51a. शीला बीमार है।
ši:la: bi:ma:r hɛ.
Shiela sick is
Shiela is sick.

51b. शीला घर पर है।
ši:la: ghar par hɛ.
Shiela home at is
Shiela is at home.

51c. *शीला बीमार है और घर पर।
**ši:la: bi:ma:r hɛ ɔr ghar par.*

All major sentence constituents, including nouns, adjectives, and adverbs, can be omitted under identity.

Omission of subject/object

52. अमित ने किताब खरीदी और ø पढ़ी।

amit-ne kita:b xari:di: ɔr ø paṛhi:.

Amit-erg book bought and ø read

Amit brought a book and read.

Omission of adjective/verb

53. उसके पास नीली कमीज़ है और मेरे पास ø टोपी।

uske pa:s ni:li: kami:z hɛ ɔr mere pass ø ṭopi:.

he-obl blue shirt is and I-poss-obl ø cap

He has a blue shirt and I have a blue cap.

Omission of adverb/verb

54. सोहन कल अपने घर गया और मोहन ø शहर ø।

sohan kal apne ghar gaya: ɔr mohan ø šahar ø

Sohan yesterday own village went and Mohan city

Sohan went to his village yesterday and Amar went to the city.

5. Lexicon

Here we list useful classified English-Hindi vocabulary for quick reference. The vocabulary is listed under different sections: (1) animals, birds, and insects; (2) flowers, fruits, and vegetables; (3) jewels, metals, and minerals; (4) miscellaneous items; (5) body parts; (6) occupations; (7) kinship terms; (8) adjectives; (9) verbs; (10) adverbs; (11) conjunctions; and (12) pronouns.

5.1. Animals, Birds, and Insects

animal	जानवर	ja:nvar / pašu
ant	चींटी	cĩ:ṭi:
bear	भालू	bha:lu:
bedbug	खटमल	khaṭmal
bird	चिड़िया / पक्षी	ciṛiya: / pakši:
buffalo	भैंस	bhɛ̃s
bullock	बैल	bɛl
butterfly	तितली	titli:
camel	ऊँट	ũ:ṭ
cat	बिल्ली	billi:
cock / rooster	मुर्गा	murga:
cockroach	तिलचट्टा	tilcaṭṭa:
cow	गाय	ga:y
crow	कौआ	kɔa:
cuckoo	कोयल	ko:yal
deer	हिरण	hiraṇ
dog	कुत्ता	kutta:
donkey	गधा	gadha:
eagle	बाज	ba:j
elephant	हाथी	ha:thi:
fish	मछली	machli:
fly	मक्खी	makkhi:
fox	लोमड़ी	lo:mṛi:
frog	मेंढ़क	mẽḍhak
goat	बकरी	bakri:
hare	ख़रगोश	xargoš
hen	मुर्गी	murgi:
horse	घोड़ा	gho:ṛa:
insect	कीड़ा	ki:ṛa:

jackal	गीदड़	gi:daṛ
kite	चील	ci:l
leopard	तेंदुआ	tendua:
lion	शेर	šer
lizard	छिपकली	chipkali:
mare	घोड़ी	ghoṛi:
monkey	बंदर	bandar
mule	खच्चर	khaccar
owl	उल्लू	ullu:
peacock	मोर	mo:r
pig	सुअर	suar
pigeon	कबूतर	kabu:tar
rat	चूहा	cu:ha:
scorpion	बिच्छू	bicchu:
sheep	भेड़	bhe:ṛ
snake	साँप	sã:p
sparrow	गौरिया	gɔrɛya:
squirrel	गिलहरी	gilhari:
swan	हंस	hans
tiger	बाघ	ba:gh
wolf	भेड़िया	bheṛiya:
worm	कीड़ा	ki:ṛa:

5.2. Flowers, Fruits, and Vegetables

almond	बादाम	ba:da:m
apple	सेब	se:b
apricot	ख़ोबानी	xo:ba:ni:
banana	केला	ke:la:
beet root	चुकंदर	cukandar
betel leaf	पान	pa:n
betel nut	सुपारी	supa:ri:
bitter gourd	करेला	kare:la:
black plum	आलू बुख़ारा	a:lu: buxa:ra:
brinjal / eggplant	बैंगन	bɛ̃gan
cabbage	बंदगोबी	bandgo:bi:
carrot	गाजर	ga:jar
cashew nut	काजू	ka:ju:
cauliflower	फूलगोबी	phu:lgo:bi:
coconut	नारियल	na:riyal

coriander	धनिया	dhaniya:
cucumber (small)	खीरा	khi:ra:
custard apple	शरीफा	šari:pha:
date	खजूर	khaju:r
fig	अंजीर	anji:r
garlic	लहसुन	lahsun
ginger	अदरक	adrak
gourd	लौकी	lɔki:
grape	अंगूर	angu:r
green chilie	हरी मिर्च	hari: mirc
groundnut	मूँगफली	mũ:gphali:
guava	अमरूद	amru:d
jackfruit	कटहल	kaṭhal
jasmine	चमेली	came:li:
lady's finger	बिंडी	binḍi:
lemon	नीबू	ni:bu:
lichee	लीची	li:ci:
lotus	कमल	kamal
mango	आम	a:m
marigold	गेंदा	gẽda:
(musk)melon	खरबूज़ा	kharbu:za:
mint	पुदीना	pudi:na:
mulberry	शहतूत	šahtu:t
onion	प्याज़	pya:z
orange	नारँगी	na:rangi:
papaya	पपीता	papi:ta:
pea	मटर	maṭar
peanut	मूँगफली	mũ:gphali:
pear	नाशपाती	na:špa:ti:
pineapple	अनानास	ananna:s
pistachio nut	पिस्ता	pista:
plum	आलू बुखारा	a:lu: buxa:ra:
pumpkin	कद्दू	kaddu:
pomegranate	अनार	ana:r
potato	आलू	a:lu:
raisin (small)	किशमिश	kišmiš
raisin (large)	मुनका	munakka:
radish	मूली	mu:li:
raspberry	रसबरी	rasbhari:
spinach	पालक	pa:lak
sugar cane	गन्ना	ganna:

sweet lime	मौसमी	mɔsami:
sweet potato	शकरकंद	šakarkand
tomato	टमाटर	ṭama:ṭar
turnip	शलगम	šalgam
walnut	अखरोट	akhro:ṭ
watermelon	तरबूज़ा	tarbu:za:

5.3. Jewels, Metals, and Minerals

aluminum	अलमूनियम	almu:niyam
brass	पीतल	pi:tal
bronze	कांसा	kã:sa:
copper	ताँबा	tã:ba:
diamond	हीरा	hi:ra:
emerald	पन्ना	panna:
gem	मणि / रत्न	maṇi / ratn
glass	काँच	kã:c
gold	सोना	so:na:
iron	लोहा	lo:ha:
jewel	जवाहर	java:har
mercury	पारा	pa:ra:
nickel	निकल	nikal
pearl	मोती	mo:ti:
sapphire	नीलम	ni:lam
silver	चाँदी	cã:di:
steel	इस्पात	ispa:t
sulfur	गंधक	gandhak
tin	टीन	ṭi:n
topaz	पूखराज	pukhra:j
zinc	जस्ता	jasta:

5.4. Miscellaneous Items

accident	दुर्घटना	durghaṭna:
acquaintance	परिचय	paricay
admiration	प्रशंसा / तारीफ़	prašansa: / ta:ri:f
age	आयू / उम्र	a:yu: / umar
air	हवा	hava:
answer	उत्तर	uttar / java:b
application	प्रार्थना पत्र	pra:rthana: patr
area	इलाका	ila:ka:

ashes	राख	ra:kh
autumn	पतझड़	patjhaṛ
baking pan	तवा	tava:
bark (of tree)	छिल्का	chilka:
barley	जौ	jɔ
basket	टोकरी	ṭo:kri:
bath	स्नान	sna:n
behavior	बर्ताव	barta:v
bell	घंटा	ghanṭa:
birthday	जन्म दिन	janm-din
boat	नाव	na:v
bread	रोटी	roṭi:
bridge	पुल	pul
center	केंद्र	kendr
charcoal	कोयला	koyla:
child	बच्चा	bacca:
church	गिरजा	girja:
city	शहर	šahar
class	दर्जा	darja:
cleanliness	सफाई	safa:i:
cloud	बादल	ba:dal
cold	सर्दी / जुकाम	sardi: / zuka:m
comfort	आराम	a:ra:m
committee	कमेटी	kameṭi:
community	समाज	sama:j
complaint	शिकायत	šika:yat
cooked rice	भात	bha:t
corn	मक्की	makki:
cough	खाँसी	khã:si:
country	देश	deš
court of law	अदालत	ada:lat
cup	प्याला	pya:la:
dance	नाच	na:c
day	दिन	din
difficulty	मुश्किल	muškil
dispensary	चिकित्सालय	cikitsa:lay
district	ज़िला	zila:
dust	धूल	dhu:l
earth	पृथ्वी	prathvi:
earthen oven	चूल्हा	cuhla:
education	शिक्षा / तालीम	šikša: / ta:li:m

egg	अंड़ा	ãḍa:
entertainment	मनोरंजन	manoranjan
enquiry	पूछताछ	pu:chta:ch
evening	शाम	ša:m
exhibition	प्रदर्शनी / नुमाइश	pradaršani: / numa:iš
fare	किराया / भाड़ा	kira:ya: / bha:ṛa:
fatigue	थकान	thaka:n
favor	कृपा	kripa:
fear	डर	ḍar
feast	दावत	da:vat
feather	पंख	pankh
fever	ज्वर / बुखार	jvar / buxa:r
frying pan	कड़ाई	kaṛa:i:
fire	आग	a:g
flag	झंडा	jhãḍa:
fog	कुहरा / धुँध	kuhra: / dhũdh
foreigner	विदेशी	videši:
forest	जंगल / वन	jangal / van
fountain	फव्वारा	favva:ra:
fun	मज़ाक / तमाशा	maza:k / tama:ša:
gift	उपहार	upha:r
grass	घास	gha:s
harbor	बंदरगाह	bandarga:h
health	स्वास्थ्य	swasthy
heat	गर्मी	garmi:
help	मदद / सहायता	madad / saha:yita:
hobby	शौक	šɔk
holiday	छुट्टी	chuṭṭi:
horn	सींग	sĩ:g
hospital	अस्पताल	aspata:l
hunger	भूख	bhu:kh
ice	बर्फ	barf
information	सूचना	su:cna:
intoxication	नशा	naša:
introduction	परिचय	paricay
island	टापू / द्वीप	ṭa:pu: / dvi:p
joke	मज़ाक	maza:k
journey	यात्रा सफर	ya:tra: / safar
kidney beans	राजमाह	ra:jma:h
kindness	कृपा / मेहरबानी	meharba:ni: / kripa:
ladle	कलछी	kalchi:

lane	गली	gali:
language	भाषा / ज़बान	bha:ša: / zaba:n
leaf	पत्ता	patta:
leave	छुट्टी	chuṭṭi:
lentil	दाल	da:l
lid	ढक्कन	ḍhakkan
lie	झूठ	jhu: ṭh
literature	साहित्य / अदब	sa:hity / adab
love	प्यार	pya:r
man	आदमी	a:dmi:
marriage	विवाह / शादी	viva:h / ša:di:
meat	माँस	mã:s
message	संदेश	sandeš
memorial	स्मारक	sma:rak
memory	याद	ya:d
mile	मील	mi:l
mistake	गल्ती	galti:
month	महीना	mahi:na:
mortar	ओखली	okhli:
moon	चाँद	cã:d
moonlight	चाँदनी	cã:dni:
morning	सुबह	subah
mosque	मसजिद	masjid
mountain	पहाड़	paha:ṛ
museum	अजायबघर	aja:yabghar
music	संगीत	sangi:t
name	नाम	na:m
news	समाचार / ख़बर	sama:ca:r / xabar
newspaper	समाचारपत्र / अख़बार	sama:ca:rpatr / axba:r
night	रात	ra:t
noon	दोपहर	dopahar
north	उत्तर	uttar
paddy	धान, शाली	dha:n / ša:li:
pain	दर्द	dard
person	व्यक्ति	vyakti:
pitcher	मटका	maṭka:
pity	दया	daya:
plate	प्लेट	paleṭ
place	जगह	jagah
potato	आलू	a:lu:
police	पुलिस	pulis

police station	थाना	tha:na:
praise	प्रशंसा / तारीफ	prašansa: / ta:ri:f
prayer	प्रार्थना / दुआ	pra:rthana: / dua:
present	उपहार	upha:r
price	कीमत	ki:mat
procession	जलूस	jalu:s
program	कार्यक्रम	ka:ryakram
port	बंदरगाह	bandarga:h
quarrel	झगड़ा	jhagṛa:
question	प्रश्न / सवाल	prašan / sava:l
rain	वर्षा / बारिश	varša: / ba:riš
rainy season	बरसात	barsa:t
regret	खेद / अफसोस	khed / afsos
religion	धर्म	dharm
rent	किराया	kira:ya:
repair	मरम्मत	marmmat
reply	उत्तर / जवाब	uttar / java:b
request	निवेदन / प्रार्थना	pra:rthana:
rest	आराम	a:ra:m
rice	चावल	ca:val
rice pudding	खीर	khi:r
river	दरिया	dariya:
road	पथ / रास्ता	path / ra:sta:
rock	चट्टान	caṭṭa:n
root	जड़	jaṛ
rope	रसी	rasi:
salt	नमक	namak
sand	रेत	ret
sandal	चंदन	candan
sea	समुद्र /समंदर	samudr / samandar
seed	बीज	bi:j
ship	जहाज़	jaha:z
show	तमाशा	tama:ša:
sickle	द्रांती	drã:ti:
sky	आकाश / आसमान	a:ka:š / a:sma:n
smoke	धुआं	dhuã:
snow	बर्फ	barf
society	समाज	sama:j
sorrow	खेद / दुख	khed / dukh
south	दक्षिण	dakšiṇ
spit	थूक	thu:k

spoon	चम्मच	cammac
spring	वसंत / बहार	vasant / baha:r
star	तारा	tara:
stick	सोटी	so:ṭi:
stone	पत्थर	patthar
storm	आँधी	ã:dhi:
sugar	चीनी	ci:ni:
summer	गर्मी	garmi:
sun	सूर्य / सूरज	su:ry / su:raj
sunshine	धूप	dhu:p
tail	दुम	dum
temple	मंदिर	mandir
tent	तम्बू	tambu:
thanks	धन्यवाद / शुक्रिया	dhanyava:d / šukriya:
thief	चोर	cor
thirst	प्यास	pya:s
time	समय	samay
tobacco	तम्बाकू	tamba:ku:
town	नगर	nagar / šahar
translation	अनुवाद	anuva:d
travel	यात्रा	ya:tra: / safar
traveler	यात्री / मुसाफिर	ya:tri: / musa:fir
treatment	इलाज	ila:j
trouble	कष्ट / तकलीफ	kašt / takli:f
truth	सच	sac
valley	वादी	va:di:
value	मूल्य / कीमत	mu:ly / ki:mat
vessel	बर्तन	bartan
village	ग्राम / गाँव	gra:m / ga:ũ
visitor	दर्शक	daršak
vomit	उल्टी	ulṭi:
wash	धुलाई	dhula:i:
water	पानी	pa:ni:
waterfall	झरना	jharna:
week	सप्ताह / हफ्ता	sapta:h / hafta:
wealth	समपति / दौलत	sampati / dɔlat
weight	भार / वज़न	bha:r / vazan
west	पश्चिम	paščim
wheat	गेहूँ	gehũ:
wind	हवा	hava:
winter	सर्दी / जाड़ा	sardi: / ja:ṛa:

woman	औरत	ɔrat
world	संसार	sansa:r / duniya:
worship	पूजा	pu:ja:
wood	लकड़ी	lakṛi:
year	साल	sal
zoo	चिड़ियाघर	ciṛiya:ghar

5.5. Body Parts

arm	बाँह	bã:h
armpit	बगल	bagal
beard	दाढ़ी	da:ṛhi:
body	शरीर	šari:r
bone	हड्डी	haḍḍi:
brain	दिमाग / मस्तिशक	dima:g / mastišk
breast	स्तन	stan
cheek	गाल	ga:l
chest	छाती	cha:ti:
chin	ठोड़ी	ṭhoṛi:
ear	कान	ka:n
elbow	कोहनी	kohni:
eye	आँख	ã:kh
eyeball	पुतली	putli:
eyebrow	भौं	bhɔ̃
eyelid	पलक	palak
face	चेहरा	cehra:
finger	उँगली	ũgli:
fist	मुट्ठी	muṭṭhi:
flesh	माँस / गोश्त	mã:s / go:sht
foot	पैर	pɛr
forehead	माथा	ma:tha:
gum	जबड़ा	jabṛa:
hand	हाथ	ha:th
(left) hand	बायाँ हाथ	ba:yã: ha:th
(right) hand	दायाँ हाथ	da:yã: ha:th
hair	बाल	ba:l
head	सिर	sir
heart	हृदय / दिल	hriday / dil
heel	एड़ी	eṛi:
intestines	अन्तडियाँ	antaṛiyã:

knee	घुटना	ghuṭna:
leg	टाँग	ṭã:g
lips	ओंठ	õṭh
liver	कलेजी	kale:ji:
lung	फेफड़ा	phe:phṛa:
mouth	मुँह	mũh
mustaches	मूछ	mu:ch
nail	नाखून	na:khu:n
navel	नाभी	na:bhi:
neck	गर्दन	gardan
nose	नाक	na:k
palate	तालू	ta:lu:
palm	हथेली	hathe:li:
rib	पसली	pasli:
shoulder	कंधा	kandha:
skin	चर्म	carm
sole of foot	तलवा	talva:
stomach	पेट	peṭ
teeth	दाँत	dã:t
thigh	जाँघ	jã:gh
throat	गला	gala:
thumb	अँगूठा	ãgu:ṭha:
tongue	जीब / ज़बान	ji:b / zaba:n
vein	नस	nas
waist	कमर	kamar
wrist	कलाई	kala:i:

5.6. Occupations

accountant	लेखाकार	le:kha:ka:r
advocate	वकील	vaki:l
actor	अभिनेता	abhine:ta:
actress	अभिनेत्री	abhine:tri:
artist	कलाकार / अदाकार	kala:ka:r / ada:ka:r
artisan	कारीगर	ka:ri:gar
barber	नाई	na:i:
blacksmith	लुहार	luha:r
boatman	मल्लाह	malla:h
carpenter	बढ़ई	baṛhai:
cartman	गाड़ीवान	ga:ṛi:va:n
clerk	लिपिक	lipik / klark

cobbler	मोची	mo:chi:
confectioner	हलवाई	halwa:i:
contractor	ठेकेदार	ṭhe:keda:r
cook	रसोइया	raso:iya:
craftsman	कारीगर	ka:ri:gar
dentist	दंत चिकित्सक	dant-chikitsak
doctor	डाक्टर	ḍa:kṭar
driver	ड्राइवर	ḍrɛvar
editor	सम्पादक	sampa:dak
employee	कर्मचारी	karamca:ri:
engineer	इंजीनियर	inji:niyar
farmer	किसान	kisa:n
gatekeeper	दरबान	darba:n
gardener	माली	ma:li:
goldsmith	सुनार	suna:r
grocer	पंसारी	pansa:ri:
hawker	फेरीवाला	phe:ri:va:la:
journalist	पत्रकार	patraka:r
judge	न्यायाधीश	nya:ya:dhi:š:
laborer	मज़दूर	mazdu:r
lawyer	वकील	vaki:l
maidservant	नौकरानी	nɔkara:ni:
mason	राज	ra:j
merchant	व्यापारी	vya:pa:ri:
minister	मंत्री	mantri:
musician	गायक / गायिका	ga:yak / ga:yika:
nurse	नर्स	nars
officer	अधिकारी	adhika:ri:
optician	ऐनकसाज़	ɛnaksa:z
peon	चपरासी	capra:si:
photographer	फोटोग्राफर	pho:ṭo:gra:phar
poet	कवि	kavi
police sub-inspector	थानेदार	tha:ne:da:r
postman	डाकिया	ḍa:kiya:
prime minister	प्रधान मंत्री	pradha:n mantri:
printer	मुदर्क	mudrak
porter	कुली	kuli:
proprietor	मालिक	ma:lik
publisher	प्रकाशक	praka:šak
salesman	विकेता	vikre:ta:
scientist	वैज्ञानिक	vɛgya:nik

sculptor	शिल्पी	šilpi:
servant	नौकर	nɔkar
shopkeeper	दुकानदार	duka:nda:r
singer	गायक /गायिका	ga:yak / ga:yika:
soldier	सिपाही	sipa:hi:
student	विद्यार्थी	vidya:rthi:
supervisor	परिवेक्षक	paryave:kšak:
sweet-seller	हलवाई	halva:i:
tailor	दर्ज़ी	darzi:
teacher	अद्यापक / शिक्षक	adhya:pak / šikšak
translator	अनुवादक	anuva:dak
washerman	धोबी	dho:bi:
watchmaker	घड़ीसाज़	ghaṛi:sa:z:
watchman	चौकीदार	cɔki:da:r
writer	लेखक	le:khak
(petition) writer	अर्ज़ी नवीस	arzi: navi:s

5.7. Kinship Terms

adopted son	दत्तक पुत्र	dattak putr
adopted daughter	दत्तक पुत्री	dattak putri:
brother	भाई	bha:i:
brother, elder	बड़ा भाई	ba:ṛa: bha:i:
brother, younger	छोटा भाई	cho:ṭa bha:i:
brother's daughter	भतीजी	bhati:ji:
brother's son	भतीजा	bati:ja:
brother's wife	भाभी	bha:bhi:
daughter	बेटी	be:ṭi:
daughter's husband	जवांई	javã:i:
father	पिता	pita:
father's brother	चाचा	ca:ca:
father's brother's wife	चाची	ca:ci:
father's father	दादा	da:da:
father's father's brother	चचेरा दादा	cacera: da:da:
father's father's brother's wife	चचेरी दादी	cace:ri: da:di:
father's mother	दादी	da:di:
father's sister	फूफी	phu:phi:
father's sister's husband	फूफ़ा	phu:pha:
father's brother's son	चचेरा भाई	ca:cera: bha:i:
father's sister's son	फुफेरा भाई	phuphera: bha:i:
father's brother's daughter	चचेरी बहन	ca:ceri: bahan:

father's sister's daughter	फुफेरी बहन	phupheri: bahan
husband	पति	pa:ti
husband's brother	देवर	de:var:
husband's brother's wife	देवरानी	dev:ra:ni:
husband's father	ससुर	sasur
husband's mother	सास	sa:s
husband's sister	ननद	nanad
mother	माता / माँ	ma:ta: / mã:
mother's brother	मामा	ma:ma:
mother's sister	मासी	ma:si:
mother's sister's husband	मौसा	mɔ:sa:
mother's father's brother	चचेरा नाना	cacera: na:na:
mother's father's brother's wife	चचेरी नानी	caceri: na:ni:
mother's father	नाना	na:na:
mother's mother	नानी	na:ni:
father's father's father	पड़दादा	paṛ da:da:
father's father's mother	पड़दादी	paṛ da:di:
mother's father's father	पड़नाना	paṛ na:na:
mother's brother's son	ममेरा भाई	mam:era: bha:i:
mother's brother's daughter	ममेरी बहन	mam:eri: bahan:
mother's sister's daughter	मौसेरी बहन	mɔs:eri: bahan
mother's sister's son	मौसेरा भाई	mɔsera: bha:i:
sister	बहन	bahan
sister, elder	बड़ी बहन	baṛi: bahan
sister, younger	छोटी बहन	choṭi: ba:han
son	बेटा / पुत्र	be:ṭa: / putr
sister's son	भाँजा	bhã:ja:
sister's daughter	भाँजी	bhã:ji:
sister's husband	जीजा / बहनोई	ji:ja: / bahno:i:
son's son	पोता	pota:
son's daughter	पोती	poti:
wife	पत्नी	pat:ni: / bi:vi:
wife's brother	साला	sa:la:
wife's father	ससुर	sasur
wife's mother	सास	sa:s
wife's sister	साली	sa:li:
son's wife	बहू	ba:hu:
stepfather	सौतेला बाप	sɔtela: ba:p
stepmother	सौतेली माँ	sɔteli: mã:
stepbrother	सौतेला भाई	sɔtela: bha:i:

stepsister	सौतली बहन	sɔteli: bahan

5.8. Adjectives

accurate	सही / ठीक	sahi: / ṭhi:k
airy	हवदार	hava:da:r
ancient	अतीक / पुराना	ati:k / pura:na:
bad	बुरा / ख़राब	bura: / xara:b
beautiful	सुंदर / ख़ूबसूरत	sundar / khu:bsu:rat
big	बड़ा / विशाल	baṛa: / visha:l
bitter	कड़वा	kaṛva:
black	काला	ka:la:
blue	नीला	ni:la:
broad	चौड़ा	cɔṛa:
brown	भूरा	bhu:ra:
cheap	सस्ता	saasta:
clean	साफ	sa:f
clear	स्पष्ट	spašṭ
clever	होशियार	ho:šiya:r / catur
closed	बंद	band
coarse	मोटा	mo:ṭa:
cold	ठंड़ा	ṭhã̄ḍa:
complete	पूरा	pu:ra:
correct	सही	sahi:
costly	महँगा	mahãga:
cunning	चालाक	ca:la:k
dear	प्यारा	pya:ra:
defective	ख़राब	xara:b
dense	घना	ghana:
difficult	कठिन / मुश्किल	kaṭhin / muškil
direct	सीधा	si:dha:
dirty	गंदा	gãda:
dry	सूखा	su:kha:
each	हर एक / प्रत्येक	har ek / pratyek
easy	आसान	a:sa:n
educated	पढ़ा लिखा	paṛha:-likha:
elder	ज्येष्ट / बड़ा	jye: šṭ / baṛa:
empty	ख़ाली	xa:li:
entire	सारा	sa:ra:
every	प्रत्यक	pratye:k

fast	तेज / तीव्र	te:z / ti:vr
fat	मोटा	mo:ṭa:
few	कम / कुछ	kam / kuch
filthy	गंदा	gãda:
fine	बारीक / ठीक	ba:ri:k / ṭhi:k
final	अन्तिम / आख़री	antim / a:xiri:
foolish	मूर्ख	mu:rkh / be:vaku:f
foreign	विदेशी	vide:ši
free	स्वतंत्र / आज़ाद	svatantr / a:za:d
fresh	ताज़ा	ta:za:
golden	सुनहला / सुनहरी	sunhala: / sunhari:
good	अच्छा	acchha:
greasy	चिकना	cikna:
great	बड़ा / महान	baṛa: / maha:n
green	हरा	hara:
handsome	सुंदर / ख़ूबसूरत	sũdar / khu:bsu:rat
hard	सख़्त / मुश्किल	saxt: / muškil
heavy	भारी	bha:ri:
high	ऊँचा	ũ:ca:
hot	गरम	garam
important	आवश्यक / ज़रूरी	xa:však / zaru:ri:
incomplete	अधूरा	adhu:ra:
independent	स्वतंत्र / आज़ाद	savatantr / a:za:d
inferior	घटिया	ghaṭiya:
intelligent	होशियार / दाना	hošiya:r / da:na:
large	बड़ा	baṛa:
last	अन्तिम / आख़री	antim / a:xiri:
left	बायाँ	ba:yã:
lengthy	लंबा	lamba:
less	कम	kam
light	हल्का	halka:
little	ज़रा / थोड़ा	zara: / thoṛa:
lonely	अकेला	ake:la:
long	लंबा	lamba:
loose	ढ़ीला	ḍhi:la:
low	नीचा	ni:ca:
many	कई / अनेक	kai: / ane:k
modern	आधुनिक	a:dhunik
more	और /अधिक	ɔr / adhik
much	बहुत /अधिक / ज़्यादा	bahut / adhik / zya:da

new	नया	naya:
old	पुराना	pura:na:
open	खुला	khula:
opposite	उल्टा	ulṭa:
orange	नारंगी	na:rangi:
peculiar	अजीब / विचित्र	aji:b / vicitr
permanent	पक्का / स्थाई	pakka: / stha:i:
pink	गुलाबी	gula:bi:
poor	गरीब	gari:b
proper	उचित	ucit
pungent	तीखा	ti:kha:
pure	शुद्ध	šuddh
raw	कच्चा	kacca:
red	लाल	la:l
remaining	बाकी	ba:ki:
rich	अमीर	ami:r
right	सही / ठीक	sahi: / ṭhi:k
ripe	पक्का	pakka:
robust	तगड़ा	tagṛa:
round	गोल	go:l
salty	नमकीन	namki:n
several	कई / अनेक	kai: / ane:k
sharp	तेज़	te:z
short	छोटा	cho:ṭa:
simple	सीधा / आसान	si:dha: / a:sa:n
single	अकेला	ake:la
slow	धीमा	dhi:ma:
small	छोटा	choṭa:
smart	होशियार	ho:šiya:r
smooth	चिकना	cikna:
soft	मुलायम / नर्म	mula:yam / naram
sour	खट्टा	khaṭṭa:
special	विशेष / ख़ास	višeš / xa:s
spicy	चटपटा	caṭpaṭa:
stale	बासी	ba:si:
stopped	बंद	band
straight	सीधा	si:dha:
strange	अजीब / विचित्र	aji:b / vicitr
strong	तगड़ा / मज़बूत	tagṛa: / mazbu:t
stupid	मूर्ख / बेवकूफ़	mu:rkh / bevaku:f
suitable	उचित	ucit

sweet	मीठा	mi:ṭha:
tall	लंबा	lamba:
tasteless	फीका	phi:ka:
temporary	अस्थाई	astha:i:
tender	कोमल	ko:mal
thick	मोटा	mo:ṭa:
thin	पतला	patla:
total	कुल	kul
true	सही / सच्चा	sahi: / sacca:
unripe	कच्चा	kacca:
vacant	ख़ाली	xa:li:
violet	बैंगनी	bɛ̃gani:
warm	गुनगुना	gunguna:
weak	कमज़ोर	kamzor
wet	गीला	gi:la:
wide	चौड़ा	cɔṛa:
white	सफ़ेद / श्वेत	safe:d / švet
whole	सारा	sa:ra:
wounded	आहत / घायल	a:hat / gha:yal
wrong	गलत	galat
yellow	पीला	pi:la:
young(er)	छोटा	cho:ṭa:

5.9. Verbs

to accept	स्वीकार करना	svi:ka:r karna:
to admit	मानना / दाख़िल करना	ma:nna: / da:xil karna:
to (be) alive	जीना	ji:na:
to ask for	माँगना	mã:gna:
to bathe	नाहना	naha:na:
to be	होना	ho:na:
to bear	सहना	sahna:
to beat	पीटना	pi:ṭna:
to become	बनना	banna:
to bite	काटना	ka:ṭna:
to boil	उबालना	uba:lna:
to (be) born	पैदा होना	pɛda: ho:na:
to break	तोड़ना	to:ṛna
to bring	लाना	la:na:
to bring up	पालना	pa:lna
to (be) broken	टूटना	ṭu:ṭna:

to build	बनाना / निर्माण करना	bana:na: / nirma:ṇ karna:
to burn	जलाना	jala:na:
to buy	ख़रीदना	xari:dna:
to call	बुलाना	bula:na:
to catch	पकड़ना	pakaṛna:
to celebrate	मनाना	mana:na:
to chew	चबाना	caba:na:
to cleanse	साफ करना	sa:f karna:
to climb	चढ़ना	caṛhna:
to come	आना	a:na:
to come out	निकलना	nikalna:
to conceal	छिपाना	chipa:na:
to conquer	जीतना	ji:tna:
to cook	पकाना / खाना बनाना	paka:na: / kha:na: bana:na:
to cool	ठंडा करना	ṭhãḍa: karna:
to cough	खाँसना	khã:sna
to count	गिनना	ginna:
to cover	ढकना	ḍhakna:
to cry	रोना	ro:na:
to cry out	चिल्लाना	cilla:na:
to cut	काटना	ka:ṭna:
to decorate	सजाना	saja:na:
to defeat	हराना	hara:na
to deposit	जमा करना	jama: karna:
to desire	चाहना	ca:hna:
to die	मरना	marna:
to distribute	बाँटना	bã:ṭna:
to divide	भाग करना / बाँटना	bha:g karna: / bã:ṭna:
to do	करना	karna:
to drag	घसीटना	ghasi:ṭna:
to draw	खींचना	khĩ:cna:
to drink	पीना	pi:na:
to drive	चलाना	cala:na:
to drive away	निकलना	nika:lna:
to earn	कमाना	kama:na:
to eat	खाना	kha:na:
to endure	सहना / बरदाश्त करना	sahna: / barda:št karna:
to enquire	पूछताछ करना	pu:chta:ch karna:
to entrust	सौंपना	sɔ̃pna:
to envy	ईर्षा करना	i:rša: karna:
to escape	बचना	bacna:

to examine	जाँचना	jã:cna:
to expect	प्रतीक्षा करना	prati:kša:
to expel	निकालना	nika:lna:
to fall	गिरना	girna:
to fight	लड़ना	laṛna:
to flee	भागना	bha:gna:
to flow	बहना	bahna:
to fly	उड़ना / उड़ाना	uṛna: (int) / uṛa:na: (tr)
to fry	तलना	talna:
to forget	भूलना	bhu:lna:
to get	पाना	pa:na:
to get down	उतरना	utarna:
to get out	निकलना	nikalna:
to get up	उठना	uṭhna:
to give	देना	de:na:
to grind	पीसना	pi:sna:
to grow	उत्पादन करना / बढ़ना	utpa:dan karna: / baṛhna:
to halt	ठहरना / रुकना	ṭhaharna: / rukna:
to happen	होना	ho:na:
to hear	सुनना	sunna:
to heat	गर्म करना	garm karna:
to help	मदद / सहायता करना	madad / saha:yta: karna:
to hide	छिपाना	chipa:na:
to hold	पकड़ना सम्हालना	pakaṛna: / samha:lna:
to increase	बढ़ाना	baṛha:na:
to inform	बताना / सूचित करना	bata:na: / su:cit karna:
to join	मिलना	milna:
to jump	कूदना	ku:dna:
to keep	रखना	rakhna:
to kill	मारना	ma:rna:
to kiss	चूमना	cu:mna:
to knead	गूँदना	gũ:dna:
to know	जानना	ja:nna:
to laugh	हँसना	hãsna:
to learn	सीखना	si:khna:
to leave	छोड़ना	choṛna:
to lie	झूठ बोलना	jhu:ṭh bo:lna:
to lie down	लेटना	le:ṭna:
to lift	उठाना	uṭha:na
to like	चाहना / पसंद करना	ca:hna: / pasand karna:

to listen	सुनना	sunna:
to live	जीना / रहना	ji:na: / rahna:
to look	देखना	de:khna:
to lose	खोना	kho:na:
to make	बनाना / तैयार करना	bana:na: / tɛya:ṛ karna:
to meet	मिलना	milna:
to mix	मिलाना	mila:na:
to occur	होना	ho:na:
to open	खोलना	kho:lna:
to (be) perturbed	गबड़ाना	ghabṛa:na:
to place	रखना	rakhna:
to play	खेलना	khe:lna:
to pluck	तोड़ना	toṛna:
to plunder	लूटना	lu:ṭna:
to possess	रखना	rakhna:
to prepare	बनाना	bana:na: / tɛyar karna:
to print	छापना	cha:pna:
to protect	बचाना	baca:na: / rakša: karna:
to pull	खींचना	khĩ:cna:
to purchase	ख़रीदना	xari:dna
to put on	पहनना	pahanna:
to quarrel	झगड़ना	jhagaṛna:
to raise	उठाना	uṭha:na:
to reach	पहुँचना	pahũcna:
to read	पढ़ना	paṛhna:
to reap	काटना	ka:ṭna:
to receive	पाना	pa:na:
to recognize	पहचानना	pahca:nna:
to refund	लौटाना / वापिस करना	lɔṭa:na: / va:pas karna:
to release	छोड़ना	choṛna:
to relax	आराम करना	a:ra:m karna:
to remit	अदा करना	ada: karna:
to reside	रहना / निवास करना	rahna: / niva:s karna:
to return	लौटना	lɔṭna: / lɔṭa:na:
to resolve	घूमना	ghu:mna:
to rise	उठना / जागना	uṭhna: / ja:gna:
to roast	बुनना	bunna:
to run	दौड़ना	dɔṛna:
to save	बचाना	baca:na:
to say	कहना	kahna:

to search	ढूँढना / खोजना	ḍhũ:ḍhna: / khojna:
to see	देखना	de:khna
to sell	बेचना	be:cna:
to send	भेजना	bhe:jna:
to set (as sun)	डूबना	ḍu:bna:
to settle down	बसन	basna:
to shine	चमकना	camakna:
to shiver	काँपना	kã:pna:
to sink	डूबना	ḍu:bna:
to sing	गाना	ga:na:
to sit	बैठना	bɛ:ṭhna:
to sleep	सोना	sona:
to smile	मुस्कराना	muskara:na:
to speak	बोलना	bo:lna: / bha:šaṇ de:na:
to spend	बिताना / खर्च करना	bita:na: / kharc karna:
to start	निकलना / आरंभ करना	nikalna: / a:rambh karna:
to stay	ठहरना	ṭhahrna:
to steal	चुराना	cura:na:
to stir	हिलाना	hila:na:
to stitch	सीना	si:na:
to stop	रुकना	rukna:
to stroll	टहलना	ṭahalna:
to study	पढ़ना	paṛhna:
to support	सम्भालना / सहारा देना	sambha:lna: / saha:ra: dena:
to suppress	दबाना	daba:na:
to swim	तैरन	tɛrna:
to take	लेना	le:na:
to take out	निकालना	nika:lna:
to teach	सिखाना / पढ़ाना	sikha:na: / paṛha:na:
to tear off	फाड़ना	pha:ṛna:
to tell	बताना / कहना	bata:na: / kahna:
to test	जाँचना	jã:cna:
to think	सोचना	socna:
to throw	फैंकना	phẽ:kna:
to tolerate	सहना	sahna:
to touch	छूना	chu:na:
to travel	यात्रा करना	ya:tra: / safar karna:
to tremble	काँपना	kã:pna:
to twinkle	चमकना	camakna:
to understand	समझना	samajhna:

to violate	तोड़ना	toṛna:
to wait	प्रतीक्षा करना	prati:kša: karna:
to wake up	जागना	ja:gna:
to walk	चलना	calna:
to wander	घूमना	ghu:mna:
to wash	धोना	dho:na:
to wear	पहनना	pahanna:
to weep	रोना	ro:na:
to weigh	तोलना	to:lna:
to welcome	स्वागत करना	sva:gat karna:
to win	जीतना	ji:tna:
to wish	चाहना	ca:hna: / iccha: karna:
to work	काम करना	ka:m karna:
to worship	पूजा करना	pu:ja: karna: / iba:dat karna:
to write	लिखना	likhna:

5.10. Adverbs

above	ऊपर	u:par
abundantly	ख़ूब	xu:b
after	बाद / पीछे	ba:d / pi:che:
after all	आखिर	a:xir
afterwards	बाद में	ba:d: mẽ
ahead	आगे	a:ge:
alone	अकेले	ake:le:
also	भी	bhi:
always	हमेशा / सदा	hameša: / sada:
among	बीच	bi:c
anytime	कभी भी	kabhi: bhi:
anywhere	कहीं	kahĩ:
at last	आखिर / अंत में	a:xir / ant mẽ
away	दूर	du:r
because	क्योंकि	kyõ:ki
before	पहले / आगे	pahle: / a:ge:
behind	पीछे	pi:che:
below	नीचे	ni:ce:
between	बीच / मध्य	bi:c / madhy
certainly	अवश्य / ज़रूर	avašy / zaru:r
constantly	बराबर	bara:bar
continuously	लगातार	laga:ta:r
day after tomorrow	परसों	parsõ:

distant	दूर	du:r
down	नीचे	ni:ce:
ever	हमेशा	hame:ša:
everywhere	हर जगह	har jagah
far off	बहुत दूर	bahut du:r
generally	प्राय: / अक्सर	pra:yah / aksar
here	यहाँ	yahã:
how	कैसे	kɛse:
immediately	तुरंत / फौरन	turant / fɔran
in front of	के आगे	ke a:ge
in the presence of	के सामने	ke sa:mne
just now	अभी	abhi:
near	पास / समीप	pa:s / sami:p
no	न / नहीं	na / nahĩ:
not	नहीं	nahĩ:
now	अब	ab
nowadays	आजकल	a:jkal
often	पायः / अक्सर	pra:yah / aksar
of course	बेशक	be:šak
only	केवल / सिर्फ	ke:val / sirf
out	बाहर	ba:har
outside	बाहर	ba:har
perhaps	शायद	ša:yad
probably	शायद	ša:yad
quickly	जल्दी	jaldi:
quite	बिल्कुल	bilkul
silently	चुपचाप	cupca:p
slowly	धीरे	dhi:re:
sometimes	कभी कभी	kabhi:-kabhi:
somewhere	कहीं	kahĩ:
suddenly	अचानक	aca:nak / eka:ek
today	आज	a:j
tomorrow	कल	kal
(in) that direction	उधर	udhar
then	तब	tab
(in) this direction	इधर	idhar
thus	यों	yõ:
under	नीचे	ni:ce
undoubtedly	बेशक	be:šak
unexpectedly	अचानक	aca:nak
upward	ऊपर	u:par

very	बहुत	bahut
well	ख़ूब	xu:b
(at) which direction	किधर	kidhar
when (interrogative)	कब	kab
when (relative)	जब	jab
where (interrogative)	कहाँ	kahã:
where (relative)	जहाँ	jahã:
whether	चाहे	ca:he
wholly	बिल्कुल	bilkul
yesterday	कल	kal

5.11. Conjunctions

although	यद्यपि / हालांकि	yadyapi / ha:lã:ki
again	फिर	phir
and	और / तथा	ɔr / tatha:
but	लेकिन / किंतु / परंतु / बल्कि	lekin / kintu / parantu / balki
hence	इसलिए	isliye
or	या	ya:
since	चूंकि	cũ:ki
so	इसलिए	isliye:
so that	ताकि	ta:ki
that	कि	ki
though	यद्यपि / हालाँकि	yadyapi / ha:lã:ki

5.12. Pronouns

any / anybody	कोई	ko:i: / kisi:
he	वह यह उस इस	vah / yah / us / is
I	मैं / मुझ	mɛʃ / mujh
it	यह / इस	yah / is
my	मेरा	me:ra:
one's own	अपना	apna:
our	हमारा	hama:ra:
she	वह यह उस इस	vah / yah / us / is
some	कुछ	kuch
somebody	कोई	ko:i: / kisi:
something	कुछ	kuch
these	ये / इन	ye / in
they	वे / उन	ve / un
this	यह / इस	yah / is

those	वे / उन	ve / un
thou	तू / तुझ	tu: / tujh
thy	तेरा	te:ra:
you (familiar)	तुम	tum
you (polite)	आप	a:p
your (faniliar)	तुम्हारा	tumha:ra:
your (polite)	आपका	a:pka:
we	हम	ham
what	क्या	kya:
who (interrogative)	कौन / किस / किन	kɔn / kis / kin
who (relative)	जो / जिस / जिन	jo / jis / jin